CIRCLE OF INTRIGUE

CIRCLE OF INTRIGUE

The Hidden Inner Circle of the Global Illuminati Conspiracy

TEXE MARRS

LTP Living Truth Publishers
1708 Patterson Road • Austin, Texas 78733

ACKNOWLEDGEMENTS

The author would like to acknowledge the very special contributions of the following persons. Without their wonderful and gracious assistance, it would have been impossible to successfully complete this book. First, a warm thanks to my wife, Wanda, for her love and her faith; to Sandra Schappert, for her creative art and graphic contributions and her keen business sense; to Kimberly Reiley, whose secretarial and editing talents are incomparable; and to the dedicated staff of Living Truth Publishers, who daily accomplish miracles: Michelle Delgado, Michael Ortega, Joe Saldaña, Gerry Schappert, and Glenda Williford. I am also extremely grateful to my ministry friends throughout the world who send me needed research materials and often write me heart-stirring letters of support and encouragement. May God richly bless each of you!

Circle of Intrigue: The Hidden Inner Circle of the Global Illuminati Conspiracy

Published by Living Truth Publishers, a division of Living Truth Ministries, 1708 Patterson Road, Austin, Texas 78733.

Scripture quotations are from the King James Version of The Holy Bible.

Cover design: Texe Marrs, Wanda Marrs and Sandra Schappert

Printed in the United States of America

Library of Congress Catalog Card Number 95-80420

Categories: 1. Current Events and Issues 2. Politics 3. Religion 4. Bible Prophecy

ISBN 1-884302-00-9

Is the Destiny of the Ten Unseen Men Revealed in Bible Prophecy?

"And the ten horns which thou sawest are ten kings, which have received no kingdom as yet; but receive power as kings one hour with the beast.

These have one mind, and shall give their power and strength unto the beast.

These shall make war with the Lamb, and the Lamb shall overcome them: for he is Lord of lords, and King of kings: and they that are with him are called, and chosen, and faithful."

—Revelation 17:12-14

Other Books by Texe Marrs

***Big Sister Is Watching You:** Hillary Clinton and the White House Feminists Who Now Control America— And Tell the President What to Do*

***Dark Majesty:** The Secret Brotherhood and the Magic of A Thousand Points of Light*

***Millennium:** Peace, Promises, and the Day They Take Our Money Away*

America Shattered

New Age Cults and Religions

Ravaged by the New Age

Mystery Mark of the New Age

Dark Secrets of the New Age

Mega Forces

TABLE OF

Contents

INTRODUCTION

The Illuminati—A World Conspiracy Forged by the Super Rich?

Is there a *World Conspiracy* forged by the super rich? Is this powerful group of wealthy conspirators the mysterious men often chillingly described as the *Illuminati?* Do these unseen men, our controllers, have a hidden agenda which dramatically endangers our homes, our families, our very lives?

These are momentous, breathtaking questions. But we must seriously consider the grim situation we now face. The conspiracy which many people today so furiously deny and which others cunningly and craftily seek to conceal is real. God's prophetic Scriptures warned us this would happen—that a small cabal of utterly wicked men, pridefully believing themselves to be divine "gods," would recklessly plot a global conspiracy in the last days.

An Alliance of Blood and Dynasty

In the pages of *Circle of Intrigue,* a prophetic drama of almost unbelievable proportions unfolds. We discover an alliance of blood and dynasty—of infidels maniacally driven by a witch's brew combination of vanity and greed to launch a series of Earth-shattering events. Indeed, their plot, if successful, will extinguish our most precious freedoms and liberties and bring disaster and chaos to every corner of the globe.

In their view, the ten men who comprise the *Inner Circle* of the Illuminati have a glorious mission to fulfill. Theirs is a quest for global dominion and for total and absolute victory over God and His chosen. They will not stop until every man, woman, and child on Planet Earth bow down before them and satisfy their sordid, animalistic cravings. Already fabulously rich, heirs of royal bloodlines and modern-day lords of ancient, monied dynasties, these ambitious and corrupt men can never get enough. Their urge to power dominates their senses and blinds their instincts. Tragically, their secret worship of the radiant god symbolized by the pyramid and its capstone with the all seeing eye drives them ever onward toward their volcanic and explosive final destiny.

Circle of Intrigue is unique in that it is the first book to fully and meticulously expose the existence of a ruling *Inner Circle* of the global Illuminati conspiracy. The *Inner Circle* of the Illuminati is the elevated capstone of the pyramid of society. Comprised of ten "Wise Men," the *Inner Circle* meets privately at palatial estates, luxurious resorts, and secluded sites around the globe, plotting the future of the world. Who are these men? Why do they collude and conspire together? Why do they hide behind different disguises? This book examines the men who are at the very epicenter of the great World Conspiracy and confirms the astonishing accuracy of Bible prophecy.

Network of Power

We will also take a close-up look at the servants of the *Inner Circle*. The Illuminati's network of power is a mosaic of the world's most famous personalities, financiers, corporate chairmen, and political figures. Through these lower-level subordinates, the *Inner Circle* is shown to secretly dominate and control America's political process. President Bill Clinton, House Speaker Newt Gingrich, Senate Majority Leader Robert Dole—these men and hundreds of others slavishly serve the haughty elitists of the *Inner Circle* and unerringly carry out their agenda for World Government and a global financial order.

Right-wing or left-wing, Republican or Democrat, there really is *not* a dime's worth of difference between the two, major political parties.

A Lawless Quest

Circle of Intrigue definitively proves and documents the lawless quest of the Illuminati. Here you will find the amazing facts about the men who lay claim to supernatural origins and have developed an occult strategy—*Ordo Ab Chao* (Order Out of Chaos)—designed to mold the world into a totalitarian New Age Kingdom by the magical year 2000.

Someday soon, the diabolical leader of the *Inner Circle* will be possessed by Satan and raised to become the Antichrist, the beast whose number is 666. This man, the "little horn" of the book of Daniel, will complete the work of Napoleon, Lenin, Hitler, and Stalin. Indeed, as this book persuasively documents, all these dictators served the same occult system—and the very same master. They, like today's Illuminati leadership, knelt before the altar of the great solar deity, whose heinous symbol is the swastika, the swirling sun sign. In *Circle of Intrigue* you will discover the true identity of this fierce, ancient—and modern—solar god whom the Illuminati adore and worship.

An Epic Struggle Between Good and Evil

Faithful and devoted students of God's prophetic Word have long known that the time would come when the world would be readied for this epic, heart-stopping, and climactic struggle between good and evil. What I unmask in the pages that follow paints a clear and convincing—if frightening and ominous—picture of the *ten kings* prophesied to reign over the Earth.

The Bible forewarned that, in the last days, just before Christ Jesus' glorious and triumphant return, there would arise a Fascist World Order, with mankind ruled over and oppressed by ten, powerful men. What's more, these ten—whom I believe to be the *Inner Circle* of the Illuminati—are prophesied to "have one mind, and shall give their power and strength unto the beast." (Revelation 17:13)

The occult blueprint for humanity designed by the Illuminati was once accurately described by one of the conspirators as "veritably the *Code of Hell.*" I agree. Indeed, in chapter eleven, I identify the shadowy, unseen *master* who is the father of this unholy scheme of the globalists. He is, I explain, the "Solar Serpent," otherwise known as Satan, or Lucifer.

We Must Expose This Colossal Plot

As Christians and true patriots, it is both our duty and our obligation to expose this colossal plot. We must shine the inspirational light of truth on the gross darkness which now encompasses our nation and the world. But in so doing, let us never forget that even before we came into existence, God had already foreordained the end of all things. Thus, the conspiracies and schemes of the Illuminati were doomed to failure from the beginning. How pitiful, then, how woefully inadequate, is their unseemly struggle to overcome the Great God who sits in the heavens! And yes, how very tragic is the destiny of these men.

In obedience to their hellish master, the Illuminati have chosen to serve the cause of unrighteousness. In their arrogance and deceit, they seek to harm and destroy God's elect, and they foolishly make war against the One who sits on the throne. In rejecting the Truth and embracing the Lie, these deceived men are bringing to pass the striking, end-times prophecy foretold in the book of Revelation:

> These shall make war with the Lamb, and the Lamb shall overcome them: for he is Lord of lords, and King of

> kings: and they that are with him are called, and chosen, and faithful. (Revelation 17:14)

I fervently believe that those who are "called, and chosen, and faithful"—those who believe in Jesus Christ and are born again through His Love and grace—have nothing to fear in the dark days which lie just ahead. We can and should look to the future with confidence, remembering that even the secret things are God's. He is and shall ever be Lord and King.

What's more, His prophetic Word promised that we would know the truth in these last days. Indeed, Christ declared, "Ye shall know the truth, and the truth shall make you free" (John 8:32). It is impossible for God's elect to be deceived. The Scriptures reveal that even though the whole world shall fall under a strong delusion and shall believe the Lie of Satan and his Illuminati, those who trust in God will not be taken by surprise. As we read in Daniel 12:10, "the wise *shall* understand."

— Texe Marrs
Austin, Texas

ONE

The Astonishing Global Power and Influence of the Inner Circle

The fourth beast shall be the fourth kingdom upon earth, which shall be diverse from all kingdoms, and shall devour the whole earth, and shall tread it down, and break it in pieces. And the ten horns out of this kingdom are ten kings that shall arise...

—Daniel 7:23-24

The ten, so-called "Wise Men" of the Illuminati are fabulously rich.... Still, they want more...and more.

—Texe Marrs

Cloaked in mystery and shrouded in secrecy, the *Inner Circle* is comprised of ten powerful men. These men meet regularly—at least twice per year—in a secluded location. Their proceedings take place in a locked and sealed suite at a swank and exclusive resort hotel, or at a private estate owned by one of their minions. Their policy decisions and agenda, kept top secret, result in the most dire and grievous consequences for ordinary citizens. Wars, revolutions, scientific discoveries, diseases, famines, financial booms—and crashes!—these are some of the life-giving *or* life-destroying decisions made at their confidential sessions. The future of Planet Earth and its almost six billion inhabitants is plotted out in the dark recesses of the minds and hearts of these ten cruel men.

Most Americans know little or nothing of the existence of the *Inner Circle* and are totally oblivious to its grand design. But those few who are aware refer to these men in awe-inspiring tones. They are said to be the Lords of Wisdom, the Custodians of the Plan, the Torch Bearers, the Unknown Men, the Wise Men, the Keepers of the Royal Secret, or even cryptically as the "One."[1]

In *Circle of Intrigue,* I introduce them under their actual title: the *Inner Circle.* The *Inner Circle* is the core group which has long guided the destiny of the Illuminati conspiracy. Led by spirit beings from another dimension—a grotesque and shadowy "otherworld"—the elitists of the *Inner Circle* are the masterminds, the organizers, and the board of directors of a gigantic and far-flung empire. It is an empire which transcends international borders and closely coordinates the efforts of thousands of the planet's best known and most influential politicians, bankers, corporate executives, social engineers, and religious leaders.

Mystical Guardians of a Holy Secret

Fabulously wealthy, enormously privileged, and vastly separated socially from the masses whom they consider to be "peasants" and "useless eaters," the men of this clandestine *Inner Circle* revel in their mental, spiritual, and racial superiority. When they meet, they deem their coming together to be an "assemblage of the gods." They claim to be mystical guardians of a great and holy secret, involving royal bloodlines and supernatural birthright.

As they view it, their supposed, higher nature and their extraordinary origins confer on them the responsibilities of *noblesse oblige.* They are convinced it is their obligation and right to be divine rulers of all mankind.

Over the centuries, these arrogant and haughty men have banded together, amassing untold wealth and material treasures. With their combined wealth has come tremendous clout and the ability to reward friends and allies and to punish enemies. Greedy and wicked, believing themselves to be beyond good and evil, the men of the *Inner Circle* wantonly contract out the assassination of enemies. They also ruthlessly bring into line courageous men and women who refuse to accede to their foul agenda.

Wayward servants like John F. Kennedy, who become rebels and "lone rangers," as well as desperate men like Mafia associate Jack Ruby and millionaire publisher Robert Maxwell, are dealt with harshly and efficiently. President Kennedy and, later, his brother, Robert, were dispatched with bullets to the head. Lee Harvey Oswald's slayer, Jack Ruby, was injected with cancer-causing carcinogens while in a jail cell awaiting trial, and the flamboyant Maxwell was taken for a cruise on his yacht, beaten and thrown overboard in a shark-infested sea.

The men of the *Inner Circle* are reprobates; they have no remorse for their crimes against humanity and rebellion against God. They feel no guilt. They are thoroughly wicked and satanic, as their perverse worship of Lucifer as "Father of Light" amply demonstrates.

A Single, Spidery Thread

For nine, momentous and event-filled years I have been tracking this evil *Inner Circle* of wickedness. I have meticulously traced its close-knit network of stooges, puppets, operatives, and agents and have been saddened to discover that, like a nightmarish octopus from the depths of a sulphurous, boiling and hellish ocean floor, its sin-scarred, gaping tentacles reach even into the corridors of the White House. Indeed, they lead us straight into the oval office of the President of the United States of America.

A single, spidery thread can be traced, originating from the lair of the *Inner Circle* and spreading its slick, sickly web across national borders into the musty halls and chambers of the Kremlin, deep inside the ornate apartments of the Vatican, and within the paneled confines of the board rooms of corporate America and its *Fortune 500*.

The *Inner Circle* maintain their great power by inventing chaos and inducing conflict, bloodshed, and carnage. They control the intelligence agencies, internal security police, and armed forces of the world's super powers. And they do not hesitate to call on these groups when necessary to restore a delicate equilibrium and to create "order out of chaos." Indeed, as we shall see, *"Ordo Ab Chao"* (Latin for "order out of chaos") is one of the most revered dictums and operating laws of these scheming men and their hierarchy of evil.

In Bible prophecy is revealed the awesome military and police power of the end-times, beast system that shall rise up in the last days. Today's emerging New World Order, with its capability for rapid delivery of armaments, aircraft, ships, nuclear-tipped and Tomahawk missiles, laser weaponry, and other high tech tools of warfare to precise targets anywhere on Earth, chillingly matches the prophetic picture of global dominance given in the book of Daniel:

> Thus he said, The fourth beast shall be the fourth kingdom upon earth, which shall be diverse from all kingdoms, and shall devour the whole earth, and shall tread it down, and break it in pieces. And the ten horns out of the kingdom are ten kings that shall arise: and another shall rise after them; and he shall be diverse from the first, and he shall subdue three kings. (Daniel 7:23-24)

The Ten Kings to Devour the Earth

Notice that, in Bible prophecy, we are told that in the last days, "ten kings...shall arise." They will set up a *global kingdom* and by force they will "devour the whole earth." I believe these ten kings are the ten men of the Illuminati's *Inner Circle.* And, indeed, their influence is global.

Through analysis of inside information collected from reliable sources and collated with corroborating intelligence data, I have been able to calculate what I believe is the ethnic and geographic composition of this exclusive *Inner*

Circle of the Illuminati. Currently, its ten members appear to be divided by nation as follows:

U.S.A. - two members
Canada - one member
France - three members
Austria - one member
Great Britain - one member
Spain - one member
South Africa - one member

As you can see, the United States has two seats on this ten-member panel of supreme elitists. Neighboring Canada provides a third member. However, six members are from the same geographic and cultural region: Greater Europe—the so-called European Community. The tenth and final member is from South Africa.

My investigation further reveals that the Rothschild family lays claim to three seats, and the Rockefeller dynasty holds two coveted seats on the *Inner Circle*. Later in this book, I will profile the reigning nobility of these two, incredible dynasties and also take a close-up look at other candidates for the prestigious *Inner Circle* of the Illuminati.

It would appear that the dynastic bloodlines of Europe—the Rothschilds, Habsburgs, etc.—have a distinct advantage based simply on their numerical superiority. However, this is far from the case. In fact, it is significant that *none of the ten men of the Inner Circle profess first allegiance to their own nation-state*. They are pure globalists—planetary citizens. They are also, uniformly, worshippers of a deity who is not circumscribed by national borders or limited by geographic considerations.

Revealingly, the men of the *Inner Circle* view themselves as descendants of a historic heritage, with human roots going back at least to Greece, Rome, Egypt, and Babylon, and spiritual origins curiously attributed to a pre-Adamic state of existence. Moreover, they believe themselves to be heirs of a royal bloodline destined to rule the Earth for all eternity.

Titans of Money and Finance

Evidence I have accumulated indicates that the *Inner Circle* and its immediate entourage of deputies and assistants is constantly working behind the scenes, pulling strings in the highest levels of governments. They manipulate stock, bond, currency, precious metals, and agricultural/commodity markets, transferring wealth, arranging promotions for favored associates, and merging the resources of huge, multinational, industrial conglomerations.

For example, in the early 1990s, France's Lord Rothschild joined forces with a Wall Street investment banker, the Australian-born billionaire James D. Wolfensohn, creating an $18 billion dollar consortium. Though a huge sum, it is, however, only a tiny portion of the wealth available to men like Rothschild and Wolfensohn. To oversee this particular enterprise, the two financiers engaged the services of American Paul Volcker, former chairman of the United States' central bank, the Federal Reserve. The choice of Volcker to become the CEO for James D. Wolfensohn, Inc., demonstrates how the influence of the Rothschild name causes ripples everywhere in the world, including the Federal Reserve banking system of the United States of America.

Significantly, shortly before this joint, transnational venture, Mr. Volcker had been sent over to Moscow to serve as banking advisor to Russia in the setting up of that country's equivalent of the Federal Reserve. We may properly assume that Volcker supervised the transfer and merger of Russia's financial institutions in accordance with instructions from the Illuminati's International Monetary Fund (IMF) and its premier lending institution, the *World Bank,* connected with the United Nations.[2]

But wait, the story's not over. In mid-1995, it was announced that James D. Wolfensohn had been nominated by his comrade, U.S. President Bill Clinton, to head this same World Bank. Dutifully, Mr. Wolfensohn was confirmed for this post by the internationalists, and so a Rothschild puppet is now President of the World Bank.[3]

Previously, this institution—a key part of the Illuminati's

Big names team up for merger windfall

Tim Castle

JAMES WOLFENSOHN and Lord Rothschild,.two internationally known financiers, have come together to establish a corporate finance business to tap what they hope will be a coming wave of European mergers and takeovers.

The firm, to be called J Rothschild, Wolfensohn & Company, will be London-based, but is looking to continental Europe to find its chief executive, and plans to open an office in Frankfurt. Its chairman will be Paul Volker, the former head of the US Federal Reserve Board, who also heads Mr Wolfensohn's New York firm.

James Wolfensohn, 58, born in Australia but a US citizen since 1980, ran corporate finance at Salomon Brothers before setting up his own merchant banking boutique in New York.

Since then, James D Wolfensohn Inc has attracted a number of blue-chip clients, including Daimler-Benz, American Express and Dupont. It has also been working with the Treuhand, the German body in charge of privatising former East German enterprises.

Recent deals include Daimler-Benz's $570 million purchase last year of 34 per cent of French software house Cap Gemini Sogeti.

Lord Rothschild, 55, had his most recent public brush with a corporate takeover in 1989 when he joined with Sir James Goldsmith in the failed £13 billion bid for British tobacco and insurance group BAT Industries.

Rothschild: Euro venture

Since he left the family bank NM Rothschild in 1980, he has played a behind-the-scenes role in a number of companies through shareholdings built up by his investment trusts.

Recently he has been busy through his finance house St James Place Capital, as a major shareholder in the troubled advertising group Saatchi & Saatchi, as well as advising on privatisations in Czechoslovakia.

The two financiers have known each other for many years.

Although they have worked together on a number of private deals, the new venture is the first time they have been publicly in business together.

The new firm will, in effect, be an extension of Mr Wolfensohn's New York investment boutique.

"If after three to five years we have 15 to 20 major clients in Europe that would be a very good result for us," said Mr Wolfensohn.

Its strategy will be to build up a number of long-term corporate relationships, earning its money through retainers, with additional fees for specific projects.

*This article in **The European** (March 5-11, 1992) details a Lord J. Rothschild venture with Wall Street billionaire James D. Wolfensohn. Lord Rothschild is of the British Rothschilds, but this clan is international in scope. Wolfensohn is currently President of the World Bank, effective 1995. While he's temporarily doing the Illuminati's bidding in that key position, Paul Volcker, former Chairman of the Federal Reserve Board, is managing the store at home—as CEO of James Wolfensohn, Inc., merchant banking firm in New York City.*

worldwide financial apparatus—had been headed by Robert Strange McNamara. And to make my point about sordid, never-ending, spider web connections, let it be noted that before his tenure at the World Bank, McNamara was America's Secretary of Defense under Presidents Kennedy and Johnson. Oh! yes—Mr. McNamara also just happens to be a member of the Council on Foreign Relations, the Trilateral Commission, the Lucis Trust, and the Bilderbergers: Illuminati groups all.[4]

Moneybag Revolutionaries

Almost every "mass movement" is begun at the instigation of the *Inner Circle,* though the liars and collaborators of the media and press depict all events and movements as spontaneous and incidental. Artificial "crises" spring up almost overnight and immediately become the focus of attention by the politicians, the bureaucrats, the media, and the social engineers.

In recent years we have witnessed movement after movement and crisis after crisis—all preplanned and carried out exactly on schedule. When the men of the *Inner Circle* give the word, millions of dollars suddenly are made available, going swiftly into the coffers of environmental crazies, feminist weirdos, occultic priests and Eastern gurus, socialist schemers, healthcare system framers, and virus-inventing laboratories. Funding, media promotion, scholarly assistance, and business acumen have also been showered on liberal and conservative "think tanks;" religious left and religious right organizations; churches and ministries; radical neo-Nazi cells; homosexual lobbying and activist networks; civil rights organizations and gun control groups.

Massive amounts of money have also been allotted to one-world and globalist groups, foundations, and organizations such as World Federalists, World Goodwill, and the United Nations and its agencies, plus the Masonic orders and the many secret societies.

Particular attention has been paid to making sure that Illuminati front groups have the money and resources necessary, not just to influence, but to *overwhelmingly control* the political flow and economic process of the nations. The top leadership of the United States government and its higher-level bureaucracies and agencies is staffed almost exclusively by committees and executive managers of the New York-based Council on Foreign Relations.

Commerce and trade between the three, most powerful, regional groupings of nation-states—America, Asia, and Europe—is arranged behind closed doors during executive sessions of the Trilateral Commission and the Bilderbergers. Meanwhile, policy, administrative, and financial decisions affecting the lives and fortunes of literally billions of global citizens are made at the World Economic Forum, an annual affair of the insiders conducted in Davos, Switzerland.[5]

Illuminati bigwigs also meet regularly at the Bohemian Grove in San Francisco, where paganistic ceremonies are interspersed with frenetic homosexual activity, political speeches, and economic deal-making.[6]

Reward and Punishment

Much of the world's business affairs are conducted at lower levels by underlings and puppets. However, these men and women follow closely the guidelines *set in advance* by the men of the *Inner Circle*. Indeed, bureaucrats and corporate officials deviate from the prescribed format and agenda only at deep peril and risk to their own political careers and personal fortunes.

The performances of their subordinates are reviewed periodically. Analyses and reports go to the *Inner Circle,* and changes are often made in government and finance according to the results. An associate like Margaret Thatcher who fails, say, to tow the line in promoting the proposed European Union to native Brits is removed from her high position as England's Prime Minister while a servant such as Bill Clinton, who succeeds in slam-dunking *Inner Circle* projects such as NAFTA and GATT through a balky U.S. Congress, is generously praised and rewarded.

If deemed essential, an unworthy, disloyal, or incompetent servant is dealt with in a most convincing fashion. President Richard Nixon quickly fell from power and was disgraced because his two, top lieutenants, Bob Haldeman and John Erchlichman, failed to bow down and kiss the rings of the Illuminati insiders.[7] The Illuminati's mouthpiece liberal press, especially the *New York Times,* did the dirty work in ousting Nixon from office while associates in Congress wielded the axe.

President Ronald Reagan, on the other hand, went smoothly along with the elitist's plans, made no fuss, did exactly what he was told, and survived two full terms—in style.

The fate of President George Bush was sealed on October 16, 1992, when the *New York Times,* an establishment-owned press, carried a full-page interview with David Rockefeller, Jr., the rising titan of the Rockefeller bloodline. In that interview, Illuminatus David Rockefeller strongly endorsed Bush's Democrat Party opponent, Arkansas Governor Bill Clinton, for the office of president.[8] The incumbent president knew the jig was up, that the *Inner Circle* had decided to elevate a younger, equally as faithful, servant to the presidency to replace a tiring and older patrician, George Herbert Walker Bush.

In the following weeks prior to the November national election, bewildered pundits noted that Bush ran a lackluster political campaign. He barely put forth a lame effort. During one presidential debate, a downcast George Bush nervously looked at his wristwatch, as if to say, "What am I doing here wasting my time?"

George Bush, nevertheless, has served the *Inner Circle* faithfully his entire life and continues to do so. As I chronicle and document in my book, *Dark Majesty,* after graduating from Yale University in 1948 as a "Bonesman" (Order of Skull & Bones, Chapter 322, Yale University), Bush launched out on his CIA adventure. He was indirectly involved in the JFK assassination as a CIA case officer stationed out of Dallas, Texas.[9]

After a brief stint in the U.S. Congress as a Republican from Houston, Texas, during which he introduced a bill to create and merge the U.S.A. into a United Nations world government, George Bush went on to serve the *Inner Circle* as Director of the CIA, Vice President of the United States, and, finally, as President.

Unquestionably, Bush's legendary acts in pursuing the Persian Gulf War, experimenting on our troops with deadly viruses and toxins, co-sponsoring and forging a New World Order with Russia's Mikhail Gorbachev, and introducing China's aging, Red Communist elite to the glorious advantages of Illuminati membership, make him an honored, senior servant. Since his retirement, Bush has been generously rewarded. He's received millions of dollars in fees and commissions doing such tasks as speaking at a reception for the Reverend Sun Myung Moon and being a "good will" emissary to Vietnam for major oil companies.[10]

Their Master's Voice: Servants of the Illuminati

I have always been intrigued and amused by the old *RCA Victor* logo which pictured a bewildered dog with its head cocked toward a loudspeaker, listening intently. The logo came with the phrase, "His Master's Voice." How much in common the Illuminati's servants have with the RCA Victor canine! Whatever their master, the *Inner Circle,* says, they always have their head cocked and their ears wide open, not to mention their pocketbooks. In the appendix, I provide the names, nationalities, and positions of a number of the servants of the Illuminati's *Inner Circle.* Also indicated is their membership in Illuminati front groups, such as the Council on Foreign Relations (CFR), the Trilateral Commission (TLC), and the Bilderbergers.

You'll find, for example, President Bill Clinton's name prominently listed. Clinton is an Illuminatus *par excellence,* though, compared to the distinguished ten men of the *Inner Circle,* he is only a lower-level functionary and lackey. Nevertheless, his ruthlessness, demonstrated lack of morals, and devotion to their deity (Lucifer), has earned Clinton membership in such elite groups as the CFR, TLC, and the Bilderbergers.

In 1987, the President, a Senior De Molay (Mason) was chosen by Scottish Rite Freemasonry as the De Molay organization's "International Alumnus of the year." Incidentally, the De Molay, a Masonic youth organization, is named after Jacques de Molay, the Frenchman who once served as Grand Master of the corrupt Knights Templar, a precursor group to today's global Masonic order. In 1314, Jacques de Molay was tried and convicted of blasphemy and treason. Among the accusations against him: that he and his Templars worshipped Baphomet, the satanic, androgynous goat-god of Gnosticism.[11]

De Molay was also found guilty of homosexual perversions and of the blasphemous act of urinating on a crucifix of Christ. What a fitting tribute, then, for Illuminatus Bill Clinton to be honored for his contributions to the De Molay organization![12]

Other servants of the *Inner Circle* of the Illuminati are Vice President Al Gore and former Vice President Dan Quayle. Gore is a Democrat and Quayle a Republican, proving the old adage that, as far as the Illuminati are concerned, "There's not a dime's worth of difference" between the two political parties. Indeed, as we shall see, a key component of the Secret Doctrine of the Illuminati is the chaos theory of "conflict between opposites." The Illuminati are masters at creating their own, fake opposition. When *real* opposition arises, the Illuminati move swiftly to preempt or co-opt the opposition forces, using money or political influence as a leverage.

In the case of Al Gore, the man from Tennessee was a long-time beneficiary of the late multimillionaire and industrialist, Armand Hammer. Hammer pumped big bucks into the lustful political ambitions of, first, former U.S. Senator Albert Gore, Sr., and now his son, Vice President Al Gore, Jr. The Gores are proprietary property of the Illuminati's *Inner Circle*.[13]

Dan Quayle, too, is an Illuminati creation. Not smart enough or sufficiently talented to make it on his own, Mr. Quayle's solid Masonic and Rockefeller connections did the trick. In 1990, Quayle was privileged to join the elite at a Bilderberger gala in Long Island, New York.[14] In 1995, Dan

Quayle acknowledged and thanked Illuminatus Laurance Rockefeller for his "contributions" to Quayle's success. (You can find a rather quaint, but significant, acknowledgement by Quayle of Laurance Rockefeller's contributions in Quayle's ghostwritten autobiography, *Standing Firm,* which perhaps should have been titled, *Standing Firm With My Monied Friends, the Rockefellers.*[15]

Many servants are found in the religious realm, as well. The so-called Religious Right is heavily funded by Illuminati sources. Many of America's most famous "conservative" Christian evangelists, as well as New Age gurus, occult leaders, and the liberal churchmen of the World Council of Churches and the National Council of Churches, are "blessed" with money and other material benefits, courtesy of the Illuminati's *Inner Circle.*[16]

A Fascist World Order

The corporate world is especially seeded with Illuminati puppets and beneficiaries. The ranks of such groups as the Bohemian Grove, the Bilderbergers, the Council on Foreign Relations, the Skull and Bones Society, and the Trilateral Commission are swollen with the names of corporate chairmen, presidents, and CEOs. Among the major executives holding membership in one or more of these elite organizations are the heads of the following multinational corporations:

Xerox
General Electric
General Motors
Prudential Insurance
Allied Chemical
Standard Oil of California
Texaco
Mobil Oil
Atlantic Richfield Oil
ITT
AT&T

Nations Bank
IBM
Pepsico
Fiat
First City Bank Corp
Bechtel
Banque de France
Siemens
John Wiley & Sons
Goldman, Sachs & Co.
Shell Petroleum
Seagrams Distilling
Mellon Bank
Chrysler Motors
NBC-TV
CBS-TV
ABC-TV
Exxon
Southern California Edison
Ryder Systems
American Express
Bank of America
Time-Warner
Times Mirror Co.
John Hancock Mutual
Nynex Corp.
Morgan Stanley Group (Bank)
Boeing Aircraft
Levi Strauss
Quaker Oats

We could go on and on listing the men who have treacherously sold their country down the river by their affiliation with and support for the globalist goals of the Illuminati, as evidenced by their membership in its branch organizations. This corrupted, interwoven, and incestuous relationship between the federal government and the corporate community—both under control of Illuminati bigwigs—is *prima facie* proof that America has become a Fascist nation. Move over

Mussolini and Hitler, here we come!

While Mussolini and Hitler were able to establish authority in only a dozen or so conquered nations in Europe and Africa, the empire of the Illuminati spans the seven continents of the globe. The men of the *Inner Circle* intend to keep it that way and are continually tightening their already iron-like grip on the world's commercial, corporate, and financial resources. To accomplish their aim of dictatorial control, they are setting up international agencies empowered with vast regulatory authority that cuts across national lines.

The World Trade Organization is Formed

One recent example is the formation of the World Trade Organization (WTO), headquartered in Geneva, Switzerland. A banker allied with the *Inner Circle,* Ireland's Peter D. Sutherland, former chairman of Allied Irish Bank, was appointed as director general of GATT (General Agreement on Tariffs and Taxes) to oversee the organizing of the WTO. After the onerous GATT bill was crammed down the throats of U.S. citizens—thanks to Illuminati servants Clinton, Dole, and Gingrich—the *Inner Circle* chose an Italian banker and politician, the suave Renato Ruggiero, to head the WTO. America's financial sovereignty now ominously lies in the hands of an Italian conspirator working for ten of the most wicked men on Planet Earth: the men of the Illuminati's *Inner Circle.*[17]

Significantly, Peter D. Sutherland and Renato Ruggiero, like their American counterpart, Bill Clinton, are members of the Bilderbergers, a group of 125 influential money men, corporate chieftains, and allied politicians tied to Illuminati interests.

Illuminati Influence in Higher Education

It is not only the corporate overlords who are intently listening to "Their Master's Voice." Illuminati influence reigns supreme on university campuses. For example, at the University of Oklahoma, former U.S. Senator David Boren serves as President. In the Senate, Boren was a socialist-oriented Democrat. He also is a patriarch of the Order of Skull & Bones and a member of the traitorous CFR. Meanwhile, we find that Tomas Able, President of California State University is CFR; so is Bernard Warren, President of City University of New York; and so are the heads of such distinguished institutions as Columbia, Cornell, Fordham, Georgetown, Duke, Harvard, M.I.T., Michigan, and Texas.

The Illuminati's Green Team

Environmental groups seem to have armies of "green volunteers." But dig deep, as one researcher did, and you discover the pervasive Illuminati influence lurking beneath the surface. Indeed, the environmental movement was founded, organized, and is now run by the *Inner Circle* of the Illuminati. No wonder such environmental heavies as Kathy Fuller, President of the *World Wildlife Fund,* is a member of the Council on Foreign Relations. Maurice Strong, Chairman of the *United Nations Environmental Programme,* is a member of the World Economic Forum, an Illuminati financial group which meets

Maurice Strong, head of the United Nations Environmental Programme, helped found the Illuminati's World Conservation Bank.

once each year in the tiny resort community of Davos, Switzerland, to help decide the world's financial future.

The seedy realm of global banking and finance and the bizarre campaign to "save our Mother Earth" join hands in one of Maurice Strong's creations, the *World Conservation Bank*. This Illuminati entity was co-founded in the late 1980s by Strong, Baron Edmund de Rothschild, James Baker (Bush's Secretary of State), and David Rockefeller, Sr. Currently, Clinton's Secretary of Interior, Bruce Babbitt, is working under the control of this World Conservation Bank. Its purpose is to force poor and impoverished Asian, African, South and Central American countries strapped by debt to relinquish title to millions of acres of valuable and prime, virgin lands to the bankers. In exchange, their huge loan balances—at exorbitant interest rates—are "forgiven."

The objective of this Fascist project is to transfer virtually all the world's remaining lands to the control of the Illuminati through its bogus World Conservation Bank. Thus, global-wide production of oil, precious metals, diamonds, timber and other resources can be restricted, keeping prices at artificial highs. Since the Rothschilds, Rockefellers, and other dynasties now own the giant, multinational corporations which produce oil, timber, and other valuable commodities, this successful scam to lock up all remaining lands via the World Conservation Bank means trillions of dollars in future profits for the Illuminati.[18]

Media Flunkies

Want to know why the media as a whole are so vehemently anti-America First, pro-Marxist and unpatriotic? You need look no further than the membership rolls of the Illuminati front groups for an "illuminating" explanation. Richard Smith, Editor-in-chief and President of *Newsweek*, is CFR; so are the brass at *US News & World Report, Time, Vanity Fair, Atlantic Monthly, The New Yorker*, and most other top magazines.

To insure that the conservative side of publishing is also

Barbara Walters, co-host of ABC-TV's ***20/20,*** *with an associate at the General Luncheon of the Council on Foreign Relations, in 1990.*

controlled, the CFR claims the heads of such magazines as *American Spectator, Forbes, Financial World, and Readers Digest.* William F. Buckley, infamous publisher of the *National Review,* is a fake conservative who has served the *Inner Circle* well as a CIA operative. Buckley is also currently a member of the CFR.

In the newspaper field, our eyes roll when we discover the fix is in there, too. The publishers of the *New York Times, Los Angeles Times, Minneapolis Star-Tribune, Wall Street Journal,* and the *Washington Post* are all members of the CFR. Many of these newspaper publishing goliaths are Trilateralists and Bilderbergers to boot.

In the TV world, we are perhaps not surprised to find that its top executives are also devoted members of Illuminati organizations. Even the news anchors at CBS, NBC, ABC, CNN, and PBS are initiated as "token members" of the CFR, the Trilateral Commission and other notorious groups. *Prime Time's* Diane Sawyer is CFR, so is *20/20* co-host Barbara Walters. Evening news anchors Dan Rather *(CBS),*

Tom Brokaw *(NBC)*, and Peter Jennings *(ABC)* are CFR stooges, along with *60 Minutes*' Ed Bradley and *ABC News*' John Scali. And we wonder why our TV news programs are packed with so much socialist, politically correct, and unAmerican garbage!

The Greed Factor

Why would legions of bankers, businessmen, educators, and media executives so enthusiastically join hands with these elite representatives of the devil, and so readily agree to subvert democracy and undermine American sovereignty? I believe the answer can only be *greed.*

Greedy men can never have enough: The Bible states that, "the love of money is the root of all evil." The ten, so-called "Wise Men" of the Illuminati are fabulously rich. They own the planet's gigantic industries and financial combines and hold title to untold millions of acres of fertile lands and natural resources. Still, they want more...and more. How profound, therefore, is this statement from God's Word, found in Proverbs 27:20: "Hell and destruction are never full; so the eyes of man are never satisfied."

TWO

Beyond Secret Societies: The Supermen of the Illuminati

For there is nothing covered, that shall not be revealed; neither hid, that shall not be known. Therefore whatsoever ye have spoken in darkness shall be heard in the light; and that which ye have spoken in the ear in closets shall be proclaimed upon the housetops.

—*Luke 12:2-3*

I have heard much of the nefarious and dangerous plan and doctrines of the Illuminati. It was not my intention to doubt that the doctrines of the Illuminati and the principles of Jacobinism had not spread in the United States. On the contrary, no one is more satisfied of this fact than I am.

—George Washington
The Writings of George Washington

There *is* a "hidden brotherhood," writes Richard Smoley, editor of *Gnosis,* the slick, philosophical magazine published by the Lumen Foundation, headquartered in San Francisco. "It consists of wise, almost omniscient figures who work in secret to further the evolution of humankind." It is beyond secret societies, he adds, though he admits, "Secret Societies do exist."

But for Smoley and others active in promoting the occult

worldview, "the brotherhood can't be equated with any one organization. It is indeed the Temple of the Holy Spirit."

"Its members," he claims, "include adepts with superhuman powers." Moreover, they are, adds Smoley, possessors of a religious "truth beyond all creeds...a truth furnishing its members with a common life that undercuts any differences in belief."[1]

Smoley does not, in his *Gnosis* article, identify this "hidden brotherhood" as the Illuminati nor does he allude to The Plan of an illumined elite to establish and preside over a World Empire. Often, men like Richard Smoley possess a measure of occult knowledge but, ultimately, are blinded to the heinous truth of Lucifer and his Illuminati world conspiracy. They cannot know because, having rejected God, they dwell in darkness.

Yet, if we have pure hearts before God, we can know the facts about the Brotherhood and Order of the Illuminati. In Proverbs 25:2 we find this intriguing passage: *"It is the glory of God to conceal a thing: but the honour of kings is to search out a matter."* In Daniel 12:10, we read that in the last days the wicked will suffer confusion and blindness, but *"the wise shall understand."* With God's promises, then, kept secure in our hearts, we dig into the dungeons of mystery to uncover the dark secrets of the Illuminati conspiracy.

Circle of Intrigue proves beyond controversy that there is, in fact, a "hidden brotherhood." Even more frightening is the hellish leadership and grotesque goals of this secretive, covert elite. They are the Illuminati, diabolical men who are engaged at this very moment in operating a world conspiracy of breathtaking dimensions. To rephrase Lincoln, it is a conspiracy of the few, by the few, and for the few.

Who do we mean when we cryptically refer to "the few?" By this I mean a tight-knit cabal of spiritually wicked, totally reprobate men bound together by blood and money in a sordid, occult covenant against the Most High God. These are men devoid of nationalist pride. Citizens of the Earth, their allegiance is pledged to their hidden masters. Thus, they secretly despise the symbols of patriotism and cloak themselves in such symbols only when necessary to deceive.

The Ultimate Goal of the Illuminati

What is the ultimate goal of the Illuminati? It is not just World Government, though they do seek to consolidate and exert all political power. Moreover, their true goal is not just more and more money, though they do possess an inordinate, virtually insatiable and mad desire to acquire and spend great wealth. The true, ultimate goal of these despicable men is to overthrow the incomparable and majestic One who sits on the throne of the universe: Jesus Christ, Lord of lords and King of kings. Make no mistake, this is a colossal and epic spiritual rebellion—a foul, filthy and thoroughly abominable attempt—doomed to failure—to defeat the very powers of Heaven and to install on the emerald throne the most evil personage ever created by the hands of God: Lucifer, the great apostate and infamous fallen star.

What mysterious ambition and curious set of desires is it that drives, energizes, and enervates the miserable men of the Illuminati to join hands and cast their lots with Baphomet, the grotesque horned and false god also known as Lucifer? How extraordinary, how strange it is to even imagine the depths of blackness which haunt the scarred souls of these awful men. What possible inducement and enchantment could make them do such a thing—rebel against the very God who created them and who loves them so much He gave His Son on the cross for their sins, and indeed the sins of the whole world?

The Quest for Power

Is it *money,* or perhaps *power,* which so captivates the minds of the Illuminati? It is an unassailable fact that the *Inner Circle* of the "Illumined Ones" possess fabulous, untold wealth. Riches, in turn, translate into power, and it was Britain's sage Lord Acton who, in 1888, wisely remarked that, "Power corrupts and absolute power corrupts absolutely."

The Illuminati bloodlines have incredible influence over a wide array of life, whether it be cultural, political, financial, industrial, religious, or educational. Taking a cursory look at just one, satanic family, the Rockefellers, gives us a glimpse of the mind-boggling extent of Illuminati control:

> The Rockefeller's Chase Manhattan bank has 25 directors and these directors in turn interlock with 100 major industrial corporations, banks, utilities, and insurance companies.[2]

The Rockefeller dynasty has also for decades controlled entire Christian denominations and many universities and colleges through foundations, including the Twentieth Century Fund, the Rockefeller Foundation, and others.

Bill Moyers, the former White House advisor to President Lyndon Johnson whose Public Broadcasting System (PBS) television program makes him a popular guru to millions of New Agers and occultists, says that "Rockefeller sits at the hub of a vast network of financiers, industrialists and politicians whose reach encircles the globe."[3]

There can be no doubt that Illuminati bloodlines, including those of such family names as Astor, Bundy, Dupont, Kennedy, Onassis, Rothschild, Rockefeller, Lord, Habsburg, Mellon, Oppenheimer, Sassoon, and Sinclair possess immense wealth and power. Has Satan given them this great treasure and power because of their loyalty and service to him? This appears to be the case for they are the joint overseers of a vast, global empire encompassing lands, diamonds and gems, precious metals, oil, timber, and gaudy estates. Their combine corporate holdings and stock shares are staggering, and their liquid cash reserves retained in banks in financial centers of New York City, London, Frankfurt, and Tokyo beggar the imagination.

A Power Over Power

Jacques Attali, an insider who has faithfully served them for decades in a variety of high-level financial positions, including the presidency of the European branch of the World

Bank, has revealed in a book—authored no doubt at *their* urging—the consummate power of these super rich men of the Illuminati.

They are, Attali confides, "linked together in a close-knit, almost dynastic network." Moreover, he says that they "constitute a parallel aristocracy planted within the heart of every regime" in the world. They are nothing less than an "elite both of wealth and culture," organized into an "austere Order with its own, implacable moral and ferocious rituals."[4]

Confirming my own in-depth research on the family bloodlines which comprise this planetary network of power and wealth, Attali writes of this aristocratic network of dynasties: "The Name is its primary riches and the Land its ultimate vanity."[5]

These facets, then, according to Attali, lend to the Illuminati insiders their fearsome power: (1) their Name; (2) their aristocratic and clannish behavior; (3) their organizing of themselves into a global Order; (4) their unique "moral code;" and (5) their "ferocious rituals."

Taken together, says Attali, these traits make the Illuminati the lords of the Earth. Though unelected, nevertheless, they preside and reign over mere elected politicians and administrators who perform the mundane, everyday tasks of government and society. In effect, Attali reports, these lords of the Earth constitute a *"Power Over Power."*[6]

The Three Circles of Power and Intrigue

But, again, it must be noted that the preeminence of the Illuminati is not due to their own Power, awesome as it is, but because they are infused and directed by a greater, occult Power which is established over them. Thus, we have an interlinking system of *three circles*. In the first circle, there is Satan, or Lucifer, and his demon spirits who comprise a spiritual hierarchy. This is the meaning of the symbolic "point of light" inside the Circle of Intrigue.

Next, just outside the Luciferian point of light, we discover an exclusive and tight-knit *Inner Circle,* made up of a handful of elite and usually unseen men who actually rule the planet. Finally, there is the "outer circle," comprised first of illumined bloodlines which are not of the first rank and then, following them, are the several thousand servants who willingly bow down and kneel before their human masters in order to gain material riches. They, too, wield a measure of influence and authority over the masses. In this latter category we find a great number of presidents, prime ministers, ambassadors, corporate chieftains, ecclesiastical potentiates, and leaders of global organizations.

Candidates and Elections are Controlled

The majority of citizens know little or nothing about The Plan of the Illuminati. In democratic nations the gullible masses are led to believe that their votes decide elections, that they choose their own leaders. What nonsense! These deluded men and women are painfully oblivious to the horrible truth: that unless a man has the endorsement of the masters who rule behind the scenes, he has no chance whatsoever of winning high office. And unless a politician covertly promises to support the goals of the Illumined Ones—which include the subversion of Christian morality, and the promotion of environmentalism, globalism, and the gradual end of American sovereignty—he or she will *never* be elected.

The rulers guarantee the outcome of elections by infusion of millions of dollars into the campaigns of their favored candidates, by their iron-fisted control of both the media and political parties, by endorsements of candidates by major organizations which they control; and, if necessary, by vote scams and outright electoral fraud.

Moreover, in the U.S.A., candidates for high offices are carefully screened and chosen by Illuminati political organizations, such as the Council on Foreign Relations, the Trilateral Commission, Freemasonry, the Bilderbergers, and the Bohemian Grove. We have only to consider the Illuminati-approved credentials of our most recent U.S. Presidents to illustrate this point. When elected, President Jimmy Carter was a Mason and also a member of the CFR and Trilateral Commission. President Ronald Reagan was at first a Bohemian. Later in his presidency, Reagan was made a 33° Mason "at sight."[7] Upon assuming the presidency, George Bush was a patriarch of the Order of Skull & Bones (a Black Lodge of Freemasonry), a former director of the CFR, and a member emeritus of the Trilateral Commission.[8] Meanwhile, President Bill Clinton is a Bilderberger, a Senior DeMolay (Freemason), and a member of both the CFR and the Trilateral Commission.[9]

Here are the Illuminati affiliations of several other influential politicians in contemporary America. Not surprisingly, each of these men have been prominently mentioned as potential candidates for the White House:

House Speaker, Newt Gingrich: 33° Mason; member of CFR and World Future Society.

Former Chairman of the Joint Chiefs of Staff, Colin Powell: Prince Hall Mason; member of CFR.

Senate Majority Leader, Robert Dole: 33° Mason.

Civil Rights Leader, Jesse Jackson: Prince Hall Mason; member of CFR.

The common thread among these men is obvious. First, they are Masons, and second, they are members of the Council on Foreign Relations. Both groups, Masonry and the CFR, promote globalism and a hidden, international brotherhood. Both are opposed to traditional, biblical Christianity. *No one can be elected as President of the United States who does not espouse these unholy and thoroughly unAmerican views.*

The Illuminati use men like Clinton, Gingrich, Dole, and Powell—as well as statesmen like Henry Kissinger, Zbigniew Brzezinski and Warren Christopher—as cannon fodder for their revolutionary objectives. They make such men temporary stars and then they cast them into obscurity, as it suits their purpose. But rarely do the "servants" break into the *Inner Circle.* Indeed, only ten men are admitted to the prestigious

Inner Circle, though many others operate on its fringes and, in so doing, wield huge powers and influence on world affairs.

The men of the *Inner Circle* are the masters; those below them on the pyramidal hierarchy are the servers. In his book *Ancient Mystic Rites,* C.W. Leadbeater, 33°, refers to this exalted circle of power as the "Council of Emperors." He notes that this term applied to a group of "men of noble birth and high culture" who, under the personal direction of Satan himself, first formulated the Rite of Perfection for the masonic fraternity.[10]

According to Leadbeater, in 1761 the Council of Emperors appointed as their Grand Inspector one Stephen Morin. Morin was charged with bringing to America the occultic rites which, later, in the 19th century, were adopted in their fullest, black skullduggery by Sovereign Grand Commander Albert Pike and the Mother Supreme Council of the World, now headquartered in Washington, D.C.

In Bondage to Lucifer

The money which they possess and the power which they wield supply the greed which fuels their existence. But Lucifer has an even greater enticement in his arsenal of weaponry which he has used to bring the men of the Illuminati into total bondage to him. His most effective, and most seductive, weapon by far is his arousal in these men of a towering and arrogant, frighteningly haughty sense of *false pride.*

There have been some men who, possessing money and power, have nevertheless escaped the clutches of the Evil One. But few men who combine money and power with a haughty and arrogant false pride can escape his seductive wiles. Did our Lord have in mind the "Kings" of the *Inner Circle* when he inspired these words in Proverbs:

> It is an abomination to kings to commit wickedness: for the throne is established by righteousness. Pride goeth before destruction, and an haughty spirit before a fall. (Proverbs 16:12, 18)

What method or tactic does Lucifer employ to arouse in these men such a heightened sense of false pride? He imparts to them an outrageous lie. The Adversary whispers in their itching ears: "Ye are gods!"

"You are divine beings," he tells them, and they listen with glee and an escalating mood of excitement. Satan further explains to these men that they are the keepers of a great, occult Secret Doctrine.

"This is the *gnosis,* or hidden knowledge," he says, "of which the profane and infantile masses know nothing. It is based on ancient wisdom—which has been preserved for eons by my legions of dark angels and by the Brotherhood. Now it is yours."

"You are giants of intellect," he soothingly assures them, "men of higher consciousness. You are the illustrious and all-powerful *New Man.* It is your destiny to rule the world and to be lords over the lower races."

The late Manly P. Hall, 33°, a man whom the *Scottish Rite Journal,* in an obituary, called "the 20th century's greatest Masonic scholar and philosopher,"[11] spoke of this Secret Doctrine and touted the superior intellect of the illumined god-man race in his eye-opening volume, *The Phoenix.* In the Secret Doctrine, says Hall, "the ageless wisdom is revealed...to those who have eyes to see." Continuing, he writes that the Secret Doctrine is an ancient but neverending story: "Out of the ashes of dead beliefs rises the deathless *Phoenix.*"[12]

The ignorant and inferior masses, Hall cynically writes, cannot fathom the true meaning and goals of The Secret Doctrine:

> No one unable to understand the elements of *The Secret Doctrine* can expect to achieve the heights to which it beckons...spiritual truths can never be brought "down" to the level of the unenlightened masses.[13]

According to Manly P. Hall, only the initiate possessing the potential to become divine can ever hope to master the mysteries incorporated in the gnostic teachings of the Secret Doctrine:

> Only through the release of his own potential divinity does the initiate become qualified to comprehend the Great Arcanum...*The Secret Doctrine* affirms the existence of a primitive knowledge perpetuated from age to age and race to race by institutions of illumined thinkers...In *The Secret Doctrine* the sanctuaries of the ancient Mysteries are made to give up many of their most precious secrets.[14]

What Hall is referring to is the strange encyclopedia of occult philosophy put together by the Russian mystic and co-Mason Helena P. Blavatsky in the late 19th century, a book which she entitled *The Secret Doctrine.*[15] Mrs. Blavatsky claimed that the contents of the book were given to her by certain "masters" or "unknown superiors."[16]

In many respects, Blavatsky's *The Secret Doctrine* is comparable to Albert Pike's voluminous *Morals and Dogma,* often called the "bible" of Freemasonry. Both books purport to be compendia of mysterious truths which lead men into a higher state of gnosis (knowledge). Through the diligent search and attainment of *gnosis,* as advocated by *The Secret Doctrine* and *Morals and Dogma,* it is claimed that the initiate of higher consciousness is transformed into deity.

The god-men thus created are said to be capable of magical powers and superior intellect. Such men, it is believed, once having been enlightened and illuminated, are, in Nietsche's words, *Supermen:* Men who are beyond good and evil.

Such men are also favored by their Deity (Lucifer) to become partakers of the Higher Mysteries and to see with the "eye of intuition." They are chosen to become One with that omniscient Supreme Being who possesses the omnipresent and omnisearching *All Seeing Eye.*

Hitler and the All Seeing Eye

Adolf Hitler fancied himself one of these New Men. He read the occult classic volume, *The Secret Doctrine,* by Blavatsky, in its entirety at least four times and kept it on a stand beside his bed.[17]

> "Hitler was always talking about this Cyclops Eye," says Rauschning, who several times heard Hitler's views about the coming Superman. "Some men can already activate their pineal glands to give a limited vision into the secrets of time," Hitler told him, obviously referring to his own experiences of former reincarnations...
>
> By summing up everything which Hitler had to say about the coming Superman, a fantastic picture emerges. The New Man would have an intrepid countenance, giant stature, glorious physique, and superhuman strength. His intuitive powers would mightily transcend mere intellectual thinking...
>
> This Superman, who would arise in our midst in such a short time, would manifest magical faculties including magical powers of speech which all lesser mortals would be powerless to disobey. All spirits between heaven and earth would obey his commands. Even the weather and the chemical combinations of the elements would be subject.
>
> Such Supermen would become the elite of the earth, the Lords of all they surveyed. Nothing would be hidden from their spirit-risen and no power on earth would prevail against them. "They will be the Sons of the Gods," said Hitler.
>
> And the key to this staggering potential in man? It would be realized through the nature and quality of the blood![18]

The Power is in the Blood

To Hitler, the secret of the *blood* was the Holy Grail. The blood was the key to the making of the New Man. Pure blood contained the supernatural power of the race destined to control and rule the world. Hitler's body, we are told, was burned and only the ashes remain. But then we recall the demonic-inspired words of Manly P. Hall. In 1960, he described the Illumined Ones who know the Secret Doctrine as akin to a fiery red Phoenix bird rising up out of the hot ashes of chaos.[19] Red, of course, is the color of blood, and it is the scarlet color worn by the whore of Babylon. The color red was also chosen by the Illuminati to symbolize Communism.

Hitler believed the key to world conquest was in the blood. And today, having traced, researched and documented the secret occult oligarchies which rule the world, I must confess that, though he exercised a twisted kind of occult logic, Hitler was right. *The dark power of the Illuminati is in the blood.* The Illuminati are generational bloodlines which have over, the centuries, acquired monopoly power over most of the wealth and commerce of planet Earth.

The False Messiah to Come

Hitler was a deceiver; yet, he himself was a hapless and tragic victim of deceit. It was the Illuminati who first spawned Adolf Hitler and fired his vain imagination with Blavatsky's *The Secret Doctrine.* He was a failed experiment, the case of a power-mad disciple who turned against his masters and sought glory on his own terms.

My study of the history and lineage of the Illuminati proves that Hitler was not the first disciple who was inspired by their blood-lust philosophy to establish and reign over a Luciferian World Order. Napoleon, Frederick the Great, Charlesmagne, Wilhelm II, Lenin, Stalin, and Mao—all these men and many others have sought to become man's global messiah.

A fascinating aside of American history is that, during his presidency, George Washington was confronted with the subversion of the United States by the Illuminati's Jacobin secret agents. This led the President, at one point, to demand that the government of France recall its ambassador to the U.S.A. because of his treacherous recruitment activities on behalf of Europe's Illuminati.[20] In 1798, George Washington wrote:

> It was not my intention to doubt that the doctrine of the Illuminati and the principles of Jacobinism had not spread in the United States. On the contrary, no one is more satisfied of this fact than I am.[21]

Ironically, Washington was himself a Mason. Apparently, his fierce opposition to the schemes of the Illuminati was yet another case of the employment by satanic agents of the Hegelian dialectic, the conflict of opposites, a strategy we will discuss in some detail in later chapters.

Today, some 200 years after George Washington admitted the existence in America of the notorious Illuminati, the *Inner Circle* of this Luciferian elite are on the threshold of introducing to the world yet another false messiah. He will take up where Hitler left off, and shall "make war with the saints" (Revelation 13). Tragically, he and the men who elevate him to the throne of world power will be consumed in their deceit. The false pride of the Illuminati and their Antichrist shall fail them, their power will vanish, and their legendary wealth shall prove worthless. The Lords of the Earth will fall and never rise again from the ashes. Then, in their anger and fear, they will turn against their hellish master and cry out, "We are but men, we are not gods. You have deceived us. We have lost everything."

If only these men were to study and believe the Holy Bible, they could be saved, for in II Timothy 3:13 we read: "But evil men and seducers shall wax worse and worse, deceiving, and being deceived."

A Flawed and Unworkable Plan

The Illuminati are deceivers, and they, too, are deceived, having foolishly been taken in by the lie of Satan that they are "gods" and, therefore, not accountable to the one, great and majestic God in Heaven. Theirs is a tragic mistake. Future history will record that the Illuminati have formulated a flawed and unworkable Plan. Even if, for a time, they gain the world, the day is soon coming when their names will be exalted no more. The end shall come and their destiny will be fulfilled:

> And he said unto me, It is done. I am Alpha and Omega, the beginning and the end. I will give unto him that is athirst of the fountain of the water of life freely. He that overcometh shall inherit all things; and I will be his God, and he shall be my son. But the fearful, and unbelieving, and the abominable, and murderers, and whoremongers, and sorcerers, and idolaters, and all liars, shall have their part in the lake which burneth with fire and brimstone: which is the second death. (Revelation 21:6-8)

The fate of the Illuminati on Judgment Day will be pitiful. But for now, these wicked men are riding the crest of temporal victory. The *Inner Circle,* the elite unit of ten diabolical men who now guide the destiny of the world, is evidently convinced that their Great Work can be accomplished. It is through their dynasties and their blood that humanity and the planet are now about to enter a dramatic and climatic New Age of misery and despair. Therefore, I believe it imperative that we unmask their activities and cast a glowing beam of light on the men who comprise this *Inner Circle.*

THREE

Blood and Dynasty: A Confidential Look at the Men Who Rule the World

For the love of money is the root of all evil...

—*I Timothy 6:10*

Money is the God of our times, and Rothschild is his prophet.

—Heinrich Heine, in Paris

When Queen Elizabeth came to lunch at Hambros Bank, a surprise was planned for her—a pile of gold, silver, and platinum worth exactly one million pounds. It was three feet high, weighed 5322 pounds, and consisted of 400-ounce and 32-ounce gold bars, sovereigns, Dutch guilders and Persian rials; silver minted in Peking, Broken Hill, Australia, Peru, San Francisco and Bunker Hill; and a few Bank of England pound notes placed on top. The Queen loved it and graciously accepted a tiny, three-ounce gold bar as a souvenir.

—Joseph Wechsberg
The Merchant Bankers

"Blood is destiny!" This is the deeply held ideology which binds the *Inner Circle* of the Illuminati. It is this strange and mysterious doctrine which compels these men to conspire together against humanity and against God. They profoundly believe that their deity—whom they disguise under such arcane name as Abbadon, Jahbulon, and the undefined "Great Architect of the Universe"—has chosen them because of their royal bloodline and divine heritage.

Their destiny, the Illuminati are persuaded, is to reign as "Kings of the Earth" and to dominate their subjects with absolute and unquestioned power and authority.

In his thought-provoking manuscript, "A Little Masonic History Book: The One Dollar Bill," Dean Grace meticulously researched the origins and meanings of the pyramid and all seeing eye on the reverse of the Great Seal of the United States. His startling conclusion is that these symbols on our one dollar bill represent a "deeply laid, conspiratorial sect that hides behind different disguises:"

> Chameleon-like, these conspirators have been known under the different labels of Marxist, Socialist, Communist; also Zionist, Masonic, and Internationalist. They live in places like London, Berlin, Rome, and New York. And they control the United Nations, Wall Street, and Washington, D.C. They finance the weapons industry and help build monuments to unknown soldiers...Membership has descended from generation to generation within the royal families of Great Britain and Europe, the Houses that control International Finance, and the hierarchies of World Judaism and Roman Catholicism.[1]

A Pyramid System of Control

"This elite World Brotherhood," Grace warns, "has most of us ensnared by the tentacles of social control, a system of control that is all-pervasive and that operates at all levels up and down the social-economic pyramid."[2] Grace believes that the men who comprise this secret network of conspiracy have positioned themselves as the elevated capstone of a controlled, global society:

> Society, like the figure of a pyramid, is arranged in layers, lots of poor people at the bottom with progressively fewer

> middle income and still fewer higher income people toward the top. And society, like the pyramid on the top of the one dollar bill, has its elevated capstone, too—an elite World Brotherhood that casts its ever-vigilant eye down on society.[3]

Could Dean Grace be correct? Are we all being watched and micromanaged by a bizarre religious and political sect which has, as its prime objective, the enslavement of all mankind? Is a group of super wealthy, cunningly ingenious men, who can trace their ancestral bloodlines back hundreds of years and consider themselves to be members of a natural aristocracy, masterminding a plot to conquer and control the world?

I believe the answer to both questions is *yes*—we are being watched and micromanaged, and this insidious system of dictatorial control is the work of a small group of men who sit at the apex of a pyramidal hierarchy of evil and deception.

"Some Animals are More Equal"

In *The Secret Doctrine,* the hellish volume which inspired Hitler to such rarified heights of inhumanity and depravity, Helena Blavatsky, the founder of *Theosophy,* concisely states the sick and twisted philosophy which has long guided the thoughts and actions of the Illuminati. She writes:

> Mankind is obviously divided into god-informed men and lower human creatures...The sacred spark is missing in them and it is they who are the...inferior races on the globe...Verily mankind is "of one blood," *but not of the same essence.* We are the hot house...having in us a spark, which in them is latent.[4]

The Secret Doctrine of the Illuminati is perfectly in line, then, with George Orwell's insightful novel, *Animal Farm.* "All animals," said the pigs, "are equal, but some animals are more equal than others!"

True it is, admits the Illuminati, that all men came from one blood, as the Old Testament teaches, but the chemistry of the ancestral blood of the superior race—its "essence" to use Blavatsky's terminology—provides the men through whose veins it flows the "spark" of divinity. They are said to be "god-informed," while all others remain "lower human creatures."

Possessing the spark of divinity, the Illuminati pridefully lay claim to being a superior, enlightened race of Wise Men. Manly P. Hall, 33°, in *The Secret Destiny of America* proclaims that these great and noble men shall lead a subservient and reluctant humanity into a Golden Age:

> Wise Men, the ancients believe, were a separate race, and to be born into this race it was necessary to develop the mind to a state of enlightened intelligence...It is this larger and coming race that will someday inherit the earth...the Golden Age will come again.[5]

The Wise Men, Hall reveals are cooperating with The Plan of the ages, vigorously pushing men ever forward toward the dawning light of a New Age by use of the Hegelian dialectical process—a system of "Universal Motion:"

> There exists in the world today, and has existed for thousands of years, a body of enlightened humans united in what might be termed, an Order of the Quest. It is composed of those whose intellectual and spiritual perceptions have revealed to them that civilization has a secret Destiny—secret, I say, because this high purpose is not realized by the many; the great masses of people still live along without any knowledge whatsoever that they are part of a Universal Motion.[6]

We are further informed by Hall that the ultimate outcome of this perpetual bloodletting and sifting of mankind, this Universal Motion, will be a World Order presided over by a great and extraordinary leader: a king of divine essence, endowed with supernatural powers. Writing in a prophetic framework, Hall glowingly describes this coming Great One:

> This king was descended of a divine race; that is, he belonged to the Order of the Illumined; for those who come to a state of wisdom then belong to a family of heroes—perfected human beings.[7]

Foreordained by God

To a democratic people such as now populate the continent of North America, the notion that there exists in the world men and women "descended of a divine race," belonging to a generational "family of heroes—perfected human beings," seems fantastic, even preposterous. However, having studied these men and their forebearers for some years now and being a student of the Scriptures, I would not entirely discard and scoff at their bold statements. While these men are *by no means divine,* they may well be set aside by God for a very special destiny! My claim is that the Illuminati are, in fact, *ordained by God* to carry out their odious and awful work. Like Judas, the betrayer of Christ, their destiny is foretold in advance. As we read in God's Word:

> For there are certain men crept in unawares, who were before of old ordained to this condemnation, ungodly men, turning the grace of our God into lasciviousness, and denying the only Lord God, and our Lord Jesus Christ. (Jude, vs. 4)

Such men, the Scriptures add, are "filthy dreamers...brute beasts" who "corrupt themselves." The Illuminati are, indeed, men who have conjured up in their imaginations a vain thing: to set up a kingdom and dominion free from the redeeming grace of Almighty God. This, of course, was amazingly prophesied; there is a historically recurring pattern of rulers who corrupt themselves by warring against God and His people—and doing so through the means of *global conspiracy:*

> The kings of the earth set themselves, and the rulers take counsel together, against the Lord, and against his anointed. (Psalms 2:2)

The Rule of the Inner Circle

In 1992 in "Washington Dateline," the president of the American Research Foundation, Robert Goldsborough, wrote that he was told personally by Mark Jones, past financial advisor to the late John D. Rockefeller, Jr., that "just four men, through their interlocking directorates on boards of large corporations and major banks, controlled the movement of capital and the creation of debt in America."[8]

About a half century previous, wealthy Massachusetts liquor magnate Joseph Kennedy, the father of John F. Kennedy, was quoted in the establishment-controlled *New York Times* as stating: "Fifty men have run America, and that's a high figure."[9]

It is entirely likely that both Mark Jones and Joseph Kennedy were accurate. My intensive research and investigation has uncovered evidence that less than a hundred men govern America, and they do so from behind the scenes. These men are not elected and, generally, are unknown to the masses. Yet, of this larger group, only a few are counted among the *very elite.*

Indeed, my conviction, based not only on years of voluminous study, but, more importantly, *confirmed by what Bible prophecy reveals,* is that, presently, no more than ten men rule the entire world. These ten men comprise the *Inner Circle* of the Illuminati. Beneath them, at a subordinate level on the hierarchical pyramid, are approximately three hundred, key, global operatives; and beneath them, in turn, we find several thousand disciples, or "New World Order Servers."

Their awesome power to influence world events and to force dramatic turns in our everyday lives make it essential that we take a close look at the handful of men who comprise this elite *Inner Circle.* Our future depends on it, for the Bible testifies of the malignant acts to be done by these men. As we are counseled in *Proverbs,* the wise and godly person foresees the evil coming and avoids it, but the ignorant and complacent disregard and discount the prophetic warnings of Scripture—and are punished!

The researcher who attempts to discover the names of the highest council of the Illuminati runs into innumerable roadblocks. A veritable labyrinth of sometimes confusing and often contradictory information presents itself. Having weathered this blizzard of disinformation and surmounted many hurdles and obstacles, I have been able to narrow my list of *Inner Circle* candidates to 13 men. Two more men are added because they are of a younger generation and appear poised to replace their older, ancestral predecessors. Here, then, are brief, biographical sketches of the most powerful men on Planet Earth today—men destined soon to impact your life forever.

The Rothschild Dynasty: A Financial International

"Money is the God of our times, and Rothschild is his prophet." These words, spoken by an awed Heinrich Heine in Paris some years ago and quoted in Joseph Wechsberg's eye-opening book, *The Merchant Bankers,* indicate the power and influence ascribed to the Rothschild dynasty based on their enormous accumulation of wealth.

In the remarkable document known as *Red Symphony,* Christian G. Rakovsky, a Bolshevik founder of Soviet Communism, reveals the existence of a Financial International which is the opposite of—and yet founded and controls—the Communist International. The power base of this Financial International, says Rakovsky, is *money and banking,* and its leadership is composed of the five brothers of the Rothschild dynasty.[10]

"Bear in mind," Rakovsky advises, "the five-pointed star, like the Soviet one, which shines all over Europe, the star composed of the five Rothschild brothers with their banks, who possess colossal accumulations of wealth, the greatest ever known.[11]

That Rakovsky, later purged and executed by Soviet Dictator Josef Stalin, was on target with his description of the untold wealth and influence of the Rothschilds is undebatable. So, too, is his calculation regarding their political leanings. The Rothschilds are now, and have been for many decades, among the principal sponsors of world revolutionary activity.

In Nigel West's *Seven Spies Who Changed the World,* Lord Victor Rothschild, who died in 1991, is named as a member of the Communist Party. Victor, also not surprisingly, headed up Prime Minister Edward Heath's Downing Street "Think Tank."[12]

Today, the Rothschild dynasty continues on many fronts its secretive manipulation of global politics and finance. For example, in South Africa recently, Baron Eric de Rothschild met privately with diamond and gold titan, Harry Oppenheimer, at Vergelegen, where as reported in the media, they enjoyed together the taste of "Chateau Lafitte 1976, a rich and heady wine."

My sources from South Africa indicate much more than wine tasting was accomplished. The Rothschilds and the Rockefellers are the major financial backers of South Africa's President Nelson Mandela and they are now building a fantastic "Lost City" near Johannesburg—a resort city to rival, or best, Monaco, Las Vegas, Atlantic City, Frankfurt, and all others combined.[13]

Meanwhile, in *The European,* sort of a European equivalent of the *Wall Street Journal* and *USA Today* combined, we find the report that Lord J. Rothschild has teamed up with James Wolfensohn, the Wall Street investment giant, to effect billion dollar corporate mergers and megadeals.[14]

From over in merry England comes the news that Norman Lamont, former Chancellor of the Exchequer (Britain's top government financial post), has landed a directorship with merchant bank N. M. Rothschild.[15]

On the continent, in Switzerland, Emma de Rothschild was recently an invited guest at the annual meeting of the secretive Bilderbergers Group, while her close relative, Charlotte de Rothschild, displayed the fabulous Rothschild family painting collection at a concert and exhibition in Frankfurt. *Elan* magazine touted the Rothschild gala this way:

> When (German Chancellor) Helmut Kohl and other distinguished guests attend a concert in Frankfurt's Jewish Museum on 28 February they will be sharing in a "Rothschild "event in many senses of the word..."[16]

The reference book, *10,000 Famous Freemasons,* lists two prominent Rothschilds, including James Meyer Rothschild (1792-1868), son of the dynasty's founder, Meyer Amschel Rothschild. James is listed as a "33° of the French Supreme Council." Nathan, a second son of Meyer, is also listed.

It was Meyer Rothschild, the founder of the dynasty, who once was quoted as exclaiming: "Give me the right to issue a nation's money, and then I do not care who makes its laws."

Charlotte de Rothschild performed as soprano in an opera at the Jewish Museum in Frankfurt, Germany on February 28, 1994. Here, the wealthy heiress is shown in front of a painting of her ancestor, banker N.M. Rothschild, and his family.

Ominously for the future of the nation of Israel, the Rothschilds virtually control that country's politics and destiny. They have given generously to building projects and to political causes. It is also believed that it was the Rothschilds who, in 1948, persuaded David Ben Gurion and other Zionist founders to adopt the magical symbol known as the *Star of David* to be the emblem for Israel's flag. Occultists know this symbol as the hexagram, the six-pointed star.[17]

My investigation documents the preeminence in the Illuminati's dominant ruling *Inner Circle* of at least four Rothschilds: Baron Edmond de Rothschild, Baron Eric de Rothschild, Lord J. Rothschild, and Baron Guy de Rothschild.

The Rockefeller Dynasty: Apollo's Disciples

A revealing statue of Apollo the Sun God, mythological precursor of the coming Antichrist, graces the entrance of the massive Rockefeller Center in New York City. The cover of *New York* magazine once showed an artist's depiction of David Rockefeller, Jr., as akin to the god, Atlas, struggling but managing to hold the entire globe on his shoulders. Except possibly for the Rothschilds, no other bloodline or dynasty on Earth is comparable to that of the Rockefellers.

Since its founding by the notorious industrialist John D. Rockefeller in the late 19th century, this dynasty has spread its greedy tentacles in all directions. Not content to monopolize the oil industry, the Rockefellers have, like their European counterparts, the Rothschilds, gone into banking. Today, with the merger in 1995 of Chemical Bank and Chase Manhattan Bank, the Rockefellers now control the largest banking combine in the United States.

The Rockefellers are into every evil avenue feasible. They donated the land on the Hudson River where the United Nations building sits. They funded the blasphemous Parliament of the World's Religions, held in Chicago in 1993. Before that epic devilfest, the Rockefellers founded the Marxist-oriented World Council of Churches and National Council of Churches. The dynasty also founded and now controls the peculiar and mysterious Rockefeller Museum in Jerusalem, which displays a model of the coming Great Temple of the Jews to be built on the Temple Mount in Jerusalem. The enigmatic *Dead Sea Scrolls* are also housed in this unusual museum.

Laurance Rockefeller seems to be today's chief spiritual guru in the family. Thanks to Laurance's financial support, the New Age movement has been able to publish and distribute such unholy books as Barbara Marx Hubbard's *The Book of Co-creation* and Matthew Fox's *The Coming of the Cosmic Christ*.

The current head of the dynasty, David Rockefeller, Sr., founded the Trilateral Commission in 1973 and has guided the organization toward its World Government objectives. He also was North American head of the Council on Foreign Relations. Notably, David Rockefeller's Chase Manhattan Bank was favored by the Kremlin to be the first American bank to open an office in Moscow.[18]

The Rockefellers have controlled every incumbent President of the United States since Woodrow Wilson. Bill Clinton is no exception. In August, 1995, the Associated Press released this fascinating tidbit of news, which was duly reported in newspapers across America:

> Bill, Hillary Rodham, and Chelsea Clinton decided to go West for their summer vacation this year. The Clintons, say White House sources, will head to the Grand Teton Mountains in Jackson Hole, Wyoming for a week or more of golf, horseback riding, and buffalo barley soup. They'll lodge at the sprawling home of Democratic Senator John D. Rockefeller IV of West Virginia.[19]

We'll have more to say about Bill Clinton and his influential friends, the Rockefellers, in a subsequent chapter.

The Rockefeller siblings are key members and policymakers of the *Inner Circle* of the Illuminati. David Rockefeller, Sr., definitely holds a coveted seat; most likely, John (Jay) D. Rockefeller IV and Laurance Rockefeller also are prime candidates for inclusion on this distinguished council. Young

Top left: *U.S. Senator Jay Rockefeller (D-WA) of the Rockefeller Dynasty gives instructions to Hillary Rodham Clinton. Hillary's fascist healthcare plan for America was the brainchild of Jay Rockefeller. Angered by its failure in Congress, Rockefeller vowed that his fascist scheme—which would consolidate all healthcare under five, Rockefeller-owned insurance companies—would eventually become law, "whether the American people want it or not."*

Bottom left: *David Rockefeller, Sr., the financial maven who now heads the fabulous Rockefeller empire, founded the notorious Trilateral Commission in 1973.*

At right: *New York's towering Rockefeller Center is graced with this statue of Apollo the Sun God. Note the torch in Apollo's hand and the satanic circle which supports him.*

Top: *United Nations Secretary-General Trygve Lie accepts check from John D. Rockefeller III in the amount of $8.5 million for purchase of the land for the UN headquarters in New York City.*

Bottom: *David Rockefeller presided over the meeting of the Council on Foreign Relations on September 11, 1989. Boris Yeltsin, then a relative unknown, was guest speaker. Later, Yeltsin was elected to the presidency of Russia.*

David Rockefeller, Jr., will, one day soon, take his exalted place among the sitting "gods" of the *Inner Circle.* He is now being groomed by his father to oversee the family's vast banking and corporate empire.

The Habsburg Dynasty: Keepers of the Holy Grail

Otto von Habsburg has been called "Europe's hidden king."[20] Son of the last Empress of Austria (Zita, who died in 1989), Otto is currently a member of the European Parliament and has used his position to launch a campaign for a new "Holy Roman Empire," complete with a monarch and a holy, united Roman Catholic church. Naturally, Otto von Habsburg sees himself or his son, Karl, age 33, as the future leader of this reborn empire. He has been quoted as saying, "The time for the (Habsburg) dynasty lies in some happier tomorrow when a new Europe...will undergo a time of resurrection."[21]

In his fascinating book, *Guardians of the Grail,* J. R. Church suggests that Otto von Habsburg is connected to the blasphemous *Priory of Sion,* a France-based secret society whose members claim to be the true, physical heirs of a sexual relationship between Jesus Christ and Mary Magdalene.[22] "The Habsburg dynasty," Church writes, "which ruled the Holy Roman Empire since the 19th century, is the direct lineage of the Merovingian bloodline. The Habsburgs are reputed to be the family of the Holy Grail offspring of Mary Magdalene."[23] The family shield of the Habsburgs is the double-headed eagle.

That the Habsburgs are deeply involved in the Black Lodge of Europe's nobility is unquestionable. Interestingly, Otto von Habsburg, whose best known royal title is Archduke of Austria, also claims the title of *"King of Jerusalem!"*[24]

In his book, *Charles V,* Otto von Habsburg declared his goal of a united Europe, based on religious and political ecumenicism, which would become a "supernatural state."[25]

Karl von Habsburg, the heir apparent, has been quoted as saying, "History shows that power flows toward that which controls the purse strings."[26]

Archduke Karl von Habsburg, heir to the Habsburg Royal Dynasty, at his 1993 wedding to Baroness Francesca Thyssen-Bonemisza. The ***London Daily Mail*** *called it "Europe's wedding of the year."*

While I make no assertions in *Circle of Intrigue* as to whom the Antichrist is or shall be, it is, nevertheless, of keen interest that, according to J. R. Church, based on the 26-letter English alphabet and the occult numbering system, the name "Karl von Habsburg" produces the prophetically significant number 666.[27]

I believe that the elderly Otto von Habsburg, born in 1912, is a member of the Illuminati's covert *Inner Circle.* At the appropriate time, his grandson, the rising Archduke Karl von Habsburg, will join the ranks of these ten diabolical men.

Juan Carlos—The Antichrist King?

King Juan Carlos was born in Rome on January 5, 1938, as a descendent of the royal Bourbon family of France (most of Europe's royalty is blood-related) and of the bloodline of the deposed King Alfonso XII of Spain, now deceased. On July 23, 1969, Spain's military dictator, Generalissimo Francisco Franco, stood before a jam-packed session of the Spanish parliament and declared, "Conscious of my responsibility before God and history, I have decided to recommend Prince Don Juan Carlos de Borbon y Borbon as my successor."[28]

Like the Habsburgs, Juan Carlos also lays claim to the title, "King of Jerusalem." He is further called the "Defender of Catholic Holy Land Interests." Also like the Habsburgs, Juan Carlos has close ties with Jewish Zionist interests. The Spanish King, accompanied by the President of Israel, Chaim Herzog, has visited Madrid's Jewish synagogue to cement these ties.[29]

In yet another remarkable similarity with the Habsburgs, some are saying that King Juan Carlos could be the Antichrist and the beast, 666. Notable among those making this claim was the late Dr. Charles Taylor, a Bible prophecy teacher from California. In 1993, Dr. Taylor's book, *The Antichrist King—Juan Carlos,* was published. It proposes that Juan Carlos meets all the specifications of the Antichrist found in the Scriptures. Prior to his death, I had several, fascinating conversations with Dr. Taylor about his study of King Juan Carlos. I do not personally find convincing Dr. Taylor's thesis that Juan Carlos is the prophesied Antichrist, but many of the prophetic parallels are certainly there.

King Juan Carlos is not only a potential member of the Illuminati's *Inner Circle,* he is also a member of *Opus Dei,* a powerful and secretive Roman Catholic order. *Opus Dei*

Spain's King Juan Carlos, pictured here with President Bill Clinton during a formal state visit in 1993, holds the royal title, "King of Jerusalem." One well-known Bible prophecy teacher has written a book claiming King Juan Carlos meets all the biblical specifications of the coming Antichrist.

(translated, "God's Work") is made up primarily of wealthy corporate chieftains in Spanish-speaking countries. Its austere discipline, loyalty to the Pope, hidden rituals, intelligence operations, and reputed criminal activities have begotten *Opus Dei* "such unkind epithets as 'Holy Mafia' and 'White Freemasonry.' "[30]

The Bronfman Dynasty: Whiskey and Money

"Edgar Bronfman, Sr., would have to be considered a candidate for the select list of unelected rulers, those anonymous few who determine America's debt and control her destiny." These are the words of Dr. Dennis L. Cuddy and Robert Henry Goldsborough in their brief, but informative, guidebook, *The Network of Power*.[31] According to Cuddy and Goldsborough, the Bronfmans of Canada have inestimable financial and political power, geometrically increased through interlocking directorates.

Edgar M. Bronfman, Sr., is Chairman and Chief Executive Officer of Seagram Co., Ltd., the giant international distillery. Together with his son, Edgar Jr., and his brother Charles, the senior Edgar Bronfman also owns over 164,000 shares (roughly 26 percent) of DuPont common stock, and he also owns a huge hunk of Time-Warner.[32]

Bronfman, Sr., is a member of the Council on Foreign Relations and, significantly, is also President of the *World Jewish Congress*. Lawrence Patterson, publisher of *Criminal Politics* magazine, identifies the elite of the World Jewish Congress (WJC) as "the real leaders of world Government:"

> The members of the Bilderberg and Trilateral groups are indeed powerful people, but it must be remembered that they stand *below* the World Jewish Congress in the hierarchy of the New World Order Conspiracy...It is from the WJC through which the orders flow—around the world to the members of the Trilateral Commission, the Bilderberg Society, the Club of Rome, and the Council on Foreign Relations.[33]

The logo of the World Jewish Congress pictures a regionalized globe, within the six-pointed Star of David, set against a black, circle background. The esoteric meaning of the Star of David symbol is examined later in ***Circle of Intrigue.***

Patterson also states that the WJC is a super secret organization and that its meetings are closed to all except members. "The secrecy surrounding the WJC Global Assembly," he reports, "far exceeds that of any Bilderberg or other conspiracy group."[34]

I do not have any evidence that the Bronfmans are Luciferians, but since the WJC is tied in with the Anti-Defamation League (ADL) and the *B'nai B'rith,* the influential New York chapter of the Masonic Lodge, it stands to reason that Edgar Bronfman, Sr., is a Mason. As a Mason, he would be instructed on the Jewish mystical system of the *Cabala* (or Kabalah) and recognize the all seeing eye as a sign of deity. Notably, the Masons promote the rebuilding of the Great Temple of Solomon on the Temple Mount in the Holy City of Jerusalem—also a goal of the World Jewish Congress.

The Bronfman family has a reputed history of organized crime activity. In the heavily documented exposé book, *Dope, Inc.,* the claim is made that, "the Bronfmans' ties to North America's crime syndicate have never been broken, but merely undergone corporate reorganization."[35] Their financial and corporate network gives this family the capability to commit crimes on a global scale.

Lord Peter Carrington: Banker and Bilderberger

Britain's Lord Carrington seems always to be in the thick of world finance, chaos and war, and political intrigue. A high-level Bilderberger, Carrington runs the historic Hambros Bank,

Edgar Bronfman, Planet Earth's top liquor producer and President of the World Jewish Congress, presents President Bill Clinton with the "Nahum Goldman Medal" at the group's tribute dinner at New York's luxurious Waldorf-Astoria Hotel on April 30, 1995.

which, with the recent collapse of Barings Bank, is more than ever a powerhouse on the European continent and, indeed, across the Earth.[36]

Carrington was sent by the British prime minister as an envoy to the Bosnia-Yugoslavia area where ethnic conflict and genocide has been going on now for some years between the Serbs, the Croats, and the Moslems. It is not clear whether Carrington was inciting the wars or attempting to mediate an end to them. The British Lord is a former Secretary-General of NATO.

Lord Carrington is the co-founder of Kissinger Associates, the Rockefeller firm in New York which enables Henry Kissinger and former Bush-Reagan Administration lackeys to run political and financial errands for the Illuminati's *Inner Circle*. In addition to being the behind-the-scenes head of Hambros, Carrington is also a director of the gigantic Barclays Bank and, reputedly, is involved with Mafia and Masonic interests throughout Europe. His Hambros Bank owned 25 percent interest in Michael Sindona's *Banca Privata*.

Sindona's financial group bankrolled the P-2 Black Masonic Lodge operation and also conducted financing for Vatican covert activities.[37]

Lord Carrington, in common with others of the *Inner Circle,* has a keen interest in making Jerusalem the future world capital. He has worked closely with the Bronfmans, the Rothschilds, and the Rockefellers, and with Israeli officials such as former Defense Minister Ariel Sharon and former Prime Minister Yitzhak Shamir, to further the Israeli cause. One of the objectives of this group is to rebuild the Jewish temple in Jerusalem.

Harry Oppenheimer: King of Diamonds

Harry Oppenheimer is deeply involved in Illuminati projects around the world. The South African billionaire coordinated the transfer of the government in his nation to Nelson Mandela and his Communist-controlled African National Congress. In 1985, Oppenheimer set up a Corporate Council for South Africa. Through secret agreements with Mandela, his puppet, Oppenheimer remains in control of South Africa.

The Oppenheimer family's mining combine made them fabulously rich. It was German-born Sir Ernest Oppenheimer (1880-1957) who first went to South Africa as a representative of Rothschild diamond interests. In 1917, Sir Ernest established the Anglo-American Corporation of South Africa, Ltd., which became a gargantuan success in the diamond trade and in gold, platinum, and other precious materials. Just two years later, in 1919, he took over the preeminent De Beers Consolidated Mines. By 1957, the Oppenheimer dynasty owned 95 percent of the world's diamond mines.[38]

Today, Harry Oppenheimer has intimate ties with the murderous Israeli spy agency, the *Mossad.* He has clandestinely worked with the United States Defense Department, which has spent some $3.5 billion to build three secret military installations in Botswana, near Pretoria and Johannesburg. In Johannesburg, the largest Jewish temple in the world is under construction, said to be a precursor to the coming

Great Temple in Jerusalem—and it is coming into being largely through the efforts and money of Oppenheimer, along with his globalist friends, the Rothschilds and Rockefellers.[39]

What's really scary is the monstrous U.S. Embassy and CIA headquarters built recently in Pretoria with Oppenheimer's blessing. This facility, architecturally shaped in the form of a grotesque, flat, Illuminati pyramid without the capstone, now oversees a continuously orbiting system of spy satellites. From the bowels of this Antichrist structure, the CIA executes the Illuminist plot to destabilize and depopulate—that is, to *murder,* Africa.

The genocide, massacres, and bloodshed in Rwanda and Burundi were stage-managed from this CIA/U.S. Embassy stronghold as are numerous other efforts by the Illuminati's *Inner Circle* to strangle Africa and bring back the "glorious days of colonialism." The men of the *Inner Circle* yearn for the bygone era when the superior and noble white race of *Money Lords* reigned over their slaves and bragged openly of their immeasurable riches of natural resources. What is

The Central Intelligence Agency conducts massive spy, unconventional warfare, and terrorist operations from this U.S. Embassy stronghold in Pretoria, South Africa. Note the mysterious, occult symbol formed by the architectural monstrosity.

ahead, thanks to the elite, is a *New, Colonial Africa,* nominally governed by controlled, mind-numbed, black servants like Nelson Mandela—under the ever-vigilant, all seeing eye, of course, of the *Inner Circle* elite of the global Illuminati.

The Royal Court: Princes and Candidates

Who else joins the Rothschilds, Rockefellers, Bronfmans, Carringtons, Oppenheimers, *et al* in the lofty, rarified air of the *Inner Circle?* My investigations have centered on men like Giovanni Agnelli, the Italian automotive magnate (Fiat Motors), and on Rupert Murdoch, the multibillionaire Australian publisher who serves as "Mr. Moneybags" for House Speaker Newt Gingrich.

My investigation has also led me to delve into the activities and power potential of Heinrich von Pierer, Chairman of Siemens, the huge German electronic combine. Another influential candidate is George Soros, a Hungarian Jew and now a British subject. This international financier, who controls the $3.5 billion Quantum Fund and others, is a mover and shaker at the exclusive World Economic Forum held annually in Davos, Switzerland.

Prince Bernhard of the Netherlands is also a figure who bears watching. In *The Invisible Government,* Dan Smoot states, "Prince Bernhard is known to be an influential member of the Societe Generale de Belgique (the multibillion dollar holding company of the Royal House of Orange), a mysterious organization...of large corporate interests from many companies." Bernhard is one of the top leaders in the ultra-secretive Bilderbergers Group.

Also as a prime candidate we must consider Prince Philip, husband of England's reigning Queen Elizabeth. Philip, who leads by default due to the stupidity and indiscretions of his son, Prince Charles, oversees Britain's powerful *United Lodge of Freemasonry,* and he presides over the secretive and monarchial *Order of the Garter.* The Prince is also director of the *World Wildlife Fund,* a premier Illuminati front group specializing in environmental propaganda, and he heads the

Giovanni Agnelli, a member of the elitist Bilderbergers, is Chairman of Fiat Motors. Fiat was much favored by Italian Fascist dictator Benito Mussolini. At top is a painting of Fiat from the 1920s. Observe the similarity with the poster (bottom) of Soviet Communism's "New Man." In fact, the Illuminati's Plan aims for a ***Fascist New Order*** *(a synthesis of Communism and Capitalism) and a god-like* ***New Man****.*

George Soros, multibillionaire investment dynamo, presents a copy of his book to Russian President Boris Yeltsin. Note the circle on the cover. Soros has many contacts inside the former Communist countries.

United Nations *Sacred Literature Trust.* (The latter is an occultic project to bring together in one location all the world's "bibles, scriptures, and holy books." The goal is to develop a *One World Bible,* which shall establish a set of common moral rules and divine guidelines for all mankind.)

Pope John Paul II, the Vicar of Rome and Pontiff for almost one billion Roman Catholics around the globe, deserves special mention. In my audiotape reports, *The Last Days of Pope John Paul II* and *All Fall Down: The Plot to Crown the Pope the Prince of Peace,* I have elaborated on the role the Pope will play in the New World Order yet to come.[40]

For now, let me simply say that the Vatican is closely allied with Illuminati interests and exists as a complementary tool of the *Inner Circle.* But, the Pope also has his own, extensive global intelligence, financial, and political network. It exists, ironically, as both an accomplice and an adversary to the Illuminati's massive operation. Moreover, the future of both the Pope of Rome and the men of the *Inner Circle* is bound up in their joint plan for Jerusalem and Israel.[41]

A Need for Further Investigation

The very nature of a successful conspiracy is that the names of the perpetrators remain unknown and hidden from view. The Illuminati conspiracy presents a maze and labyrinth to even the most seasoned of investigators. Through the grace of God and with His help, in this book I uncover the names of many of the conspirators, trace their activities, and expose their dark, occult philosophy and Plan. In a follow-up book to *Circle of Intrigue,* I intend to report my subsequent findings. With divine help, I will flesh out and unmask the men of the *Inner Circle* and will continue to expose to the light their notorious schemes, plots, and crimes.

The Royal Court: Jesters and Pretenders

For those readers who may be disappointed that I have not named or proposed as members of the *Inner Circle* such men as Ross Perot, Ted Turner, Mikhail Gorbachev, Paul Volcker, Henry Kissinger, Alan Greenspan, Robert McNamara, Peter Peterson, James Wolfensohn, Robert Rubin, and others, as well as the current crop of world politicians—Clinton, Chirac, Major Kohl, Chrétian, *et al,* please be assured: I am well aware of their insider connections. And I am aware of

Former Secretary of State Henry Kissinger has alliances with a number of Illuminati chieftains. It was David Rockefeller, Sr., who made Kissinger a political star.

the loyal labors of these men in support of the Illuminist agenda.

But these ambitious men are mere stooges and puppets. They must do their master's bidding. They have been generously rewarded in the past for doing so. Later in this book, we will take a look at some of their crimes and operations.

It is these pitiful, slavish men—the Clintons and Yeltsins, Bushs and Gingrichs of this world—whom Alice Bailey, founder of the Lucis Trust, refers to in her revealing book, *Esoteric Psychology (Vol. 1)*. She writes that "adaptation to the group need and purpose are much treasured by the Order which they serve, for in their hands lie the future of the Brotherhood's monumental tasks of restructuring the world."[42] Further, she accurately describes them as "servers," commenting:

> These servers...are knowers of the Plan, and in every organization they constitute the new and slowly evolving group of World Servers. In their hands lies the salvation of the world.[43]

Through the Lenses of the Ten Kings: A Global Vision

By examining the major dynasties and families which, already, tenuously control the world but who seek *total global domination* by the year 2000, we begin to grasp a panoramic vision of the objectives this wicked group have in mind for our future. The men of the *Inner Circle* have mapped out a Plan to achieve World Government, even a World Empire, with historic Jerusalem as its capitol. They exalt Zionism and envision a rebuilt Great Temple of the Jews; but, in fact, they honor neither the Torah and Mosaic Law nor the Messiah, Jesus Christ. They view humanity as "useless eaters," as stepping stones to their quest for global dominion.

What they have in mind for biblical Christians, patriots, and nationalists is almost too gruesome to contemplate. Israel and the Jewish people will also suffer if the schemes of these men are successfully executed by the year 2000, or shortly thereafter. Orthodox Judaism will eventually be snuffed out (see II Thessalonians 2) as the world's great religions are unified and synthesized with the occult sects to form a heinous and mind-boggling *Beast Religious System*. This is the meaning of the omnipresent and ever-popular New Age slogan: "unity in diversity."

Through their puppets, the world's political leaders, the ten kings of the *Inner Circle* (see Revelation 17) shall make promises, but they will not keep them. They will flatter the citizenry of Israel and arouse a dangerous sense of ethnic pride and arrogance in Jews around the world. They will easily deceive pseudo-Christians and bedazzle the vastly enlarged New Age community. Then will come the great and overpowering disillusionment. Chaos will spread like a ravaging cancer over the face of the Earth. The anointed leader of the *Inner Circle* will come on the stage, vowing to set things right, to establish "order out of chaos." And then the end shall come.

FOUR

Assemblage of the Gods: The Rise of the Ten Wise Men of the Inner Circle

And the ten horns which thou sawest are ten kings, which have received no kingdom as yet; but receive power as kings one hour with the beast.

—*Revelation 17:12*

For earthly princes lay aside their power when they rise up against God, and are unworthy to be reckoned among the number of mankind. We ought, rather, utterly to defy them.

—John Calvin
Institutes of Christian Religion

For many years now I have been researching and investigating the bloodlines and dynasties of the Illuminati. Not surprisingly, my investigation has unearthed the ancient pagan worship, satanic ritual, and the unholy, "sacred" architecture and art of these wealthy and influential families. The Rockefellers, the Rothschilds, the Vanderbilts, the Astors, and the Habsburgs believe themselves to be much, much more than mere mortals. They are convinced that they are *gods*.

On November 4, 1994, David Meyer visited the Biltmore estate in Asheville, North Carolina. Meyer, formerly an occult astrologist, is now a biblical Christian dedicated to exposing and rooting out the evils of satanism and the corruption of the New Age movement. He wrote of his fascinating observations concerning the Vanderbilt family's Biltmore estate in his *The Last Trumpet* newsletter:

> I had known for a long time that this 250 room mansion was the world headquarters for Illuminism, and I finally found an opportunity to visit the place where the elite gather to rule the world. Some of the rooms are open to the public and many are not. Cameras are also forbidden...One of the first rooms that we came to had a large plaque which said *"The Assemblage Of The Gods."* On the walls of this massive temple-like room were large tapestries depicting the various satanic principalities such as Pan, Zeus, and Poseidon...In witchcraft and especially its Illuministic upper levels, tapestries are sacred, because they believe time is woven in a tapestry and that they belong to the eternal spirit realm...I also noticed something very unusual about the massive table centered in the room. On each side of this table were 13 chairs of ornately carved wood. These chairs had no arms on them, but the chair at each end of the table did. I know enough about witchcraft to know that this is a table of two covens with a High Priest on one end and a High Priestess on the other.[1]

David Meyer's comments on the table and seating arrangements (13 chairs) as indicating witchcraft activity is intriguing and significant. My investigation shows that the Illuminati is led at the top by a Council of Ten Wise Men. These men I call the *Inner Circle*. Underneath this olympian group of supposed god-men, in concentric circles, are several thousand faithful initiates and disciples. These men and women are the servants of Satan, and they frequently form themselves into witchcraft covens and groups of "13."

In 1995, my wife, Wanda, and I also had the opportunity to visit the huge, ornately decorated and magnificently appointed Biltmore Estate. I saw the demonic gargoyles perched on its exterior ledges. Inside, I observed the satanic faces and also those of the goddess carved into the wood of furniture. In the lavishly done library, the towering ceiling was painted in frescos like Michelangelo's Sistine Chapel in the Vatican in Rome, displaying such features as the bare-breasted goddess. The rituals of the Masonic Lodge were also recorded on walls, ceilings, and in paintings. A stifling air of spiritual darkness pervaded the sprawling mansion and its grounds.

My experience in visiting the Biltmore has been repeated in castles and mansions of the elite we have visited on Long Island, New York, in San Simeon, California, in Paris, France, in Bavaria, and in many other places. What we are dealing with are filthy rich, powerful dynasties who almost uniformly scorn Jesus Christ and Christianity as the province of lower-class fools and buffoons. The scions of the Illuminati bloodlines believe themselves to be far above the religion of the pitiful, lower consciousness masses. These men are persuaded by their Luciferian demon guides that they are *titans and gods*—divine personages destined to rule the earth.

The supposed class superiority and higher consciousness of these pompous and haughty elitists is well noticed by the lower-class men and women who would ride the coattails of the Illuminati hierarchy to temporal world power. Such men as Bill Clinton and Newt Gingrich would kiss the ground these "gods"—the Rockefellers, Rothschilds, and the others—walk on, if they were ordered to do so.

For a time during the 20th century, as the middle class gained ground and were led to believe that *they,* not the super rich, held the reigns of power in democratic societies, it was supposed that these dynastic families were receding in authority and influence. That turns out to be gross propaganda, spread by the media controlled by the Illuminati bloodlines. In fact, the super rich have *gained* in authority and influence.

The Ruling Class and the New Caste System

The New Age leadership fully recognizes from where the fount of global power springs. William Irwin Thompson, a

New Age authority who has authored such books as *Evil and World Order* and *At the Edge of History,* recently commented that this ruling class of the elite has become tremendously powerful in recent years as a "process of planetization" has occurred.

> There is a ruling class at the top that communicates through oral means, face to face...and at the bottom there is an underclass.[2]

According to Thompson, the developing class system is "almost like a return of the Vedic (Hindu) caste system."[3] (That being so, one wonders who the "untouchables" are to be in the new, caste system? The Christians?)

The "oral" class now in authority, says Thompson, "has the right accent, and has wealth...The rich get richer and the poor poorer, and the smaller ruling class just rules the masses through *pageantry* and *illusion."*[4]

The ruling class to which Thompson refers, the Illuminati, retains its great influence and authority by the passing out of favors. To their own go the plums of highest political office, the CEO and chairman positions in the giant, multinational corporations, and so forth.

I am thus reminded of the complaint found long ago, in October 1873, in a Yale University student newspaper called *The Iconoclast.*[5] It seems that students at Yale who were not of the privileged class had investigated a curious secret society, the *Order of Skull & Bones,* made up of only a handful of fellow students but supported by a bevy of wealthy alumni backers, that, apparently, ran the entire school and dictated collegial policies. In their newspaper, the dissident students mentioned that they were taking a risk because of the potential retribution that might be visited upon those who *dare* to oppose or unmask the secret society and its undue influence. Nevertheless, they felt it an obligation to expose the elitism of *Skull & Bones:*

> What right, forsooth, have *fifteen* men
> to lord it over all?

What right to say the college world
shall on their faces fall?
If they have grounds on which they base
their claim as just and true,
We challenge them to set them forth exposed to
public view,
That all may know the reasons why this oligarchy proud
Elect themselves as lords supreme o'er us, the
"vulgar crowd."

We offer no objections to their existing clan, —
No one disputes with them this right, we question but
the plan
On which they act, — That only he who wears upon his
breast their emblem, he for every post shall be
considered best.

We wish this understood by all. Let none who read this say
That we are moved by petty wrongs or private spite obey;
It is for principles of right that we with them contend,
For principles which they've ignored, but which we
here defend.

O fellow students, who with us revere these classic halls,
Shall none assert the right to act as to each seemeth best,
But cringe and fawn to him who wears a **death's head** on
his breast?
Nay, let all rise and break the spell whose sickly
glamour falls
About all that originates within those brown stone walls.

And if they will not hear our claims, or grant the justice due,
But still persist in tarnishing the glory of the blue,
Ruling this little college world with proud, imperious tones,
Be then the watchword of our ranks — Down, Down With
Skull and Bones!

The grotesque Order of Skull & Bones, which I examined in voluminous detail in my book, *Dark Majesty,* is a Black

The Order of Skull & Bones operates as a Black Lodge of Freemasonry. This is its logo.

Lodge of international Freemasonry. Bonesmen, as its members refer to themselves, claim their initiation ritual to be of a special race and caste, while all those outside the Order are denigrated and described as "vandals and gentiles." I demonstrate in my book that the influence of Skull & Bones extends far beyond the hallowed walls of Yale University. Its power is in its clannish alumni. The present membership of this odious secret society includes former President George Bush, columnist William F. Buckley, Senator John Kerrey, and many others. However, the Order of Skull & Bones is only one of numerous fraternities, secret societies, orders and organizations used by the Illuminati to recruit its future "talent."[6] Moreover, I do not believe that its members comprise but a few of the *Inner Circle* of the Illuminati.

Wise Men and Magicians

Interestingly, the "Patriarchs" of Skull & Bones are often referred to as the *Wise Men*. Indeed, an entire book has been written about them, entitled *The Wise Men*.[7] Its author is Walter Isaacson, a member of the Council on Foreign Relations (CFR). It should be noted that many bonesmen go on to become members of the CFR.

The regal men of the *Inner Circle* of the Illuminati seem to enjoy being called the "Wise Men." In 1982, the Planetary Commission for the World We Choose, a top New Age globalist organization, announced the meeting of a "World Council of Wise Persons." The announcement said the meeting was to be held at the headquarters of the United Nations in New York City, and the participants would "share their vision and insight into moving humanity over the next threshold."[8]

It may be that the description of the Wise Men appeals to these men because of the Bible's gospel message about the Wise Men, the Magi from the East who saw the star in the sky and came laden with gifts, looking for the Christ child. The top echelon of the Illuminati see themselves in much the same way, as Magi (magicians) from the East (referring to their pagan religions) looking for the coming of their own Christ figure—the New Age messiah and king (i.e., the Antichrist). Their gift to him shall be the entire planet Earth, complete with all its riches and all its worshipful humanity.

Ten Notorious Men Prophesied to Reign Over the Earth

The Bible magnificently prophesies the ascension to global power of an elite cabal of exactly *ten* co-conspirators in the last days. In Revelation 17:3 we are told of the vision of "a scarlet coloured beast, full of names of blasphemy, having...ten horns." Elsewhere in *Circle of Intrigue,* I examine the meaning of the scarlet color of *red*. For example, I point out that the family shield of the Rothschild dynasty has the color red. Indeed, their name, Rothschild, literally means "red-shield." Red was also the color chosen by the Illuminati to symbolize their Communist regimes in Russia and China. But here, let us concentrate on the *ten horns* of the red beast. Revelation 17:12-14 gives the interpretation and meaning of the ten horns:

> And the ten horns which thou sawest are ten kings, which have received no kingdom as yet; but receive power as kings one hour with the beast. These have one mind, and shall give their power and strength unto the beast. These shall make war with the Lamb, and the Lamb shall

> overcome them: for he is Lord of lords, and King of kings: and they that are with him are called, and chosen, and faithful. (Revelation 17:12-14)

What we thus have is confirmation of ten "kings" who will be men of vast political and economic power in the last days. (Also see Revelation 17:15). They rule over the entire Earth and are of "one mind." In other words, they think alike, they believe alike, and they act in complete unison.

Moreover, in their unity, they *conspire* together to "give their power and strength unto the beast."

The beast, whom they shall support with all their power and strength, is none other than the Antichrist, Satan incarnate. In Revelation 13, he's described as a beast rising up with "ten horns." Upon these ten horns are "ten crowns." Again we discover *ten men,* ruling as divine kings over all the Earth and serving the beast, the Antichrist who in Revelation 13:18 is revealed as the man who has the number 666.

It is made clear, also, that these *ten men* do more than simply obey and support the beast in his conspiratorial aims. *They literally worship him, and they worship the dragon, Satan,* who gives this evil 666 leader his sinister power:

> And they worshipped the dragon which gave power unto the beast: and they worshipped the beast, saying, Who is like unto the beast? who is able to make war with him? (Revelation 13:4)

In Revelation 13:8 we find out two more essential facts about this last days Antichrist beast (666). First, we are informed that he despises true Christians and goes all out to destroy them and to undermine and diminish their godly influence. Second, we again have confirmed the fact that his rule is *global* in scope:

> And it was given unto him to make war with the saints, and to overcome them: and power was given him over all kindreds, and tongues, and nations. And all that dwell upon the earth shall worship him, whose names are not

> written in the book of life of the Lamb slain from the foundation of the world. (Revelation 13:7-8)

Prophecy thus provides a remarkably clear picture of Satan's end-times world conspiracy. It is led by a wicked man, empowered by Satan, who wields authority over all nations and all people with the exception of Christians. This demoniac individual, known as the beast, has an *Inner Circle* of *ten men* who rule with him. These ten men are of *one mind* and give their power and strength unto the beast.

It is invariably the case that *occult* doctrine and philosophy, though distasteful and grotesque, parallel Bible prophecy. This is because the devil is forced to carry out to the letter his mission, so that God's greater Plan for world redemption can be fulfilled. That is why the beast will be identified with the number 666 and why he and his Illuminati use symbols, images, and marks. Satan cannot invent his own numbering system or refrain from using symbols to represent his work—he is restricted by God's prophetic Plan as found in the Scriptures.

This is likewise true of Satan's employment of a *ten man* hierarchy as the *Inner Circle* of his Illuminati. He is compelled to do so, and therefore, occult doctrine and philosophy follow on the heels of Bible prophecy.

The Power of the Number Ten

A few examples will suffice. J.C. Cooper, a well-known mystic and author, writes in her *An Illustrated Encyclopedia of Traditional Symbols* of the meaning in the occult world of the circle and the significance of the number ten:

> God is a circle whose center is everywhere (Hermes Trismegistus). As the sun it (the circle) is the masculine power, but...as the encircling waters, it is the feminine... The circle is typified by the number ten.[9]

In *A Dictionary of Symbols,* published by a Theosophy press, J. E. Cirlot explains:

> The circle or disk is very frequently an emblem of the sun...It also bears a certain relationship to the number ten, symbolizing the return to unity from multiplicity.[10]

When we recall that Lucifer lays claim to being the Sun God, we then understand the meaning of the circle as the sun. In occult numerology, the number ten represents this circle and also represents the unbroken, eternal unity of all things under Lucifer. That, after all was his idle boast in Isaiah 14:12, to conquer God and to reconcile all things—heaven, earth, and hell—unto himself. The circle of ten, then, symbolizes the Kingdom of Satan. The point within the circle, an especially malignant Illuminati mark, stands for the dominance of Lucifer, the point of light, over his ten man *Inner Circle.*

It is a fascinating fact that in divine biblical numerology,

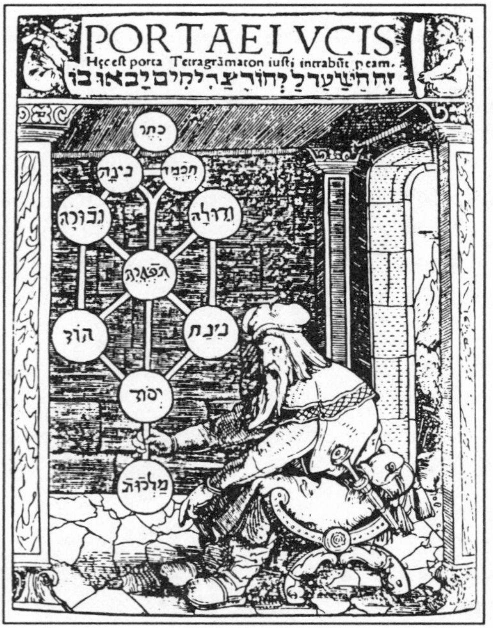

This 5th-century, occult, Cabalist treatise illustrates the mystical Tree of the Sephiroth as the divine "Portal of Light." Note the **ten** *aspects formed as circles.*

as opposed to devilish interpretations, the number ten is the number of *Testimony*. In his excellent book, *Biblical Mathematics,* evangelist Dr. Ed Vallowe notes that the number ten signifies the responsibility of man under the law to keep the commandments and bear a testimony for God. Vallowe writes:

> God gave the TEN commandments to man for him to bear Testimony before God and man. There were TEN Plagues upon Egypt and Pharaoh during the days of Moses. (Exodus 7:12) Abraham prayed for TEN righteous people within the wicked city of Sodom. He wanted a TESTIMONY FOR GOD. In the parable of the TEN virgins, it gives the legal number necessary for a Jewish function or wedding.
>
> We have the TEN servants to whom were entrusted TEN pounds and one was rewarded by being given authority over TEN cities. (Luke 19:13, 17)
>
> TEN powers become powerless against the LOVE OF GOD: "For I am persuaded, that (1) neither death, (2) nor life, (3) nor angels, (4) nor principalities, (5) nor powers, (6) nor things present, (7) nor things to come, (8) nor height, (9) nor depth, (10) nor any other creature, shall be able to separate us from the love of God, which is in Christ Jesus our Lord." (Romans 8:38-39)
>
> TEN vices which exclude from the Kingdom of God are listed in I Corinthians 6:9-10. "Know ye not that the unrighteous shall not inherit the kingdom of God? Be not deceived: (1) neither fornicators, (2) nor idolaters, (3) nor adulterers, (4) nor effeminate, (5) nor abusers of themselves with mankind, (6) nor thieves, (7) nor covetous, (8) nor drunkards, (9) nor revilers, (10) nor extortioners, shall inherit the kingdom of God."
>
> The Tithe is a TENTH of our earnings belonging to the Lord. We are commanded to "Bring ye all the tithes into

the storehouse, etc." (Malachi 3:10) The Tithe is our TESTIMONY of faith unto the Lord.

TEN times we read in Genesis One, "GOD SAID" Here we have the TESTIMONY from the Lord concerning His Creation, and Power.

TEN Psalms begin with Hallelujah. (Psalms 106, 111, 112, 113, 135, 146, 147, 148, 149, 150) Here the Psalmist is giving his TESTIMONY of Praise unto the Lord.[11]

But, says Vallowe, when Satan and his human agents rebel against the Law, the Commandments, and against the Testimony of God, tragedy results as men conspire with the Evil One to bring about a human World Order based on deception and chaos: "A TEN kingdom confederation is the last phase of human sovereignty upon this earth. This will take place during the tribulation period. (Daniel 2 and 7; and Revelation 13 and 17)"[12]

The Little Horn of the Antichrist

The book of Daniel provides another important piece of the prophetic puzzle. Again we find that a New World Order is to arise in the last days. The same picture as we found in the book of Revelation materializes—*the beast with ten horns.* But in Daniel 7:7-8, 23-25, we discover also the manner and sequence of events in which the beast is energized and comes to power. From the midst of the ten horns comes yet another, "little horn:"

> And the ten horns out of this kingdom are ten kings that shall arise: and another shall rise after them; and he shall be diverse from the first, and he shall subdue three kings. And he shall speak great words against the most High, and shall wear out the saints of the most High, and think to change times and laws: and they shall be given into his hand until a time and times and the dividing of time. (Daniel 7:24-25)

This little horn is a person, for we are told that "in this horn were eyes like the eyes of man, and a mouth speaking great things." (Daniel 7:8)

This little horn of Daniel is the Antichrist. He is full of Satan and his soul is possessed by the devil. Prophecy tells us he is different ("diverse") from the first ten horns and that in acquiring his great power over them, the Antichrist beast plucks up three of the ten horns by the roots. He subdues three of the ten kings.

Now, since Revelation 17 tells us that all ten of the kings are loyal to the Antichrist (little horn), so much so that, being of one mind, they give their strength and power unto him, why would he forcibly *remove* and *subdue* three of them?

I believe the answer is found in the *Hegelian dialectic,* which we will study in some detail later in this book. These ten men rule over ten kingdoms, or nation/regions, of the Earth. For some reason, three of these nation/regions are to be *sacrificed* so that the Antichrist's goal of world conquest can be achieved. The Royal Secret of the Illuminati is "Equilibrium: Order Out of Chaos." Through chaos, and from the resulting death, bloodshed, and catastrophe, three of this planet's ten, last days kingdoms will be sacrificed, so that equilibrium and world order can be achieved.

Currently, the leaders of the G-7 (U.S.A., Japan, Germany, France, Italy, Great Britain, Canada) regularly meet and set agendas and objectives to carry out the dictates of the Illuminati. This grouping will certainly be increased to nine to accommodate Russia and China. Then will come the tenth member, which may be Israel once the Antichrist moves his headquarters to Jerusalem. This, in fact, has long been a key element in the secret Plan of the Illuminati.

It is important for us to understand that whatever will be the composition of these ten kingdom powers, the "little horn" will come up from "among them" (Daniel 7:8). He will arise *after* them and be different, or "diverse," from the ten. Is this a prophecy foretelling the Antichrist being propelled to power through the mechanism of the United Nations? This possibility is reinforced by the Scripture which reveals that the little horn "shall devour the whole earth, and shall tread it down, and break it in pieces." (Daniel 7:23)

Global Law is Coming

The Bible prophesies of the beast that, exercising global power, he will "think to change times and laws." Already we are facing the threat of a tidal wave of international treaties and agreements. Plans are now in progress for a World Environmental Agency, an International Criminal Court, and a Global IRS, the latter agency to be a taxing authority under the direction of the United Nations. What's more, the nations of the Earth are rapidly converting their armed forces into subordinate units under United Nations command authority. In 1993, by executive order (Presidential Decision Directive 25), President Bill Clinton directed U.S. military officers to obey United Nations authority and willingly serve under UN commanders, be they from Turkey, Brazil, Greece, China, or Russia! Meanwhile, all U.S. military units were ordered to remove "U.S.A." insignia and markings from

The Illuminati intend to empower the United Nations to police the world and destroy national sovereignties.

aircraft, missiles, tanks, armored personnel carriers and other equipment, as well as from all facilities and real estate in the possession of the Department of Defense.

An order to remove the "U.S." insignia from the U.S. Air Force dress blue uniform, however, had to be lifted after a rebellion set in among officers and enlisted men. The Clinton administration and its pro-United Nations puppet, the Polish-born Chairman of the Joint Chiefs of Staff (JCS), General John Shalikashvali, fearing a mutiny, countermanded their directive which had called for removal of the "U.S." insignia and other patriotic markings from the uniform.

Interestingly, in the U.S. Army, Christian and Jewish chaplains have been ordered to wear on the breast of their uniform a chaplain's insignia which displays the symbolic "sun rays" most prominently. This blasphemous act appears to be intended to suggest the authority of Lucifer, the Illuminati's Sun God, over the symbol of Christianity (the cross) and Mosaic Judaism (the tablets of Moses).

A Conspiracy of the Rich

In a booklet I wrote in 1990 entitled, *How Will We Know the Antichrist?*, I explained that the beast has a great advantage over the men of the *Inner Circle* who are destined to serve him. He is blessed by Satan, the dragon, who gives him his terrible power. That he rises to the pinnacle of world prominence by conspiracy is revealed in Daniel 11:23 which states, "He shall work deceitfully: for he shall come up, and shall become strong with a small people." In other words, the Antichrist beast rides to the crest of global authority through the deceitful efforts of a small group of co-conspirators.

Hitler was at the helm of a great nation of many people, Germany, when he became conqueror of much of Europe in the 30s and 40s. But he was first catapulted into high office by the secret societies who helped him fund and organize his fanatical Nazi party. His power came from a *small band* of thugs and social misfits. Hitler worked deceitfully and rose up and became strong with a "small people."

The same is true for Russia's Vladimir Lenin, whose Bolsheviks (later called "communists") were funded and organized by the same group of international financiers who backed the rise of Adolf Hitler. Never did Lenin and his successors have the popular support of the masses. The strength of the tiny band of Bolsheviks (a "small people") came from their conspiratorial activities ("work deceitfully").

Now, as we rush through the 1990s and move furiously toward the new millennium, a small but powerful contingent of evil men are again hard at work. This *Inner Circle* of ten men, considering themselves to be "philosopher kings" of divine blood, are furiously working to prepare the entire Earth for the expected arrival of their great leader. He will be the little horn who comes up among them. Working deceitfully, he will project an image that he is a man of peace, a strong man of integrity riding a white horse (Revelation 6). But the Bible reveals his *true* character:

> He is a proud man, neither keepeth at home, who enlargeth his desire as hell, and is as death, and cannot be satisfied, but gathereth unto him all nations, and heapeth unto him all people. (Habakkuk 2:5)

The ten men of the *Inner Circle* of the Illuminati, like their esteemed leader, are "proud men." They believe they are higher consciousness Wise Men endowed with divinity. They pretend even to be gods, superior lords fully deserving of our worship and admiration.

What should be our response to so bold and blasphemous a claim? John Calvin, in his commentary of the book of Daniel (1561), had some choice reflections on how Christians should view such men, who deign to be an "assemblage of the gods." He declares:

> For earthly princes lay aside their power when they rise up against God, and are unworthy to be reckoned among the number of mankind. We ought, rather, utterly to defy them (conspuere in ipsorum capita, lit., 'to spit on their heads') than to obey them.[13]

FIVE

“Ordo Ab Chao”—The Great Work of the Illuminati

The Royal Secret... the Secret of the Universal Equilibrium... shall at length make real, the Holy Empire of true Masonic Brotherhood.

—Albert Pike, 33°
Morals and Dogma

The perpetrators of revolution have learned one thing well. They must control all sides.

—*Christians Awake Newsletter*

There are two great forces in the world... Each is directed from the same boardroom.

—James Knox
American Focus

The Great Work of the Illuminati—the transformation of mankind on planet Earth—will be substantially completed in the decade of the 1990s. That was the prediction of this century's most wicked occultist, Britain's Aleister Crowley, the man who relished calling himself “The Beast, 666.”

In his sinister volume, *The Book of the Law,* published in 1904, Crowley testified that a demon spirit identified as “Horus” gave him this prediction. Horus also told Crowley that the 1940s would be a decade of chaos, bloodshed, and war—a startling prediction that came true with the chaos and flames of World War II.

Thriving on Chaos

Apparently, Crowley's spirit guide, Horus, thrives on chaos. Indeed, all demonic powers are enchanted with chaos, for it is through chaos that Satan's objectives are met. Satanic doctrine teaches that, ultimately, the New World Order can be established in society only after a time of *planned,* great world turbulence and chaotic disorder. It is this very concept—"order out of chaos"—which is at the foundation of all Masonic doctrine.

Significantly, Masonic initiates elevated to the 33° are given a "jewel" to wear proudly. This jewel is decorated with the sign of three, interlocked triangles, representing both the unholy trinity and the number 666. The jewel is also inscribed with the Latin inscription *"Ordo Ab Chao,"* interpreted as *"Order Out of Chaos."*[1]

The Royal Secret of Freemasonry, the True Word of a Master Mason, is the word *Equilibrium*—signifying that order shall be established by the Masonic society's god-man leader once the chaos is quelled and universal order is established. (Students of the World Conspiracy will recognize this philosophically as the working of the *Hegelian Dialectic.)*

Crowley was a knowledgeable Mason, and, as such, he knew well the Royal Secret—that global Equilibrium, or Synthesis, was to be achieved as a direct result of chaotic events to occur during the final decade of the 20th century. Then would emerge the New Civilization—the birth of a global society led by a small band of spiritually superior men. Satanically energized god-men, to be exact.

The Conflict of Opposites: Toward a Holy Empire

What is the high-level Masonic initiate chosen for world service told of the meaning of the Royal Secret, the word

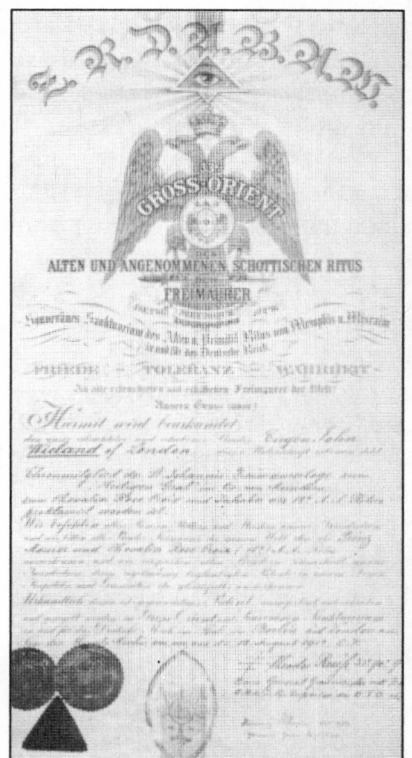

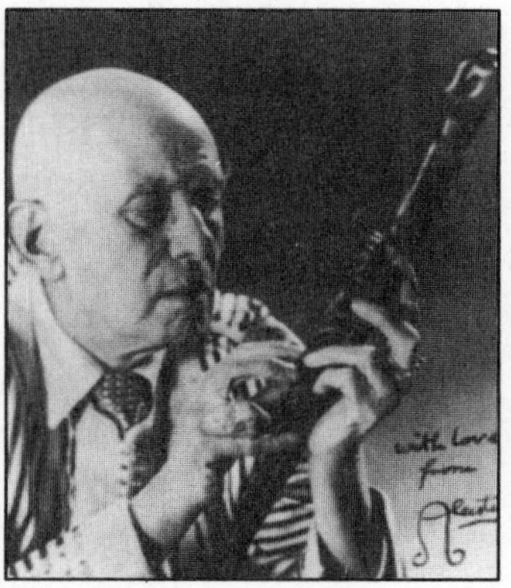

Left: *The occultic* ***Ordo Templi Orientis****, like their* ***Scottish Rite*** *cousins, have long employed the symbols of the Double-Headed Eagle and the All Seeing Eye, as shown on this Masonic Charter (1912).*

Top right: *British satanist Aleister Crowley, whose spirit guide told him of the Great Work of the Illuminati.*

Lower right: *Masons rising to the highest, 33rd, degree receive this "jewel" which they wear with pride. Observe the Latin phrase, "Ordo Ab Chao" (Order Out of Chaos).*

Equilibrium? He is instructed that the Illuminati is continually creating and fostering *two* opposing forces which clash and compete. Chaos is produced by the friction between these two, polar ideologies or groups. And it is through chaos that The Plan for global domination and the self-realization of deity is executed. The heated battle that ensues results, finally, in Equilibrium—the syncretic balancing of the two opposing forces. In all occult systems since the beginning of time, this system of achieving Equilibrium through the planned conflict of opposites is found.

International Masonry's most distinguished scholar and occult teacher, its former Sovereign Grand Commander Albert Pike, wrote of Equilibrium in his lengthy and authoritative volume, *Morals and Dogma of the Ancient and Accepted Scottish Rite of Freemasonry.* His statement came at the very end of his classic book, frequently touted as the "Bible" of Freemasonry. There, on page 861, Pike discloses the ultimate goal of the international Masonic order and, indeed, of its hidden, overseer group, the Illuminati:

> The Royal Secret, of which you are a Prince, if you are a true adept... is that which the *Sohar* (an occultic and cabbalistic text) terms The Mystery of the Balance. It is the Secret of the Universal Equilibrium.... Such, my Brother, is the True Word of a Master Mason; such is the true Royal Secret, which makes possible, and shall at length make real, the Holy Empire of true Masonic Brotherhood.[2]

The goal, Pike revealed, is World Government—a "Holy Empire"—ruled by the princes of the unity-in-diversity New Age World Religion. Pike relates this goal to the teachings of the Sohar, a Babylonish book of the Kabbalah, the ancient system of magic and mysticism first adopted by apostate Jews taken captive in Babylon and brought back with them to Israel. The Kabbalah (also known as "cabala") contains the seed doctrines of Luciferianism which have, thanks to the secret societies and orders of the Illuminati, by now been disseminated to all corners of the globe.

Ten Signs of the End of the World

In a video recently produced, I provided ample evidence that planned chaos now confronts us on a grand scale. That video* was entitled *Ten Signs of the End of the World.*[3] These are the ten signs which I discussed and which document the success today of Satan's ages-old plan to "reinvent the world" and "create a New Civilization:"

1. A New World Order is being created, with Israel and Jerusalem readied to become capitol of the world and the throne of Antichrist. (Matthew 23:2; II Thessalonians 2; Revelation 11:8; Revelation 18:24)

2. Commercial and political Babylon now exist. (Revelation 18; James 5; and Zechariah 5)

3. False christs and false prophets emerge and deceive millions. (Matthew 24; Revelation 13)

4. The worldwide, Mystery Babylon religion of Satan is revived. (Revelation 17)

5. The financial control of world economies and the taking of the Mark are made possible. (Revelation 13)

6. The Word of God is being attacked and ravaged. (Revelation 22:19-20; I Timothy 6:3)

7. Bible prophecy is today horribly mocked and scorned by supposed "Christian" leaders. (II Peter 3; James 4)

8. The Gospel is being shamelessly marketed like soap. (Romans 6:17-18; Isaiah 56:11; II Peter 2:3; I Peter 1:7)

---

* *available for $22 from Living Truth Ministries: phone toll free 1-800-234-9673 or write to 1708 Patterson Road, Austin, Texas 78733*

9. False teachings multiply, and the spiritual death of the apostate Christian establishment is in evidence. (II Timothy 4:3; I Timothy 4:1-2; II Peter 2)

10. Demonic communications abound as insatiable satanic agents devour mankind. (Genesis 6; Revelation 18:2; Revelation 16:13; II Thessalonians 2:1-4)

It is for his fidelity to this satanic plan that Vice President Al Gore, a Mother Earth worshipper and closet occultist, is touted by the press for his professed goal of "reinventing government."[4] Meanwhile, those in the know understand clearly why House Speaker Newt Gingrich, an Illuminati insider, has endorsed the techno-fascist, New Age book, *Creating A New Civilization,* by Alvin and Heidi Toffler.

The 1990s have, indeed, turned out to be banner years for evil. To further their cherished goal of reinventing the world, the men of the Illuminati have sponsored numerous events designed to "raise global consciousness." For example, America's First Lady, Hillary Clinton, went over to Copenhagen in March, 1995, for the United Nations' *World Summit on Social Development.* There, meeting with 120 heads of state and UN Secretary-General Boutros Boutros-Ghali, Hillary smilingly announced that America's taxpayers would immediately shell out an additional $118 million to assist "social development" (meaning, *revolution*) around the globe.

In September, 1995, yet another U.S. delegation headed by Hillary Clinton trekked to Beijing, Red China, for the UN's *World Conference on Women.* This disgusting affair was followed by one even more odious—a Mikhail Gorbachev gala, held, appropriately enough, in gay San Francisco from September 27 to October 1.

At Gorby's bash, an impressive array of world leaders met to further the Illuminati's plans for the New World Order. Attendees included former President George Bush, former Prime Minister Margaret Thatcher of Britain, President Vaclav Havel of the Czech Republic, CNN magnate Ted Turner, and former Japanese Prime Minister Yasuhiro

Hillary Rodham Clinton and UN Secretary-General Boutros Boutros-Ghali, at the World Summit on Social Development.

Nakasone. The meeting was officially called the *State of the World Forum.* The Gorbachev Foundation—U.S. taxpayer funded, naturally—headquartered in Presidio, California, heralded the event as "the birth of the FIRST GLOBAL CIVILIZATION."[5]

Within weeks of Gorby's meeting came two other premier, Illuminati-sponsored events. In early October, Pope John Paul II addressed the UN's General Assembly. Commemorating the 50th Birthday of that august—and satanic—body, the Pope spoke on the subject of "how tolerance can promote world religious unity." This demonstrated his support for the UN's designation of the year 1995 as the "International Year of Tolerance."

Israel's ambassador to the UN was no doubt thrilled to hear this message of his friend, the Pope. Indeed, the Jews celebrated their own international gala—an extravagant 3,000 year birthday party in October to mark Jerusalem's trimillennial anniversary.

Bloodshed and Chaos on a Massive Scale

Meanwhile, chaos on a bloody scale has been in abundance. In the 90s, massacres and genocide in Bosnia, Rwanda, and Burundi shocked the world's conscience. The FBI, CIA, BATF, and other Big Brother agencies staged "terrorist" bombings, sniper attacks, burn-outs, and killing fields around the U.S.A., including grim events at the New York Trade Center, the Oklahoma City federal building, and the Branch Davidian complex in Waco, Texas.[6] They pinned it on the cults and the dreaded patriot militias, of course, and on "terrorists" and fundamentalists of all stripes—Christian and Moslem. Naturally, most of these staged death events were scheduled to occur according to the Satanic Ritual Calendar.[7]

A clue to the occult significance of such events is given in the Masonic textbook, *A Bridge to Light* (published in 1988 by the Supreme Mother Council, Scottish Rite). In its pages we are again reminded of Pike's theory that crisis and turmoil shall "make possible, and shall at length make real, the Holy Empire of true Masonic Brotherhood."[8] Yes, according to the Masonic wisdom, out of chaos shall come order: thus, *Ordo Ab Chao*.

This, of course, is an occult teaching and a reality of which the profane, lower-level Masons know nothing, for the truth is kept hidden from them and veiled in symbols and arcane doctrine. But it is religious dogma *par excellence* for the men of the *Inner Circle* and for their Illuminati henchmen.

The higher-level initiates are well aware that in the working of The Plan, death and bloodshed—unparalleled *chaos*—are prescribed. John Randolph Price, president of the Planetary Commission and organizer each year of a massive and worldwide "Instant of Cooperation" event, has proclaimed that the "Divine Plan" requires chaos to cleanse and purge the world before a bright, new era can emerge:

> This New Age *will be*. A new heaven on Earth *will be*. Preparations are being made now, and *out of chaos* will

> come the beginning of peace on earth, a New Order for Mankind.[9]

It's interesting to note that this quote by John Randolph Price is found in his book, entitled *The Superbeings*. In that book, Price quotes certain spirit entities from beyond as revealing to him a coming New Age kingdom on Earth—a New Age to be led by highly evolved and "illuminated" superbeings.

Invented Crises Lead to Opportunity

The Secret Doctrine of the Illuminati, known by them as "Ordo Ab Chao"—order out of chaos—is confusing and nonsensical to uninitiated, logical-thinking persons. It is based, as we shall see, on the scientific concept that "iron sharpens iron" and on the political dictum that "crisis leads to opportunity." What Satan's legions have realized for many generations now is that when the masses of people become frightened, harried, and beset by bloody chaos, they tend to turn to their leaders and plead, "Fix things—do something—NOW!" This frantic desire for security creates opportunities for the Illuminati. They work to *invent* chaos, to generate anger and frustration on the part of humans and thus, take advantage of peoples' desperate need for order.

In the 1920s in pre-Nazi Germany, communist agitators and demonstrators took to the streets, threatening the security of the people. Then Hitler sent out his Brownshirt thugs to confront the communists. The resulting explosion of discord caused the German people to cry out for a leader who could re-establish *order out of chaos*. Hitler was their savior, the man on the white horse, promising *"Ordo Ab Chao."*

Satanic secret societies, of course, controlled both the Marxist, communist forces and their Nazi opposition. In other words, chaos was created *on purpose* so that order (and control) could be established. Facing the dire results of a threatening chaos, the multitudes are more than willing to empower a savior—the knight in shining armor—to put down the forces of chaos and re-establish order. Out of revolutionary chaos comes the opportunity for The Plan of the Illuminati to be realized.

Conspiracy writer Nesta Webster was one of only a few keen observers who has suggested that the power of tyrants resides in this Masonic doctrine. In *World Revolution,* Webster outlined the operational plan of the global conspirators. Theirs, she wrote, is "a systematic attempt to create grievances in order to exploit them."[10]

Sinking the Lusitania

Again and again, the controllers have artificially created a crisis and then come up with a *prepared in advance* solution. In 1917 the ship *Lusitania* was sunk in the Atlantic with the loss of hundreds of passengers. President Woodrow Wilson, an Illuminatus, blamed the tragedy on German U-boats. His intent was to bring the United States into the war on behalf of British secret societies and Freemasonry. His problem—and that of his co-conspirators—was that the American masses abhorred and were opposed to war. Indeed, to win election the previous year, Wilson had promised he would *never* send American boys to fight a European war.

It is now believed by some capable historians that the British sank the Lusitania themselves and blamed German U-boats to allow Wilson to use the sinking as a pretext to commit U.S. troops and forces to battle against Germany. Other historians say that the cargo hold of the Lusitania was filled with weapons made in America and headed for Britain to be used in the war effort. In either case, the facts were covered up. President Wilson stirred up the public by lying and inflaming public opinion to hate the Germans. In this way, the angry masses were propagandized and persuaded to send U.S. troops overseas to fight World War I.

The Illuminati intended to use the chaos of the war to further their globalist plot. Thus, following the allied victory, President Wilson and his behind-the-scenes White House mentor, Col. House—who later helped found the Council on

Foreign Relations—promoted the concept of the *League of Nations,* a predecessor of today's United Nations. The League of Nations was touted as a fledgling World Government necessary to end all future wars.

The Illuminati were unable to convince the American public to back their League of Nations scheme. However, in 1913, earlier during Wilson's administration, the elitists succeeded in two other long-cherished goals. First, their lackey, Woodrow Wilson, and his conspiratorial colleagues rammed through the Federal Reserve Act, creating the bankers' dictatorial Federal Reserve Board. Next, they tacked on the Sixteenth Amendment to the Constitution, putting the albatross of an income tax and an IRS agency around the necks of the citizenry.[11]

Chaos and Crises by Design

Here are some other examples of contrived crises and created chaos used by the Illuminati to advance their nightmarish scheme for Orwellian World Government:

* *War Invented:* On December 7, 1941, the Japanese attacked Pearl Harbor. History now reveals that President Franklin D. Roosevelt, 33° Mason, and his traitorous colleagues *knew in advance* that the attack would occur. The War Department had broken the Japanese code. But FDR had committed the U.S. to intervene in World War II and a pretext was needed to cause the American people, very isolationist and anti-war, to willingly back a declaration of war.[12]

* *More War Invented:* In August, 1964, President Lyndon B. Johnson claimed that North Vietnamese P-T boats had lobbed artillery shells at a U.S. ship off the coast of Vietnam. LBJ won almost a unanimous vote of Congress as the Gulf of Tonkin Resolution was passed granting the President extraordinary powers to pursue the air and ground war against the Communist foe. Years later, it was discovered that the North Vietnamese had never attacked the U.S. vessel. The incident was a tragic hoax—a contrived crisis.[13]

* *Diseases Invented:* In the 1980s, the media began sounding the alarm that a dreaded virus, HIV or AIDS, threatened the lives of tens of millions of Americans. Evidence, however, indicates that the U.S. Army's biological warfare laboratories may well have created the AIDS virus and that the United Nations World Health Organization *(WHO)* may have engineered its spread in Africa and elsewhere. The results could have been anticipated: fear, anxiety on the part of the masses, and the empowerment of the homosexual lobby. But an even more ominous consequence may lie in store in coming years if the *Inner Circle* decides to use viruses to decimate and depopulate the Earth.[14]

* *Environmental Crisis Invented:* In 1966, a classified government study, *The Report From Iron Mountain,* recommended that a global environmental crisis be contrived to engage the masses in a holy war to save Mother Earth.[15] The Illuminati saw that the environmental scare could also be used to further their Plan for World Government by international treaties (the *Convention on Biological Diversity).* This would destroy private property rights and enable the creation of a World Environmental Agency which would erode American sovereignty and enforce global law.

Corporate overlords tied in to the Illuminati network immediately began pumping millions of dollars into environmental organizations such as the Sierra Club, Greenpeace, the Nature Conservancy, and others, creating today's massive Mother Earth propaganda lobby. By keeping America's vast forests of timber from being harvested and huge reserves of oil from being extracted, the Fascist, corporate overlords of the Illuminati have also artificially kept prices of these natural resources sky-high. The environmental movement is a financial bonanza for the rich![16]

* *Overpopulation Crisis Invented:* Also in the 1960s, the Rockefellers and other Illuminists decreed that a disastrous "overpopulation problem" existed, although there was absolutely no scientific evidence whatsoever for this conclusion. Millions of dollars were pumped into organizations such as

the National Organization for Women (NOW), Planned Parenthood, and Zero Population Growth. Again, draconian bureaucratic measures of control were propagandized as necessary to solve this created crisis, including mass abortions and euthanasia.[17]

* *Healthcare Crisis Invented:* In 1992, co-Presidents Bill and Hillary Clinton, acting on behalf of the Rockefellers, declared by fiat the existence of an imaginary healthcare "crisis." Their proposed solution was to socialize America's entire healthcare system and bring it under stiff, Fascist government control. Fortunately, their attempt failed, but trust me—this scheme will be resurrected. It's too lucrative a scheme to lay fallow for long.[18]

* *The Crime Crisis Invented:* Also in 1992, the "crime problem" became a major focus of the controlled media. Despite FBI statistics which actually showed decreases in serious crimes, the public was fed dramatic "case" stories by the media about the victims of crime.[19] Always, *handguns* and the artificial category known as *"assault weapons"* were portrayed as the enemies of America. According to the Illuminati-inspired propaganda, violent criminals weren't the problem—just guns. Result: Congress passed the *Brady Bill* and President Clinton successfully demonized the National Rifle Association (NRA) and other Second Amendment groups. America is moving fast down the road toward a police state as the BATF, FBI, DEA, IRS, Secret Service, Customs Service, and dozens of other police agencies are targeting owners of guns for harassment and extinction.

* *Terrorist Crisis Invented:* In 1993 and 1995, so-called "terrorist" bombs caused devastation and loss of lives at the World Trade Center in New York City and at the federal building in Oklahoma City. Shocking news reports, covered up by the controlled media but accurately reported by alternative, patriot media, indicate government involvement in both of these horrendous tragedies. Result: The Illuminati conspirators stirred public outrage against patriotic militia

and other America First groups and pushed anti-terrorist bills through Congress.

Meanwhile, in federal court in New York City, during the trial of the Arabs accused of planting the bomb at the World Trade Center, the prosecution was stunned when the defendants introduced a tape recording which implicated the FBI itself in the monstrous bomb attack. In the tape recording, an FBI infiltrator is overheard offering the Arabs the bomb device and explosive materials. On the witness stand, this same FBI operative admitted that the FBI had provided the explosives and the bomb used by the Islamic plotters, and he confessed that he had been paid the sum of one million dollars to go undercover and deliver the deadly materials to the terrorists.[20]

* *Anti-Semitism Crisis Invented:* Throughout the 60s, 70s, and 80s, and on into the 90s, numerous radical groups advocating racial conflict and anti-Semitism were unearthed by the media. The media constantly bombarded us with frightening tales of KKK lunatics, neo-Nazi haters, and so forth. Then, evidence began to leak out that almost without exception, *every one* of these arcane and violent groups were set up by federal authorities. When such groups were "outed" and exposed, it was always federal infiltrators and affiliated non-governmental agencies who were responsible.[21]

It now can be concluded that, while there are no doubt some haters in every society, the U.S.A. included, the most visible of hate organizations featured so prominently in the newspapers and on TV news programs are government founded and funded. Result: The Illuminati has been incredibly successful in getting the public to accept outlandish gun control laws, hate and thought-crime legislation, and the empowerment of the FBI and other investigatory agencies.

A gestapo police state has been created in America, complete with the awesome powers to tap phones, break down doors, terrorize the citizenry, plant or destroy evidence, confiscate property, and even to murder innocent victims—all in the name of justice.[22]

* *Ethnic Cleansing Crisis Invented:* In the early 1990s, following the dismantling of the Iron Curtain and the ending of the "Cold War Crisis" (an Illuminati coordinated feat!), conflict, bloodshed, and chaos broke out in former Yugoslavia as the Croats, Serbs, and Moslems staked their individual claims to land and territory. Sensing a unique opportunity to demonstrate to the whole world both the danger of ethnic nationalism and the need for empowerment of a United Nations military assault force, the Illuminati began to covertly arm and agitate the Serbs and Croats. Concentration Camps were set up and stories of mass rape and torture became staple on Cable News Network (CNN) and on other establishment media.

Result: The artificial cry went out: "If only we could stop this evil nationalism, end separatist religious strife, and empower the United Nations, the carnage and atrocities such as we find in Bosnia would never again plague the world!"

Chaos is Good for Us

It is plain to see that modern history provides account after account of the Illuminati and its agents interfering in the affairs of men and nations. World Goodwill, an Illuminist organization connected to the United Nations organization, opined that, nevertheless, the many world crises and chaos could be used "for good"—to create conditions making possible the New Age, New World Order:

> We are living in one of the great crisis eras in all human history. Issues of peace and war, poverty and abundance, of racial, political, and industrial conflict face us on every side. Religious divisions and the clash between age and youth are likewise present, and underlying all is the basic conflict between material and spiritual values, between self-interest and world service. And yet, there is universal recognition that humanity is entering a New Age...and only the men and women of goodwill (*the Illumined Ones*) can guarantee a successful outcome. Countless movements based

> on goodwill (*Illuminist*) are attempting to create a better world...and carry out sustained and united world service.[23]

It is revealing, too, that World Goodwill and its affiliated parent organization, the Lucis Trust, are promoters and distributors of what they call the "Prayer for the New Age." Its official title is *The Great Invocation* because it invokes the "Hidden Ones" to come forth from their "world centre" to establish "world unity." *The Great Invocation* was read from the podium to kick off the Earth Summit, a huge environmentalist extravaganza held in Rio de Janeiro, Brazil in August, 1992.

Among the dignitaries at that gala environmental event were then U.S. President George Bush, Russian President Boris Yeltsin, Britain's Prime Minister John Majors, and various United Nations officials. They all sat solemnly as *The Great Invocation* was read, which included the notorious, yet mysterious, stanza, "Let Light and Love and Power restore the *Plan* on Earth. Om-Om-Om."

Two Opposing Forces, One Master

In 1969 in *Christians Awake Newsletter,* a fascinating article was published. Here are a few of the insights expressed in this phenomenal article:

> The perpetrators of revolution have learned one thing well. They must control all sides. For every action there must be an opposite and equal reaction. Hence today, we are witnessing classic world revolution.
>
> Revolution is like politics. There are always two sides. These two sides are controlled, inspired and guided so that these two sides finally merge into a planned and predicted conclusion.
>
> When the American people hear the word "Russia" they have been conditioned to think Communism. The world

> Communist hoax depends on it for its existence. Likewise, the giant military establishment in the United States depends on the Russian hoax. And finally, the fraudulent and shameful IRS tax tyranny depends on it.

What the patriotic author of this perceptive article was trying to tell us is that the Communist threat was, and is, a hoax. Yes, the Stalinists butchered millions and purged millions more. Yes, they conquered Eastern Europe and erected an iron curtain. But it was nothing more than Grand Theater. All along the Capitalist (Thesis) versus Communist (Antithesis) standoff was a staged drama of the super rich conspirators.

They first financed Vladimir Lenin and helped him and his Bolsheviks overthrow the Russian czar. Then they proceeded to contain, and yet feed, the monster until, finally, in the 1980s they could find no advantage in continuing their amusing and profitable game of global opposites. The Illuminati told Gorbachev the jig was up. The time for *synthesis* had arrived. Poof! Like magic, the gigantic, supposedly menacing Communist behemoth President Ronald Reagan had once labeled the "evil empire," promptly fell apart, right on cue. The illusion was no longer needed. The pageant was over. On to a *new game* for the Illuminati.

Fascism Arrives in Time for the New Millennium

That new game, of course, the new *synthesis,* is a treacherous combining of the most unscrupulous characteristics of both Capitalism and Communism. And what do you get when you merge Soviet Communism with American Capitalism? You get *Fascism*—a totalitarian socialist state in which, together, the state and a filthy-rich, corporate elite lord it over a docile and suppressed, woefully deceived populace. It is *Fascism* which lies in store for America and the world if the Illuminati get their way.

That is the reason why Gorbachev came to the United States and was given the historic Presidio Army installation as headquarters for his Gorbachev Foundation. It is why

President Bill Clinton travels regularly to Moscow and why America is propping up Russia with its tax dollars. Fascism is why the KGB and the CIA now cooperate to jointly harass U.S. and Soviet citizens, and why former Communist rulers still preside over the governments of the former Republics of the U.S.S.R.—Georgia, Ukraine, Chechnya, and the others. It is also the reason why the U.S.A. is fast becoming a socialist bulwark. We are becoming more Sovietized with each passing day. *Synthesis* of Communism and Capitalism is occurring.

Only a few, astute Americans familiar with the globalist and Hegelian aims of the Illuminati ever really understood what America's so-called "War on Communism" was really all about. James Knox, publisher of *American Focus* newsletter, is one such man. Here is his incisive analysis of the "Capitalist vs. Communism" dialectic set up by the elitists to alchemically transform mankind:

> There are two great forces in the world...Each is directed from the same boardroom. One is Capitalism and the other is Communism...While unrestrained Capitalism rapes natural resources and condemns the weak to poverty, it does provide a climate of opportunity and added value to sustain a society. But it does not lend itself to the absolute dictatorial world control dreamed of by powerful and arrogant men...
>
> To evolve a society of subjects working for an elite corps of rulers or even a single ruler, Communist/Socialist movements were created to counter Capitalism. In the late 19th century Hegel had postulated that the most desirable social order would develop out of the *interaction of opposing forces,* by first identifying a *thesis* (Capitalism), creating an *antithesis* (Communism) and, by controlling their relationship, elicit the new desired *synthesis* of man's purpose (Fascism).
>
> Herr Hagel was surely an Illuminati, for it was they who created and underwrote Communism to commence the 80-year old trek to World Fascism.[24]

Knox's analysis is right on target. The *synthesis* of Communism and Capitalism—the combining of these two, great competing systems vying for world domination—is *Fascism*. Fascism is the ideal system for the Illuminati. Through Fascism, the Rothschilds and the Rockefellers and their many, eager disciples intend to transform the planet into a totalitarian Brave New World. What's more, says Knox, the anointed leaders of the Illuminati "will personify the gods and the lifestyles of classical mythology."[25] They will be masters of a new Babylon, Rome and Egypt.

Fascism, Knox writes, is ideal for the Illuminati: "It was created as a one-party system, not democratic but oligarchic and dictatorial." Fascism, as practiced by the Nazis, left industry, commerce, and property in the hands of individuals and corporations. Nevertheless, the government, the state, was the ultimate orbiter of authority.

In the new, 2000 AD version of Fascism designed for implementation in the New World Order, the upper echelons of the corporate elite *are* the state. They are to possess absolute power. Industry and commerce are to be regulated by the state solely for their benefit. Private property is, for all practical purposes, to become state property, though its title may remain in the hands of individuals. Commerce will either be regulated to enrich the Illuminati overlords or it will be regulated out of existence.

In the view of the Illuminists, Capitalism gave too much power to the middle class and even to the little people. Communism gave too much power to the bureaucracy and the politicians. Fascism is best because it relegates the bulk of power to the few, the privileged elite—the *Illuminati*. Thus, we should have, from the perspective of the conspirators, the best of both worlds: Communism *and* Capitalism. *We shall have a Fascist New World Order.*

Hitler and Mussolini Improved On

Hitler and Mussolini's Fascism was tentative, flawed, incomplete. Besides, it left out the possibility of a Zionist

At left: *When Mikhail Gorbachev visited the United States in 1992, he was flown from city to city on this airplane owned by multimillionaire publisher Malcolm Forbes, which, appropriately, is named "Capitalist Tool." Malcolm Forbes, a homosexual, is now dead of AIDS.*

At right: *President Ronald Reagan called the U.S.S.R. the "evil empire." Then on cue, the evil empire supposedly just vanished.*

At left: *This revealing picture is from the Fall 1992 issue of* ***Foreign Affairs****, the official journal of the Council on Foreign Relations. William G. Hyland, Editor-in-Chief, is shown pointing out to CFR visitor Mikhail Gorbachev an original copy of the very first issue of* ***Foreign Affairs*** *which has notes written in it by Lenin's own hand.*

At right: *President Reagan confers with Gorby.*

superstate headquartered in Jerusalem. Moreover, even though Hitler and Mussolini were initially funded by the Illuminati and their work guided by the secret societies (*Vril, Thule,* etc.), the two dictators unexpectedly became "free-lancers."[26] They rebelled against their creators and threatened to set up their own World Empire, apart from the greedy hands of the Illuminati.

Still, the Hitler-Mussolini era had been an approved Illuminati project, an experiment to determine how effective a Fascist system could be in controlling the masses. In this respect, it was an overwhelming success. Hitler's *Third Reich* lasted just twelve years, but though it was terminated by the Illuminati short of its goals, the Third Reich experience proved conclusively to the financiers and other elitists that Earth was like a ripe plum for the taking. With enough propaganda and preliminary spadework, men everywhere could be manipulated through deception to become slaves and cogs of a Fascist World Empire.

Operating on this key premise, for decades until the mid-80s the masters of the Illuminati Conspiracy cleverly used the ominous specter of atheistic Communism and the induced fears of a nuclear first strike by the Soviets to persuade the citizenry to enthusiastically support the corporate boondoggle known euphemistically as the "military-industrial complex."

After an enormous amount of blood (and money) had been sucked out of the citizens to build this military-industrial complex, it was decided that the myth of the invincible Communist superstate would be ended. Its time was up. Its usefulness at an end. No longer did a majority of people believe in the Communist threat. It was painfully apparent that the Communist states were technical failures with bankrupt economies led by incompetent bureaucrats and commissars.

Now a new enemy had to be chosen—a new set of hate targets promulgated. That new enemy, the horrible new monster chosen for eventual elimination by the Illuminati, is *Nationalism.* Patriots everywhere would be demonized and caricatured as holdovers and misfits of a cave man, Neanderthal era. Global Citizens would, on the other hand, become role models and exemplars.

Nationalism is the Dark Menace

Today, as we near the dawning of the Third Millennium after the first coming of Christ Jesus, the Illuminati's final stage of struggle is between *Nationalism* (thesis) and *Universalism* (antithesis). The outcome is slated to be the *New World Order* (synthesis), a global state in which individual nations are accorded only perfunctory status, possess almost no power, have no separate autonomy, and, essentially, are subservient to the authority of a *Supreme Council of Wise Men.* The ten men who make up the *Inner Circle* of the Illuminati comprise this *Supreme Council.* Soon, their great leader will show himself as a world savior, a man who can bring "order out of chaos." He will be Antichrist, Satan in human flesh.

Christians Awake Newsletter predicted back in 1983 this coming of a Fascist superstate which would be held up as a "Kingdom of God" on Earth:

> On the stage we have the *thesis,* which is something called Communism. Then we have the *antithesis* or something called anti-Communism. The thesis and the antithesis appear to be opposites and they appear to be in total ideological struggle.
>
> Finally, they merge into the *synthesis,* as planned. The synthesis or final form is to be a world superstate which is monopoly capitalism (fascism) which is a world monopoly of capital and wealth under a benevolent facade—a "Kingdom of God on Earth."[27]

This revolutionary method—the systematic working of thesis vs. antithesis = synthesis, is the key to understanding world history. Once an understanding of this diabolical system of the combining of opposites is attained, then all other things come clearly into focus. The working of this dialectic process, this conflict of opposites, is the reason why we continue to suffer wars and rumors of wars. It is why, no matter who is in power in Washington, D.C.—Republicans or Democrats—the citizenry gets shortchanged and the will of the majority is ignored. *Ordo Ab Chao* explains the need for Big Brother governments to sponsor terrorism, incite racial violence, and inspire ethnic hatred. Through chaos, the Illuminati Plan prospers.

If we are to successfully counter the Great Work of the Illuminati we must first comprehend their philosophy of creating and perpetuating crises to achieve "order out of chaos." Only when we decipher their methods and understand their alchemical processing of humanity can we escape being manipulated by the Illuminati and breathe free as intelligent and loving human beings.

But can we succeed in this endeavor? Can we thwart the Illuminati's attempts to control us? While we may or may not be able to prevent their Plan of an Antichrist global order from being achieved, I am convinced that, if we trust in God, we *can* personally withstand this seductive philosophy, *Ordo Ab Chao,* which heavily permeates society and, unceasingly, structures governmental actions everywhere. In fact, it is God who has promised us that if we trust in Him and rely on His Word, we will *not* fall prey to the lie (II Thessalonians 2) and we *will* understand:

> Many shall be purified, and made white, and tried; but the wicked shall do wickedly: and none of the wicked shall understand; but the wise shall understand. (Daniel 12:10)

SIX

Political Alchemy and Conspiracy: Right-Wing and Left-Wing, Republican and Democrat—They're All the Same!

The ***New Age*** *magazine is...the official publication of the Supreme Council, 33rd degree, Ancient and Accepted Scottish Rite of Freemasonry...This Council claims to be the Mother Council of the World...The cover of the April 1988 issue of that magazine...shows the then President Ronald Reagan along with three other Masons. The President is holding a framed certificate that had been presented to him by...C. Fred Kleinknecht, Sovereign Grand Commander...The magazine then produced a letter that the President had written to "Illustrious Brother Kleinknecht." It read in part: "I am honored to join the ranks of sixteen former presidents in their association with Freemasonry."*

—Ralph Epperson
The New World Order

"No matter which political party is in power, nothing ever changes." How many times have we heard this complaint? Is it true? At the core, is there really no difference between the two major parties, Republican and Democrat? History provides the startling answer that totally defies the common wisdom.

The Nixon and Ford Eras: Rockefeller Reigns

From 1964 to 1974, Republican Richard M. Nixon occupied the oval office in the White House. During that era, one bureaucracy after another was created. The federal budget zoomed upward, deficits blossomed. Onerous anti-constitutional laws, such as the Environmental Protection Act, were passed, restricting the rights of private property owners and taking away their lands without compensation as required by the Constitution.

For his chief foreign policy advisor, Nixon chose Henry Kissinger. *U.S. News & World Report* explained why: "It was on the advice of New York Governor Nelson Rockefeller who described Mr. Kissinger as 'the smartest guy available,' that Mr. Nixon chose him for his top advisor on foreign policy."[1]

In fact, politician Richard Nixon was always a puppet of the Rockefeller dynasty. To prove his loyalty to their globalist aims, on July 9, 1947, freshman Representative Richard Nixon (R.-CA) introduced House Concurrent Resolution 68 indicating:

> ...that it is the sense of Congress that the President of the United States should immediately take the initiative in calling a General Conference of the United Nations pursuant to (U.N.) Article 109 for the purpose of making the United Nations capable of enforcing world law...[2]

President Gerald Ford, Nixon's successor, kept Kissinger on board as Secretary of State and chose Nelson Rockefeller as America's first, unelected vice president. Nelson Rockefeller replaced the incompetent Spiro Agnew who was ousted due to financial scandals.

Both the Ford and Nixon administrations were run by cabinet officials and bureau heads who were members of the unAmerican, pro-New World Order Council on Foreign Relations (CFR). President Ford is himself a member of the globalist CFR as well as a 33rd degree Mason.

The Carter Era: Rockefeller Reigns

Democrat Jimmy Carter took office in 1976. He immediately made Zbigniew Brzezinski his chief foreign policy advisor and made him head of the National Security Council. Who was Brzezinski? He just happened to be a CFR member and was also co-founder, with David Rockefeller, Sr., of the Trilateral Commission. "The top 19 positions in the Carter cabinet were held by individuals who had been members of David Rockefeller's Trilateral Commission."[3]

Indeed, as Governor of Georgia, Jimmy Carter was himself a charter member of Rockefeller's Trilateral Commission. In London, England in 1976, Carter met privately with Lord Rothschild and David Rockefeller and was told he would be given their "green light" to successfully run for the presidency that year.[4]

The Reagan Era: Rockefeller Reigns

When Republican Ronald Reagan campaigned for president in 1980 he vowed things would be different. No CFR or Trilateral Commission members would be invited into his administration. But what really happened? Immediately, Reagan chose as his vice-presidential running mate Skull & Bones man George Bush. Bush had been a director of the CFR and a Trilateralist. As a young congressman from Texas, he once introduced a bill to end American sovereignty and transfer powers to the United Nations. Bush was a key member in Rockefeller's Zero Population Growth (ZPG) organization, a group supporting mass abortion and depopulation of the Earth.[5]

In almost every cabinet post, President Ronald Reagan, Republican President, appointed a New World Order, Rockefeller clone. His Secretary of Commerce, Secretary of State, Secretary of Treasury, Secretary of Defense, and Director of the Central Intelligence Agency were all members of the CFR and the Trilateral Commission.

The sellout to the *Inner Circle* of the Illuminati continued unabated during the Reagan administration. Federal spending ballooned and budget deficits went through the roof. Forfeiture bills providing for the unconstitutional seizure of the peoples' property were passed and enforced—without benefit of protection of the law. The BATF, FBI, IRS, and EPA continued their marauding, thug-like criminal behavior. There were the banking and savings & loan fiascos. Nothing changed under the Republicans—in fact, things got worse!

Some die-hard Reagan fans say that, during his eight years in office, their "conservative" hero was tricked and deceived by the establishment insiders who surrounded him. He was not responsible, they claim; others did the dirty work. However, the fact is that Ronald Reagan began to compromise from the moment he received the Republican nomination for President of the United States. Indeed, it is likely the "Gipper" from Hollywood was compromised long before that, back during his stint as an ad pitch man for multinational corporation General Electric on TV's "Death Valley Days."

In any case, President Reagan was honored for his service to the Illuminati in the final months of his presidency. Ralph Epperson, in his insight-filled book, *The New World Order,* details Reagan's initiation to the exalted 33rd degree of Freemasonry. In a letter he addressed to "Illustrious Brother C. Fred Kleinknecht, Sovereign Grand Commander," the President thanked the Supreme Mother Council for the "honor" bestowed upon him and stated: "I am honored to join the ranks of sixteen former presidents in their association with Freemasonry."[6]

When he assumed the post of America's Chief Executive in 1980, Ronald Reagan was *not* a Mason at all. But tellingly, in 1988, he was made a full, 33rd degree Mason all in one, fell swoop. The Masons call this being raised and elevated "at sight" in their lodges. It is a rare occurrence. The globalists of the *Inner Circle* were happy, indeed, with this man's performance in office.

The Bush Era: Rockefeller Reigns

We know of the dismal record of George Bush—about his fervent push for the New World Order, about his sickening support of 1992's occultic Earth Summit in Rio de Janeiro, about the many environmental restrictions passed during his four-year term taking away the peoples' property, about the savage criminality of the CIA, FBI, BATF and other federal law enforcement agencies, about FEMA concentration camps being constructed, about the hundreds of millions of taxpayer dollars spent on lewd and blasphemous "art" by George Bush's National Endowment for the Arts. All this occurred during Bush's *Republican* administration.

We know also about George Bush's sitting idly by as law enforcement agencies brutally suppressed, arrested, and sometimes tortured pro-life demonstrators. We should also recall the billions of foreign aid money Bush and his cohorts sent to Russia, Israel, Egypt and elsewhere, while the American homeless population grew, factories were moved overseas, and millions of Americans were put out of work. And, of course, we recall the vast increases in federal taxes—in spite of Bush's "Read my lips—No new taxes!" pledge.

The Clinton Era: Rockefeller Reigns

Democrat Bill Clinton is more of the same. Seventeen of his top 19 cabinet officials are members of either the Trilateral Commission or the CFR. Clinton himself is a member of those Illuminati-controlled groups and is also a Bilderberger.[7] Again, taxes are increased, and the FBI, BATF, IRS, and other agencies continue their unconstitutional snooping and murderous attacks on the people and then cover up their crimes. Billions of the peoples' money go to Israel, Russia, Egypt, even to Yasser Arafat's Palestine Liberation Army. Billions go also into the gold-lined pockets of Jordan's treacherous Moslem monarch, King Hussein, Saddam Hussein's cousin and neighbor. Under Democrat Bill Clinton, as under Republican George Bush, Russia's Boris Yeltsin is allowed to rape and butcher his own people in Chechnya and elsewhere, and American troops are still under NATO and United Nations' command.[8]

Bill Clinton, like his predecessor, George Bush, is "owned"

by the Rockefellers and does their bidding. His licking their boots would be an embarrassment, *if* this vile man was capable of being embarrassed. Bill Clinton is a man with a deep hole in his soul.

Six Presidents—One Master

This, then, is the horrendous record of our six most recent presidents: Nixon, Ford, Carter, Reagan, Bush, and Clinton. Verifiably, each was a lackey and a flunky, bowing down to the New World Order establishment, and meticulously carrying out to the nth degree the entire Illuminati agenda and Plan. The terrible and awful truth is that for many years now, in the United States of America, there has been only *one* political party: the party of *money,* the one party funded and closely controlled by the *Inner Circle* of the Illuminati.

How can this be? *Why is it that the Inner Circle wins no matter who is elected to high office?* And if the Illuminati have, for term after term, controlled every modern U.S.A. President, not to mention the leaders of the Senate and the House of Representatives, why do they bother to carry out the illusion that the people have a choice? Why not end the charade and cease all this political party bickering and posturing?

Good questions, and there are answers. The answers are found in the Secret Doctrine of the Illuminati. We must focus our attention on the use by the elite of the process of *political alchemy,* as exemplified by the *Hegelian dialectic.* This alchemical process is our key to understanding why right-wing or left-wing, Democrat or Republican, nothing really changes, and America continues to hurdle forward into the Brave New World of totalitarian despotism.

Mr. Hegel's Theories: Winning Through Conflict

George Friedrich Wilhelm Hegel (1770-1831) is most often credited with developing the Illuminist philosophy that has

Zbigniew Brzezinski meets in the library of the Council on Foreign Relations. Brzezinski, who helped David Rockefeller, Sr., found the Trilateral Commission, was National Security Advisor in the Carter Administration.

Dole and Clinton Strike a Deal on World Trade Pact

Escape Clause for Congress Is a Key

By DAVID E. SANGER

The ***New York Times*** *(November 24, 1994) details how Senate Majority Leader Bob Dole and President Clinton teamed up to establish the Illuminati's World Trade Organization (WTO).*

Presidents Richard Nixon, a "conservative" Republican and Jimmy Carter, a "liberal" Democrat, were both controlled by David Rockefeller, Sr.

become widely known as the *Hegelian dialectic.* Hegel believed that only through "Reason" (a Masonic concept) could man attain freedom. To Hegel, history is a three-step process of change: *Thesis, Antithesis,* and *Synthesis.*[9]

In the first instance, *Thesis,* Hegel proposed that crises occur and fears by the masses mount up. The people become angry and occasionally hysterical about present conditions. Opposition is generated to solve the misery, fear, and sometimes panic experienced by the people. This opposition becomes the *Antithesis.* Then, in the third step of this social process, a *Synthesis,* or compromise solution, is found to the problem. Equilibrium is temporarily achieved based on this clash and conflict of opposites: Thesis vs. Antithesis.

This state of Equilibrium becomes the new Thesis, of course, and this reignites the cycle. Once again opposition is encountered, and so conflict and chaos continue with more optimal states of Equilibrium progressingly achieved.

An understanding of Hegel's dialectical process gave the Illuminati the idea of priming the pump, so to speak. Why not *invent* crises? Why not *create* grievances? Why not work secretly to instill fear in the people, to create turmoil? Why not set up and control your own opposition? In this way, changes favorable to they, the rulers, the Illuminati, could be *engineered* and *caused.*

In fact, Hegel was a Masonic collaborator who conveniently provided the theory that would be used by the Illuminati with such devastating and deadly effectiveness for almost two centuries. Not only that, but Hegel surely knew that in the Masonic lexicon, "Reason," which Hegel taught could bring men freedom, is, in reality, simply an esoteric, Illuminist codeword identifying the hidden master whom occult Masons worship and adore.

In her epochal volume, *The Secret Doctrine,* Helena Blavatsky, the mother of Theosophy, revealed the name of this hidden master. "Reason," she wrote is none other than the "Serpent of Wisdom." In other words: Satan![10]

Hegel, then, was a Satanist. That he advocated a Fascist, totalitarian state is also a fact. In a perceptive article entitled, "The Hegelian Counterfeit," Franklin Sanders unmasked the awful truth about Hegel's totalitarian leanings:

> Searching for the source and object of this freedom, Hegel stumbles upon the state as the embodiment of the divine on Earth. This was not terribly original, as the Greeks had beat him to it by 25 centuries. At the same time, he tries to resolve the ancient philosophical problem of which is more ultimate: the one or the many by submerging the individual (the one) into the state (the many)...Hegel finds the unity of individual satisfaction and freedom in conformity to the social ethos of an organic community.[11]

A Grand Synthesis: Igniting a Great Fire

In other words, the Hegelian principle seeks to reassure us that the world is steadily evolving, through a series of dialectical struggles, toward a *Grand Synthesis* in which men will be free and happy because they willingly and enthusiastically serve their universal master, the superstate.

Oh, how the Illuminati must have loved this bright fellow, for, by his philosophy, Hegel paved the way for *World Revolution.* To signify their unqualified acceptance of the Hegelian principle, the Illuminati and subsidiary Masonic orders adopted as their motto the Latin slogan, *Ordo Ab Chao*—Order Out of Chaos.

Then, during the French Revolution of the 1790s, the concept of *igniting opposition* to the establishment and, thereby, dynamically escalating the revolutionary process, was rushed into practice. During that bloody era of guillotines and debauchery, the Hegelian dialectical process was expressed very cogently and powerfully by one of the Illuminist conspirators, Sylvain Maréchal. In his popular book, *Voyages de Pythagore* (1799), Maréchal invented the revolutionary phrase, "Seize the Moment" (also known as "Seize the Day," or, in Latin, *Carpe Diem*), when he wryly suggested:

> It is necessary to seize the suitable moment...With the smallest spark a great fire can be ignited.

So enamored were the Illuminati with the works of Hegel that one of Maréchal's contemporaries, the Russian Alexander Herzen, shockingly proposed that, thanks to Hegel, a "New Christianity" could take shape, made possible by "the absolute knowledge revealed by Hegel." Finally, said a euphoric Herzen, a "future society" can be constructed.[12]

"Hegel," Herzen wrote in 1839, is the *New Christ* bringing the Word of truth to men..."[13]

History Not by Accident

Today, the average citizen is abysmally ignorant about this horrendously malignant satanic doctrine and theory of Hegel's. The media and the education establishment provide not a clue to the actual operation of society and the real history of the world. Instead, we are fed the bunk notion that history is not by design but by accident. Revolution, we are told, is never planned but seems to just spontaneously "happen." We are also repeatedly reminded of the evil leaders who have arisen in various epochs of history, and we are instructed that these wicked men were either left-wing (Stalin) or right-wing (Hitler). Politicians are said to be liberal (Kennedy) or conservative (Nixon).

Meanwhile, meticulously planned events continue to transpire to drive mankind inexorably forward into the vague and hazy New Age future—the New Civilization—which our media and educators assure us will be to our benefit. Politicians and their media cohorts alike continue to confuse and irritate us with labels like conservative and liberal, right-wing and left-wing. Arab terrorists, we are told, are left-wing while militias and patriots are scathingly described to us as right-wing. These labels are designed to confuse and mislead us.

We would be well advised to heed the sage words of Antony Sutton, a conspiratorial authority who, in his excellent book, *America's Secret Establishment,* advised:

> Above all the reader must...put to one side the descriptive cliches of left and right, liberal and conservative,

> communist and fascist, even republican and democrat... They are confusing in our context unless seen as essential elements in a game plan.[14]

Rather than employ such artificial and confusing terms, Sutton cautions readers that they should, instead, always focus their attention on the *process* of politics and world affairs. It is, he warns, the *Hegelian Dialectic process* which is being used "to bring about a society in which the state is absolute;" i.e. all powerful.[15]

We must also understand that Hegel's theories were not new. The Greeks proposed similar theories as did the ancient Chinese. The conflict of opposites propelling man's destiny is also essentially the same system that atheist Charles Darwin borrowed to propose his *Theory of Evolution*. Darwin's flawed theory held that there is the organism (thesis) which clashes with the opposing forces of nature (antithesis). Out of this conflict and the resulting chaos comes a *new order* of things—a new, perfected species (synthesis). That, in essence, is Darwin's unscientific and illogical theory. The adherents of Darwinism, supported by the Rockefeller and Rothschild-designed educational establishment, cling tenaciously to the discredited theory of evolution because, if they face up to the fact that Darwin was wrong, the whole house of cards of the Illuminati might come crashing down.

Chaos Theory and Communism

German Karl Marx, in the 1860s, was inspired by Satan to adapt this same scheme to his own theories of economic and political revolution. In his books, *The Communist Manifesto* and *Das Kapital (The Capitalists),* Marx put forth the concept of "dialectical materialism." Man's evolutionary path, Marx predicted, would inevitably lead to utopian socialism: that is, to *Communism.*

The real reason for Marx's adoption of Hegel's dialectical process and for his belief in "scientific evolution" was his hatred toward Jesus Christ and the Christian Church. There is ample evidence to prove that Karl Marx was not only a member of a socialist Illuminati society known as the *League of Just Men* and that he was supported financially by this group, but that he was also a zealous student of the occult and a Satanist. "My object in life," Marx once said, "is to dethrone God and destroy Capitalism."[16]

Of Guillotines and Rebellion

Many of Marx's ideas came out of the fertile, Illuminist soil of the French Revolution of 1789. That bloody era of guillotines and rebellion, of the worship of the Masonic Goddess of Liberty and of urinating and defecating on Christian crosses and on church pews, was a time of supreme testing for Satan's chaos theory.

The French Revolution, which followed by exactly 13 years (a supernaturally significant number) the signing of the American *Declaration of Independence,* was the conscious product of an unholy Illuminati conspiratorial plot. It began with the creation of grievances—with blatant lies about the King and Queen (Marie Antonette *never said* "Let them eat cake"). Soon, the conspirators inspired a mob to storm the Bastille to "free the political prisoners."

Some in the crowd must have been startled to find a grand total of only *three* surprised and delighted drunks and vagrants. *There were no political prisoners!* Nevertheless, the rioters looted the Bastille, captured the guns and explosives found in its armory—their *real* objective in the first place—and France proceeded headlong into a chilling Reign of Terror virtually unmatched in human history in its barbarism.

Lenin, Stalin, and Mao, we are told, took Marx's writings one step further, contending that the inevitable could be speeded and helped along by a "Vanguard of the Proletariat"—a nucleus or small band of dedicated and superior revolutionary men prodding and leading the sleepy, unconscious masses ever forward into the bright New Age of World Communism.

It is easy to discern that in this curious addition to Marxist theory was the seed gospel of the Illuminati. It has long been the occult view that the Great Work—the illumination of mankind and the creation of a Holy Empire—could be achieved, even accelerated by a systematic process of world revolutionary activity.

Alchemy at Work Today

It is this process of dualism and chaos production that, today, is resulting in so much bloodshed and chaos—from Iraq and Somalia to Bosnia, Haiti, and in the Middle East. In country after country, the Illuminati precipitate and promote crises so that *order can come out of chaos* and the Holy Empire can steadily emerge from its present shadows.

What is being played out on the world scene is, in effect, *alchemy*. In the medieval ages, sorcerers, magicians, and esoteric philosophers suggested that baser metals like lead could be transmuted into gold. They also believed that, through alchemy, man in his old age could be transformed into youth. Regenerated.

The quaint beliefs of the alchemists were expressed in many books and treatises. But in fact, these writings were philosophically disingenuous hoaxes. What these evil occultists were really stating was not some new way to produce gold and become materially rich. *They were elaborating the satanic principles of world revolution.*

The alchemists had bought into the theory of man's progress to self-divinity. Their doctrine was that man could achieve perfection through his own efforts. He could become "god." Transforming lead and baser metals to gold through a magical formula and renewing youth (Ponce de León's "Fountain of Youth" myth, for example) were mythical expressions of the desire to conduct occultic experiments designed to catapult base, inferior man to godhood and to return the decaying Earth to a state of pre-evolutionary perfection.

The alchemists were, in reality, revolutionaries—the Marxists and Hegelians of their day. They sought to return man and Earth to the blissful state of their origin. Through "chaos" they would hasten the evolution of man to his original, divine status before the Adamic fall.

In sum: the goal of the alchemists was to undo God's work. In the Garden of Eden, God had placed a curse on the Earth and upon man, but the alchemists believed that their deity (Lucifer) could reverse nature's decay, overcome man's limitations, undo the curse, and effect *regeneration.*

Fallen and unregenerate man, then, has since Babylon and even before, ever proposed that freedom from God and self-divinity could be attained through *chaos.* At first, it was thought that man's perfection—the wringing of order out of chaos—could be achieved through natural evolution—via a gradual metamorphosis. But later, the idea spread that evolution could be speeded up and *induced*—that is, created—by chaos. *E*volution gave way to *r*evolution.

Satan's revolutionary disciples girded themselves for battle. Their ageless foes were God and His people. Their weapon was to be revolutionary activism and creative destruction—*Ordo Ab Chao.* The global conspiracy took on a new, more forceful dimension.

Torchbearers for World Revolution

As the 1960s and 1970s unfolded, the Illuminati-sponsored New Age movement gained millions of followers. One New Age leader, John Randolph Price, founder of the Planetary Commission, began to tout a coming Utopia to be ushered in by Illumined superbeings. These Illumined superbeings, Price's spirit guides explained to him, have long been instrumental in man's progress toward an "Aquarian Age of Spirituality on Planet Earth." They are torchbearers for *world revolution:*

> The revolution has begun...the pace is quickening. Throughout the world, men and women are joining in the uprising (and rising up) and are coming forward to be counted as part of a new race that will someday rule the universe.

> Now we can co-create the future according to the Divine Plan.[17]

Examining the writings of men like Price, we can see how profound are the prophecies in the Book of Daniel which tell us that the last days Antichrist, the beast with the number 666 (see Revelation 13) will win his kingdom through "flattery."

What blatant flattery it is to promise that a man can be "counted as part of a new race that will someday rule the universe!"

Imagine the false pride that is heightened in the breast of small-time operators such as Newt Gingrich, Jimmy Carter, Henry Kissinger, and Bill Clinton when they are assured that by cooperating with the *Inner Circle* of the Illuminati, they can divinely "co-create the future" and become torchbearers for the world revolution.

"Power, fame, money—godhood—it can all be yours," the puppets of the Illuminati are told. That's flattery on a grand scale, just as was prophesied in the Scriptures.

Inspired by such rhetoric and mesmerized by the magic of demon spirits who constantly overshadow their everyday existence, the puppet leaders of this world go boldly forth to create chaos and destruction. They do so fully expecting that out of chaos will come the New Civilization, the New World Order. It is to be a paradise on Earth, a Shangri-la world state.

The world is to be shaped and molded like some global drama, a drama in which these leaders have been promised they will be allowed to play a significant part.

In *The New International Economic Order,* co-Mason Alice Bailey describes the globalist hopes and aspirations of the Illuminati in glowing, god-like terms as the building of a *new creation:*

> In the destruction of the old world order and in the *chaos* of these modern times, the work of the *new creation* is going forward; the task of reconstruction, leading to a complete reorganization of human living....[18]

Hillary Clinton's Politics of Meaning

In yet another occult treatise, *Discipleship in the New Age,* Bailey revealed that the God of the Illuminati, whom she cagily referred to as the "universal creative aspect," has designed The Plan so that there will be a world "transition from chaos to ordered Beauty." This, she explained, is the "politics of meaning." Bailey further describes this coming time of universal love and harmony as "The One Life."[19] How fascinating is the fact that, in 1993, during a speech at the University of Texas at Austin, America's First Lady, Hillary Clinton, echoed Illuminati prophet Alice Bailey. What Americans, as global citizens, must do to transcend the current world situation, Hillary Clinton proposed, is to adopt an entirely new way of thinking: a "politics of meaning."[20]

Psychopolitics: Alchemy and Genocide, Soviet-Style

A prime example of the activism on the part of Illuminists who advocate chaos theory is found in the revealing words of Laventi Beria, Stalin's ruthless chief of security. He, too, believed in a "politics of meaning." He, too, like Hillary Rodham Clinton and her husband, Bill, was a dedicated promoter of Marx's and Lenin's dialectical materialism. In the 30s, 40s, and early 50s the vicious secret police terrorized Soviet Russia. Especially during the savage reign of Beria, all of Russia quaked in fear. Millions of victims were forcibly evicted from their homes and sent to Siberian mines and to gulag camps; countless thousands more were horribly tortured and brutalized. A deadly pall and cloud of silence settled over the land.

Beria used not only terror but chaos. His weapons were those of occult alchemy. In one infamous speech given at V. I. Lenin University, Beria revealed the basis of his alchemical methods, which he called "Psychopolitics." Here is a portion of that speech:

> Students at the Lenin University, I welcome your attendance at these classes on *Psychopolitics.*

> Psychopolitics is an important if less known division of geo-politics. It is less known because it must necessarily deal with "mental healing."
>
> By Psychopolitics our chief goals are carried forward. *To produce a maximum of chaos in the culture of the enemy is our first most important step.*
>
> Our fruits are grown in chaos, distrust, economic depression, and scientific turmoil. At last a weary populace can seek peace only in our offered Communist State; at last only Communism can resolve the problem of the masses.
>
> A psychopolitician must work hard to produce the maximum chaos in the fields of "mental healing." He must recruit and use all the agencies and facilities of "mental healing." He must labor to increase the personnel and facilities of "mental healing" until at last the entire field of mental science is entirely dominated by Communist principles and desires.[21]

As Beria's remarks make clear, the dastardly goal of state-created social chaos and confusion is the conquest of the mind. Through planned chaos and especially through the planting of double-mindedness and induced contradictions, an entire population can be controlled and enslaved. Worse, all of humanity can be driven insane. It is no small thing that the Apostle James, in the Holy Bible, taught that, "A double-minded man is unstable in all his ways."

What greater mission could Satan, his horde of demons, and his Illuminati pursue than to rule over a planet populated by mind slaves—robotized men and women driven to despair, fear, and depravity by the planned actions of the promoters of chaos and contradiction.

Russia's bloody chief of secret police, Beria, called his alchemical tactics "mental healing." Now, decades later, many of us are well aware of the sinister efforts of the Central Intelligence Agency, the FBI, the Tavistock Institute, and other Big Brother government groups to induce chaos to control the minds of men and women. We know the facts about the CIA's top secret *MK-Ultra Project* and about the CIA's monstrous *Project Monarch.* We who have studied know also about the psychedelic LSD experiments of intelligence operatives Aldous Huxley, Gerald Heard, and others. And we know of the horrors of Soviet mental institutions and "hospitals," where dissidents were taken, force-fed and injected with psychoactive drugs, and turned into little more than vegetables and dimwits.

Assault on Human Freedom

Now today, the governments of this world, inspired by the Illuminati, continue their vicious campaigns against human freedom. Increasingly, our prisons and mental institutions are used as experimental centers for the new psychopoliticians. Psychiatry and analysis, brain surgery, shock treatment, and chemotherapy—these have become inhuman tools wielded by brutal madmen who work to destroy individuality and mold us all into mindless drones forever willing to obey the dictates of the state. The Illuminati have mandated that the world is to be lobotomized through an alternating process of induced double-mindedness, chaos, pain, and pleasure.[22]

Psychopolitics—defined as "the art and science of asserting and maintaining dominion over the thoughts and loyalties of individuals, bureaucracies, and masses, and the effecting of the conquest of the opposition as well as enemy nations through mental healing"[23]—has become the chosen vehicle for the alchemical transformation of the United States and the world.

In 1937, that monstrous agent of Communism, Laventi Beria, ordered that, "The entire weight of all psychopoliticians in the nation should be pressed into service."[24] Today, as we speed toward the year 2000 and a new millennium approaches, we see irrefutable evidence that Beria's admonition is not only being heeded but is being amplified by other, modern-day "Berias" in every nation of the globe.

In America, Beria's Luciferian doctrine of Psychopolitics has almost become a religion—a shibboleth of faith subscribed to by politicians, psychologists, medical doctors, sociologists, historians, and yes, by clergymen, everywhere. Producing Luciferian chaos, discord, and confusion in the minds of men and women is America's burgeoning growth industry.

Two Shall Become One

The main principle of alchemical chaos theory is that the apparent *two* shall ultimately become *one*. Satan and his goddess—the whore of Babylon—shall become one. The masculine and feminine shall become one: the hermaphrodite. The left and right brain hemispheres of man will be integrated as one. The two great world systems in the end-times, Communism and Capitalism, shall be merged into one. The two dominant factions of Christianity, Catholicism and Protestantism, shall become one.

Finally, and most significant, the thrones of God and Satan shall be united, so that only one Supreme Deity shall preside over the cosmos. Satan stupidly and imperiously aspires to this high position. Fortunately, his is an impossible mission which will merely seal the Evil One's final defeat and destruction (see Isaiah 14).

The Sign of the Double-Headed Eagle

This grotesque, Hegelian dialectic goal of Satan—to reconcile and unite heaven and hell—is found symbolically represented in the most sacred and revered icon of international Freemasonry: the *double-headed eagle*. Note that, in Freemasonry, the majestic, soaring eagle, which the Bible depicts as a sign of God and His Holy Spirit, becomes *a two-headed beast* with one body. In the Old Testament it was Dan who refused the ensign of the serpent assigned him and his tribe by God. Instead, Dan rebelliously chose the eagle to be his banner. To this day, the perverted black bird

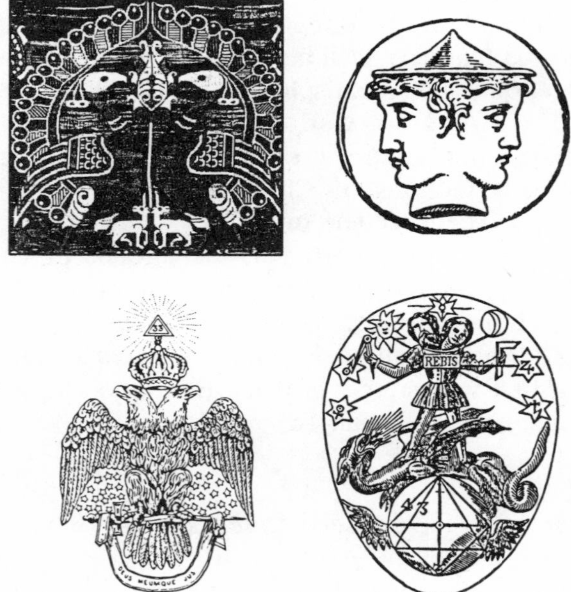

"Ordo Ab Chao," the alchemical ***Secret Doctrine*** *and* ***Great Work*** *of the Illuminati, is reflected in these illustrations from various historical eras and cultures. Each reflects the perpetual "conflict of opposites," the dialectical process used to integrate and unify society and eventually establish a World Order. At bottom left is the double-headed eagle of Freemasonry.*

of darkness known as the double-headed eagle has been adopted by evil sects connected with the Illuminati and its predecessors.

Europe's premier dynasty, the House of Habsburg, which provided the emperors for the Holy Roman Empire for five hundred years, chose as its shield the double-headed eagle. So, too, did the Russian czars (the world "czar" is Russian for Caesar). Now today, the current rulers of Russia, under the direction of the ten men who make up the *Inner Circle*—the *Circle of Intrigue*—of the Illuminati, have once again taken for their nation's symbol the mighty, double-headed eagle. Few realize that this adoption of the double-headed beast as their national symbol has ominous meaning for the future of Russia and, in fact, of the whole world.

The American Theater of Alchemy and Illusion

It is not only in Russia and overseas that the great, alchemical end-game of the Illuminati is being played out. In the United States, the Hegelian forces are in full battle array. We are deceived by the media and the politicians into believing that we have *two* major political parties, the Republicans and the Democrats. The former party is said to be conservative, the latter, we are led to believe, is liberal. But these labels, liberal and conservative, mean nothing. As events have proven again and again, both of the major political parties are 100% globalist, 100% anti-American sovereignty, and 100% anti-U.S. Constitution.

Alabama Governor George Wallace, running for President of the United States on his American Independent Party ticket in 1968, said of the two political parties: "Not a dime's worth of difference." Of course, he was right.

In 1994, when the issue of GATT and the establishment of a World Trade Organization (WTO) came before the U.S. Congress, the American people were vastly opposed to it. But this was a key project of the Illuminati. Even though House Speaker Newt Gingrich, Republican, frankly admitted the bill would undermine and eventually abolish American sovereignty, he went all out to get GATT approved.

So did his U.S. Senate counterpart, Majority Leader Robert Dole, a fellow Republican. Meanwhile, President Bill Clinton, a Democrat, promptly signed the bill into law—over the objections *not* of the opposite political party, but of the majority of the American people!

On issues affecting the goals of the Illuminati and their intention of setting up a Holy Empire and extinguishing United States nationalism, there is only *one* political party: the party of *Power and Money*. That party is owned and operated by the Illuminati.

Consider: Republican Newt Gingrich is a member of the Illuminati's traitorous Council on Foreign Relations. So is Democrat Bill Clinton. So was Republican George Bush. Republican Robert Dole is a Mason. So is Newt Gingrich. So, too, is Bill Clinton, and so, also, is George Bush.

A young and ambitious Newt Gingrich supported liberal candidate Nelson Rockefeller for President of the United States. Later, Rockefeller interests rewarded upcoming politician Newt with the money and influence necessary for him to be elected to the U.S. Congress from suburban Atlanta, Georgia. Next door, in Arkansas, Bill Clinton was the fair-haired boy swept into office by Governor Winthrop Rockefeller and the big guns of that state's Rockefeller Foundation.

A tender-aged George Bush was first made a U.S. Congressman from Houston, Texas. Then, he served his Illuminati superiors faithfully as United Nations Ambassador, Director of the CIA, and as the U.S.A.'s *Chargé de Affairs* to China. In 1980 Bush was chosen by the Republican Party as its nominee for Vice President. Later, Vice President Bush was elected President with the full blessing and considerable help of David Rockefeller, Sr. But in October of 1992, David Rockefeller, Jr., the rising scion of the Rockefeller fortune, gave a full page endorsement to Democratic presidential candidate Bill Clinton in the establishment's official newspaper, the *New York Times*.[25] That was the Illuminati's signal that George Bush was *out;* Clinton was *in*.

Is it any wonder that observers noted that in the weeks following Rockefeller's endorsement of Bill Clinton, George

Bush ran a lackluster political campaign, one demonstrably lacking in inspiration and energy? Old George knew his time was up. He had been a faithful mule and water-carrier for the Illuminati's *Inner Circle* boys for many years. But now they had chosen a new and younger star to put the finishing touches on their Great Work: William Jefferson Clinton.

Contrived Illusions and Pageantry

We can see, therefore, that no matter which political party is in power in Washington, D.C., the Illuminati are in control. What we have is the working of a masterful shell game. Democrats (Thesis) vs. Republicans (Antithesis) = Illuminati Rule (Synthesis). On the surface, it appears that politicians of each party strive mightily to contest each other, vigorously competing and vying for power and authority. But it is all mirrors and smoke. This is the Hegelian conflict of opposites.

Once in office, whether in the White House or on Capitol Hill, nothing really changes. The political chieftains of either party do not put America first. They and their judicial appointees continue to subvert and dismantle American sovereignty. Whether Republican or Democrat, the politicians continue to undermine the Constitution; they continue to endorse the plunder of the federal treasury by the Federal Reserve, they continue to globalize our U.S. Armed Forces, they empower gestapo federal police agencies, and they diligently and unceasingly move us ever closer toward United Nations control.

The ideological chaos and feigned clashes and conflict of the two political parties is all an illusion. It's a form of sophisticated pageantry, a contrived drama. *The real interests served and advanced by the leaders of America's two major political parties have for decades been, and are today, those of the Illuminati.*

If we are to successfully battle and defeat the machinations of the Illuminati, we must understand their satanic doctrine of *Ordo Ab Chao*—creating Order Out of Chaos. Much of our energies are too easily dissipated by the myth that our enemies are foreign nations, foreign leaders, foreign ideologies, foreign aggression. In fact, the Illuminati have no nation; they are universalists. They have no separate religion; they are Luciferian. And they have no quarrel with each other, though they seem at times to disagree on small points. In reality, they are united in their common goal of world conquest.

Identifying the Great Enemies of Freedom

The late Taylor Caldwell, the tremendous thinker who gave us her novel, *The Captains and the Kings,* and other books exposing the conspiracy, said it best back in May of 1974 when she warned:

> Do not believe for an instant that the world's conspiring elite in every nation have so much as a serious quarrel among them. They have just one object: control through tribute. Your slavery, through tribute, and mine...Behind this attack are the self-styled elite, secure in their own power and riches...
>
> To be effective we must direct our attacks on the real criminals, the wealthy, and powerful and secret elite of all the world—the conspirators laboring day and night to enslave us.[26]

The conspirators of whom Taylor Caldwell wisely warned us are today the implacable foes of patriotic and god-fearing men and women in every nation and community on planet Earth. Worse, they are God's enemies and are rebels against His Kingdom. They promise freedom and liberation through something they call "Reason." In fact, their Reason is merely a device enabling these wicked men to deify their own consciences and intellect and dethrone the absolutes found in God's Word, the Holy Bible.

Taken Into Bondage

As we have seen, the Illuminati cleverly and with ruthless motion ever employ the Hegelian process of the "conflict of opposites" to foment chaos and discord. They *invent* chaos and artificially inflame passions, rousing peaceful men to commit abominable acts of murder and sedition. But future history will record that this shall be their undoing. Seeking to enslave other men, they themselves have been taken into bondage by Lucifer, their counterfeit lord and god.

Willingly being made slaves, these men lustfully and continuously seek after more and more "light." Never will they be filled because, in their ignorance, the Illuminati are unaware that they are travelling down a dark, dark road to self-destruction. Vaingloriously, they stumble along in their quest for the Holy Grail. They grope for light, pressing toward the impossible goals set for them by the one whom they depict as possessing the "single eye"—the deceptive beast with the all seeing eye. It is he who directs their steps and fulfills their awful destiny.

The pitiful and soulless philosophy of the Illuminati is contained in this foul stanza, found in the Lucis Trust manual, *Discipleship in the New Age (Vol. II):*

> In neither pain nor joy is liberation found.
> In neither dark nor light will the spiritual sun appear.
> The pair of opposites distract the eyes of men.
> Only the single eye directs the steps of the initiate upon the Way.[27]

Let us not admire these wicked men who, in their rebellion and pride, worship the beast who has the all seeing, single eye. The Illuminati and their *Inner Circle* are men without a future. True, they are rich. Fabulously so. But with their riches come a curse, because, instead of obedience to God, they revile our Lord and persecute His children, the saints:

> Do not rich men oppress you, and draw you before the judgment seats? Do not they blaspheme that worthy Name by the which ye are called? (James 2:6-7)

But the saints of God, the "little people" so-called, though spitefully used and abused by the elitists of the Illuminati, are rewarded for eternity by the One true God, while the rich shall not see the Promised Land:

> Let the brother of low degree rejoice in that he is exalted: But the rich, in that he is made low: because as the flower of the grass he shall pass away. For the sun is no sooner risen with a burning heat, but it withereth the grass, and the flower thereof falleth, and the grace of the fashion of it perisheth: so also shall the rich man fade away in his ways. (James 1:9-11)

SEVEN

Inside the Magic Circle: Reward and Punishment in the Age of the Illuminati

But these, as natural brute beasts, made to be taken and destroyed, speak evil of the things that they understand not; and shall utterly perish in their own corruption; And shall receive the reward of unrighteousness...

—*II Peter 2:12-13*

"You are a great leader who will bring ***order out of chaos.****"*

—Newt Gingrich's horoscope
in *U.S. News & World Report*

"All of us will ultimately be judged on the effort we have contributed to building a New World Order."

—Senator Robert F. Kennedy

"There gather each day, between the hours of eleven and twelve o'clock...the active men whose efforts make Standard Oil what Standard Oil is...Reports are presented...republics and empires made and unmade."[1]

The above statement is from *Everybody's Magazine*, a popular mass magazine published at the turn of the century. In the article in which it is found, entitled "Frenzied Finance," investigator Thomas Lawson explores the incredible and awesome power of a small *circle* of men who closely control and manipulate the world's economies. They elevate to the highest seats of power prime ministers, presidents, and kings, said Lawson, and they remove from the pinnacles of power those whom they deem unworthy—that is, those who fail to slavishly obey their dictates and desires.

The *initiated* members of this small band, or coterie, of the super rich, Lawson reported, realize that theirs is an exclusive, secret and *religious* society based on internal loyalty, privacy, and a fierce system of rewards and punishments:

> Each member, before initiation, knows its religion to be reward for friends and extermination of enemies. Once a man is within the *magic circle*...punishment for disloyalty is sure and terrible, and in no corner of the Earth can he escape it, nor can any power on Earth protect him from it.[2]

The "magic circle," as Lawson called this close-knit conspiratorial group, controls both the Republican and Democrat parties. Politicians are in awe and are frightened to death of the magic circle. The men who lead it know and track "every twist and turn" of every Republican and Democrat, much as a gambler addicted to horse racing keeps a "dope sheet" on thoroughbreds. Moreover, the magic circle, Lawson warned, is "at the receiving end of the greatest information bureau in the world." They have "an agent in every hamlet in the country."

The Dangerous Conspiracy Must Be Ended—At Once!

Lawson's ominous research report on the chilling power of this select group of ruthless men was not mere speculation. It was based on fact. Only a brief, seven years later, in 1911, the Supreme Court of the United States ruled that "the Rockefeller's Standard Oil Company must be dissolved—at once!" Not mincing words, the Court, which, *at that time,* had not yet been subverted and conquered, emphatically stated: "For the safety of the Republic we now decree that the *dangerous conspiracy* must be ended by November 15, 1911."[3]

Unfortunately, as I stated in my book exposing secret societies, *Dark Majesty: The Secret Brotherhood and the Magic of A Thousand Points of Light,* following this important ruling, the Rockefellers and their dynastic conspiracy did not just fade away or ride off peacefully into the sunset. Their wealth and power continued—and continues—to expand at an alarming rate:

> While the Supreme Court of the United States attempted to dismantle the conspiracy put together by the international Rockefeller dynasty, the attempt, unfortunately, did not succeed. Over the years the Rockefellers have grown more and more wealthy and more cunning in the manner in which they employ their wealth to control the affairs of this world. The current head of the Rockefeller dynasty, David Rockefeller, Sr. (his son, David Rockefeller, Jr., is waiting in the wings to take over), was once labeled by *Time Magazine* as "the prime mover in banking that controls the course of world economic affairs and history."[4]

Over the years, the Rockefellers have callously plundered America and greedily guided for their own, selfish ends this nation's political, financial, and yes, even religious, destiny. This corrupt family of Illuminati hellions helped organize and fund the World Council of Churches. Their laboratories and research centers have conducted peculiar "psychological" and biological research.[5] The Rockefellers donated the land in New York City on which the United Nations building sits. In 1973 David Rockefeller, Sr., currently the patriarch and godfather of the family's fortunes, founded the globalist and conspiratorial Trilateral Commission.

Clinton and Perot Succeed—With a Little Help From Their Friends

One key family member of the Rockefeller dynasty, the late Winthrop Rockefeller, former governor of the state of

Arkansas, carefully watched over young Bill Clinton's upbringing and political career. Meanwhile, another dynasty blood relative, Nelson Rockefeller, former governor of the state of New York, through his puppets in the media, engineered the disgrace and ouster by resignation of then President of the United States Richard M. Nixon. He also supervised the exposure of the Nixon's hopelessly corrupt and fellow criminal associate, Vice President Spiro Agnew. This coup landed Nelson Rockefeller the vice-presidency, by choice of the U.S. Congress and not by popular vote.[6]

As vice president, Nelson supposedly served under President Gerald Ford, a 33° Mason who owed to the Rockefellers the success of his entire political career. In reality, Nelson Rockefeller and his aides were giving orders to Ford.

As governor of the state of New York during the 60s, Nelson Rockefeller brought a number of politicians and businessmen under his wings. Ross Perot, Jr., was apparently among them. Perot's fledgling start-up corporation, Electronic Data Systems (EDS), was given a dramatic financial shot in the arm when Governor Rockefeller arranged for the company to receive a New York state contract worth up to one billion dollars!

In 1992, when Perot ran an independent campaign for President of the United States, I believe he did so under the close direction and control of Rockefeller and associates. To put it bluntly, Ross Perot is in their debt—and in their pocket.[7]

George Bush also owes a political debt to his benefactor David Rockefeller, Sr. As President of the United States, Bush made sure the door to the White House's oval office was always open for the Trilateralist and CFR pals of the Rockefellers, and he ever did their bidding.[8] Bush's "New World Order" rhetoric was the creation of the Rockefeller political machine.

In 1980 at the Republican Party's national convention, Rockefeller threatened to stifle Republican Ronald Reagan's bid for the presidency unless the Californian chose George Bush as his vice-presidential running mate. Reagan had solemnly promised during the primary campaigns that he would *not* select anyone as his running mate who had been connected with Rockefeller's CFR and Trilateral Commission. In fact, George Bush had been on the board of directors of the CFR and was a faithful member of the Trilateral Commission to boot. Nevertheless, Reagan shocked many of his more conservative admirers when he named Bush as his V-P running mate.[9]

In return, the Rockefeller coalition rewarded the Great Communicator by showering Reagan's presidential campaign organization with money. Moreover, they ordered their underlings in the media to tout and praise Reagan.

Predictably, Ronald Reagan won the election in a cakewalk victory over his befuddled and hapless opponent, Jimmy Carter. Carter, too, was a Rockefeller stooge, but he had lost the dynasty's confidence, and the nation's, by his indecisiveness, lack of leadership, and incompetence. These flaws limited Jimmy Carter's usefulness to the *Inner Circle*.

The truth about the Rockefellers is that they still, *today*, control the global oil industry. The companies which Standard spun off way back in 1911—Mobil Oil, Exxon (renamed), Standard Oil of California, Sohio, Conoco—are all controlled by interlocking, Rockefeller dictorates. The Rockefellers also pull the strings at many top banks and Wall Street firms, including Chase Manhattan Bank in New York, the nation's largest. David Rockefeller, Sr., formerly was chairman of the board of Chase Manhattan and he still directs the firm's activities from behind the scenes.

My investigation underscores the truth that the Rockefellers, in concert with Europe's Rothschild family, represents one of the most powerful Illuminati bloodlines on the planet. The combined net worth of the Rockefellers and the Rothschilds is incalculable, though some analysts say it could be in the *trillions*. However, don't look for their family fortunes to be listed in one of the several magazines such as *Forbes* and *Fortune* which periodically list the world's richest men. Most of the wealth of these global titans is hidden in secretive trusts and in a blizzard of shadowy, difficult-to-trace financial combinations.

There are, of course, other bloodlines, other high-level members and initiates of the Illuminati. Several almost rival the Rockefellers and Rothschilds in their wealth and awesome hierarchical influence. Each of these bloodlines has its loyal puppets and sycophants. The Bill Clintons, Newt Gingrichs, and Bob Doles; the Rush Limbaughs, Dan Rathers, Pat Robertsons, and Jack Kemps, are nothing more than either willing or unwitting stooges and convenient accomplices for their more powerful and occultic overseers. If America's President Bill Clinton, Britain's Prime Minister John Major, or France's President Jacques Chirac failed to carry out a single mission directive from the *Inner Circle* of the Illuminati, their lives would be shattered. Certainly their political career would come to an abrupt end. It's not nice to mess with the men who comprise the devil's dirty and diabolical Circle of Intrigue.

The Recruitment Process

The *Inner Circle* of the Illuminati has developed a sophisticated and intensive system for the recruitment, training, discipling, and supervision of candidates for key positions in their far-flung, global empire. Talented and gifted young men are often chosen at an early age and groomed by handlers.

This system of recruitment is modeled after that of Illuminati founder, Adam Weishaupt. As Nesta Webster, in *Secret Societies and Subversive Movements*, remarked:

> In order to give a good appearance to the Order, Weishaupt particularly indicates the necessity for enlisting esteemed and "respectable" persons, but above all young men whom he regards as the most likely subjects. "I cannot use men as they are," he observes, "but I must first form them." Youth naturally lends itself best to this process. "Seek the society of young people," Weishaupt writes to Ajax, "watch them, and if one of them pleases you, lay your hand on him." "Seek out young and already skillful people....Our people must be engaging, enterprising, intriguing, and adroit. Above all the first." If possible they should also be good-looking—"beautiful people, *cateris paribus....*"[10]

Weishaupt explained that "beautiful people" are more fitted to the work of the Illuminati because:

> Such people have generally gentle manners, a tender heart, and are, when well practised in other things, of the greatest use in undertakings, for their first glance attracts; but their spirit *n'a pas la profondeur des physiognomies sombres*. They are, however, also less disposed to riots and disturbances than the darker physiognomies. That is why one must know how to use one's people. Above all, the high, soulful eye pleases me and the free, open brow.[11]

Pathways to Success: Circles Within Circles

One pathway to success by ambitious men eager to impress the Illuminati's *Inner Circle* is provided by the Rhodes Scholarship Program. U.S. President Bill Clinton, like hundreds of other politicians subservient to The Plan of the elitists, was a Rhodes Scholar. The Rhodes Scholarship Program has for decades been an important avenue used by the Illuminati to train its more promising corps of disciples. Current Rhodes Scholarship alumni active in the Clinton administration—each of whom is well trained in the revolutionary tactics of Marxism and Hegelian dialectics—include Secretary of Labor Robert Reich, healthcare maven Ira Magaziner, State Department official Strobe Talbott, and presidential advisor George Stephanopoulos.

All of these men are beneficiaries of Cecil Rhodes' huge endowment fund bequeathed to provide scholarships to Oxford for young, bright inductees chosen by Illuminati agents as capable of becoming future "helpers" and "servants."

Britain's multimillionaire Cecil Rhodes was an associate of Lord Rothschild. He spent millions to organize his part of the New World Conspiracy. Rhodes and other English power-brokers formed a secret society in 1891 patterned after Illuminati founder Adam Weishaupt's subversive pattern of the Jesuit Order and their *"circles within circles."* The "inner circle" included Rhodes himself, Lord Milner, and two other wealthy philanthropists. Subordinate circles are made up of those whom the lordly class consider the plebeian, peonage, profane class. Its ranks include the politicians, unionists, and others who slavishly serve the inner circle.[12]

One lower-level initiate of Rhodes was Lord Balfour who, as Great Britain's Prime Minister, did the Illuminati's bidding and wrote the "Balfour Declaration." This political document set the stage, eventually, for the return of the Jews and the establishment of a Zionist state of Israel, long an important Illuminist objective.

Wilson's League of Nations

Following World War I, Britain's Cecil Rhodes and the Rothschild bankers worked closely with America's Rockefellers and their underling, President Woodrow Wilson. Wilson's top aide, Colonel Mandell House, worked under the supervision of Illuminati bankers and financiers Paul Warburg and J. P. Morgan to formulate the ill-fated League of Nations, a predecessor of today's United Nations.

Nathaniel Rothschild also instructed other agents in the United States, including Jacob Schiff, to assist President Wilson and Colonel House. The failed League of Nations was an early attempt to set up the Illuminati's New World Order.

Interestingly, the occultic efforts of Colonel House, President Woodrow Wilson, and their Illuminati "masters" in putting together the League of Nations is partially chronicled by leading occultist Foster Bailey in a published lecture entitled, *Changing Esoteric Values*. Bailey, a 33° Mason, is also author of such books as *The Spirit of Masonry* and *Running God's Plan*. He is a member of the Lucis Trust, which was incorporated in New York in 1924 as Lucifer Publishing. Bailey's Lucis Trust books are published by subsidiaries in Kent, England, New York, and Geneva, Switzerland.

On page 58 of *Changing Esoteric Values* we find this remarkable discovery:

> Some of you will perhaps remember information given us about the way the old League of Nations came into existence. One of the Masters at a conference in the Hierarchy made a suggestion toward the improving of the relationships between nations in line with the new-age needed co-operation. It was considered useful. The Masters thought about it and therefore the disciples in the Ashrams (secret lodges—Ed.) who were close to them and had achieved some telepathic relationships, also thought about it. Eventually one disciple picked it up and said, "I will do something about it." He then formulated a plan of physical plane action and this was considered. The whole field was studied as to what would be practical and could possibly be achieved and the disciple was given the green light, so to speak, and went to work.
>
> In the case of the League of Nations that disciple happened to be COLONEL HOUSE. He worked with all those he could influence, and the sixth ray disciple WOODROW WILSON took the exoteric lead and the League of Nations was born. Thus an Hierarchical effort was anchored on the physical plane by a disciple and responded to by those who could catch the vision and wanted to serve their fellowmen. This example illustrates an Hierarchical technique.[13]

Don Bell, publisher of the excellent *Don Bell Reports* newsletter, confirms Foster Bailey's account of how the Illuminati hierarchy founded the League of Nations. Furthermore, he exposes the Masonic connection and warns that the later formation of the United Nations and the more recent efforts to empower the UN are a direct result of this continuing plot for a World Government:

> When World War I began, House spent most of his time in Europe, as personal representative of President Wilson. There he had ample opportunity to meet with the "Hierarchy" and perfect the plan which later was to be championed personally by Woodrow Wilson, the "sixth Ray disciple" of the "Hierarchy."

Now, let us note how Masonic records treat this story: On June 28, 29, and 30, 1917 a World Masonic Congress was held at Paris. Representatives of all Masonries attended, with the exception of the British. That Masonic Congress gave birth to the various International Parliamentarian Associations which are much in the news these days, with American Senators and Congressmen travelling all over the world to attend their various conferences. It was the World Parliamentarians Association which made that new world map, showing America being policed by foreign troops, in conjunction with a new World Government set-up.

At this same World Masonic Congress in 1917, the general guidelines for a League of Nations were approved and adopted.

The League of Nations came into being on January 10, 1920, when the Treaty of Versailles incorporating the first 26 articles of "The Covenant of the League" was ratified. The League failed, primarily because the United States Senate refused to ratify the treaty, and the League could not succeed without official United States participation. However, in Scriptural terms, the Beast that was wounded unto death was to live again, under the new name of The United Nations. Because the UN is really fulfillment of the old League, it is necessary that we understand its beginnings.[14]

Fed Reserve and Income Tax Treachery

President Wilson's inability to convince the U.S. Senate to go along with his plot for World Government under the guise of the fledgling and preliminary League of Nations, was his downfall. For years he had been under harrowing stress and pressure to fulfill the Illuminist agenda. In 1913, he and congressional puppets of Rockefeller and Rothschild had steered through an unwitting U.S. Congress the monumentally deceptive *Federal Reserve Act,* establishing dictatorial control by the Illuminati of America's entire money and banking system.

The same year, 1913, Wilson and co-conspirators in the House of Representatives lied and perjured themselves by declaring that the Sixteenth Amendment to the U.S. Constitution had successfully passed through two-thirds of the state legislatures. The Sixteenth Amendment unlawfully crammed the income tax down the workers' throats and was the catalyst for today's gestapo tactics of Big Brother's Internal Revenue Service (IRS). In fact, only a handful of state legislatures had approved the Sixteenth Amendment, not the two-thirds needed for ratification. But the confiscatory policy of the IRS was a major goal of the Illuminati's *Inner Circle,* and a little thing like "truth" was not allowed to interfere with their schemes.[15]

In 1917, President Wilson and his Illuminist handlers engineered the sinking of the ship the *Lusitania* in the Atlantic, inflaming the U.S. public and causing Congress to declare war on Germany. Through this bogus conflict the Illuminati hoped to establish the League of Nations as the embryo for the World Government of the beast to come. But when Wilson failed abominably in 1919 and a stubborn U.S. Senate refused to implement the *Versailles Treaty* and have the U.S.A. join the organization, suddenly, the President's usefulness to the *Inner Circle* was over.

Within months, it was announced that Wilson had suffered a "paralytic stroke." Mostly lying in bed, weak and incapacitated, others ran the affairs of the presidency in his name until his term of office expired. Later, to satisfy the public's questioning of just who had been in charge in the White House, the cooperative media erroneously spread stories that Wilson's wife, Edith, was running things during the chief executive's debilitating "illness." Insiders knew better.

Together, this Euro-American coalition of conspirators used what they called "Round Table" groups to found such heinous criminal establishments as the Federal Reserve Board, the Council on Foreign Relations, and, in Great Britain, the Royal Institute of International Affairs, that nation's equivalent of America's Council on Foreign Relations.

Networking Front Organizations

In fact, the Illuminati are keen advocates of organizations. Over the years they have set up literally thousands of front groups. Some are sham organizations, operating in name only. Others, like the World Federalists, World Goodwill, the Trilateral Commission, the Aspen Institute, the Carnegie Institute for International Peace, the Rockefeller Fund, and the Club of Rome exercise considerable power and influence.

One particularly nefarious and loathsome Illuminati group is the *Order of Skull & Bones,* also known as the *Skull & Bones Society.* In *America's Secret Establishment,* his excellent treatise exposing this "deathhead corps," Skull & Bones researcher Antony Sutton declares:

> The Order (of Skull & Bones) has either set up or penetrated just about every significant research, policy, and opinion-making organization in the United States. In addition to the church, business, law, government and politics...persistently and consistently enough to dominate the direction of American society...for a century...[16]

Among the elite alumni of Skull & Bones we find former President George Bush and columnist William F. Buckley, who both masquerade as conservatives. We also find such Illuminati bloodlines as the Browns, Harrimans, Dulles, Whitneys, Lords, Paynes, Lovetts, Pillsburys, Bundys, Weyerhausers, Astors, and, of course, the Rockefellers. Their common training ground was Yale University where, not incidentally, both Hillary and Bill Clinton went to law school and were watched over with meticulous and infinite care by their Illuminati sponsors.

Governmental organizations set up at the behest of the Illuminati, especially of the international variety, are ever proliferating. In recent decades we have seen the emergence of the United Nations, the International Monetary Fund, the International Labor Organization, the International Bank of Settlements, UNESCO, the World Bank, the European

Monetary Institute, and the World Wildlife Fund. Quite recently, the World Trade Organization was founded, with headquarters in Geneva, Switzerland, and a World Environmental Agency is on the way.

Through such intelligence and police agencies as the United States' CIA, the Israel's Mossad international spy organization, Britain's MI-5 and MI-6 spook agencies, Europe's Interpol, and the FBI, the Illuminati are busily and greedily extending their Big Brother tactics throughout the globe.

These police and spy groups, in and of themselves, are powerful. They possess the capability to mete out severe punishment to critics and dissenters of such fervent Illuminati goals as environmentalism and so-called "free trade." Punishment ranges from mere intimidation and harassment, to arrest, conviction, and incarceration on trumped-up charges.

Countless innocent men and women have been assassinated by these governmental agencies, with the CIA, Mossad, and Britain's intelligence agencies being most active in carrying out "terminations with extreme prejudice."

The list of individuals assassinated by Illuminati enforcement agencies is a long one—and it is growing. The name of Vince Foster, the Bill and Hillary Clinton crony who served as their Associate White House Counsel, is located on that list. Foster was reportedly a clandestine CIA operative who assisted in the laundering of the hundreds of millions of dollars the CIA's cocaine cartel netted from its drug-running operation out of the tiny airport in Mena, Arkansas. That is why his murder has been covered up and the facts suppressed by Congress and the media.[17]

Foster was reportedly "hit" when it was found out that he was freelancing. In other words, he was holding back some of the cash for himself. That's a no-no in the shadowy and gritty underworld of CIA narco-intrigue. So, Mr. Foster was lured away from his office for a nonexistent "meeting" and dispatched by CIA executioners. Then, his body was neatly laid out on a field in Marcy Park, Maryland, just one exit down the expressway from the turn-off leading to the CIA's headquarters in Langley, Virginia.

The message of the Vince Foster assassination was intended to make an impact on other, potential miscreants tempted to reserve for themselves a disproportionate share of the criminal booty of the Illuminati network. All were put on notice that betrayal of trust will be harshly dealt with and severe punishment meted out by the enforcers.

Generous Rewards for Faithful Servants

On the other hand, the rewards for faithful service to the Illuminati's *Inner Circle* can often be most generous. But loyalty and fealty to the goal of the Illuminati—the *Great Work*—must be continually manifested. Moreover, an underling's loyalty and zeal must be demonstrated externally so that those in the outer circle will see that faithful service pays off handsomely and has its rewards.

An interesting and instructive example of an external act of loyalty being demonstrated by a lower-level servant can be found in the case of Robert Dole, Republican and Senate Majority Leader. In exchange for his many years of consistently loyal service to the Brotherhood, Dole was informed in late 1994 that he would be given substantial support from the network in his bid for the presidency. But, Dole was told, in return he would have to perform an external act to be witnessed by the outer circle of the Illuminati, a group made up of the several thousand members of the Council on Foreign Relations (CFR) as well as a number of other front groups.

A compliant and hopeful Senator Dole was most happy to oblige. Thus, in the Spring '95 issue of *Foreign Affairs,* the premier Illuminati publication—the flagship periodical of the CFR itself—Robert Dole is listed as a contributing author. Senator Dole wrote for publication an article, entitled "Shaping America's Global Future." Actually, of course, it was ghostwritten *for* the Senator by CFR insiders. In this article, the man chosen by the elitists to masquerade as one of their fair-haired boys, "conservative" presidential candidates gushingly lavished praise on the United Nations, the Marshall

Plan, the World Bank, and the International Monetary Fund (IMF), all of which, naturally, were and are Illuminati projects. After this embarrassing bit of pandering, the Senator from Kansas really hit his stride by lashing out at the enemies of the globalist conspirators: the dreaded "isolationist" and America Firsters. "America must remain firmly engaged in the world," Dole admonished.

This was the external signal, disseminated in the most authoritative establishment journal published in the world today, that let insiders everywhere know that, first, "Dole is one of us," and second, "We are to aid and abet his political fortunes."

This is not to say that Dole will become President of the U.S.A. Other loyal disciples also seek that rich, political plum. But Dole has passed many important preliminary tests, and whether or not he is ever inaugurated as President, he will be richly rewarded—either in the political arena or in a life of plush retirement—for his loyal, abiding support of the globalist aims of his benefactors.

Gingrich Proves Loyal to Ordo Ab Chao

House Speaker Newt Gingrich is another servant whose successful political career has been sparked by his loyalty to the goals of the Illuminati's *Inner Circle*. As the Republican leader of the U.S. House of Representatives, Gingrich pushed the *North American Free Trade Act (NAFTA)* through the House of Representatives. NAFTA is an Illuminati project designed to merge the nations of the Americas and end American sovereignty. Gingrich next ram-rodded a $40 billion Mexico bill which was a bonanza for Illuminati anglo bankers otherwise at risk due to the collapse of the Mexican peso, and he helped set up the new World Trade Organization by pushing through the *GATT* legislation.

The Georgia congressman also supported the continuation of massive foreign aid billions to Illuminati client states Israel and Egypt. Perhaps most important, Gingrich helped to cover up such atrocities as Bill Clinton and the CIA's involvement in cocaine dope running through Mena, Arkansas and the FBI and BATF 1993 massacre and holocaust of the innocent Branch Davidians in Waco, Texas.

Because of his demonstrated talents in service to their cause, Newt Gingrich is targeted for continued advancement. The decision of the men of the *Inner Circle* to promote and enhance loyalist Newt Gingrich's political and financial fortunes was signalled in the premier establishment publication *U.S. News & World Report* in its July 3, 1995 issue.[18] There, in an article headlined "Gingrich's March Through Georgia—The House Speaker's Stock is Rising," the reader is told that the congressman's horoscope reveals the following:

> "You are a great leader who will bring *order out of chaos.*"

In an accompanying photograph, Gingrich is pictured standing with a young man wearing a t-shirt bearing the message *"Ordo Ab Chao." Ordo Ab Chao,* Latin for "Order out of Chaos," is the motto of the highest initiation, 33°, of Freemasonry. This phrase symbolizes the ages-old quest, the Great Work of the Illuminati: the goal of Lucifer to conquer God, and unite heaven, hell, and Earth, through an end-times New World Order.

Newt Gingrich, a Mason and member since 1990 of the conspirators' Council on Foreign Relations, was told that he has been chosen to be a "great leader who will bring order out of chaos." In other words, he is chosen to be a prime servant of the *Inner Circle,* and will play a leading role—he'll be at the forefront of those promoting Satan's diabolical Plan for global dominion and universal hegemony.

Whatever the Atlanta congressman's other faults, Newt Gingrich's ability to deliver on key planks contributing to the *Inner Circle's* fanatical goal of a totalitarian New World Order has endeared him to his occultic masters. As Robert Kennedy, former attorney general of the United States and U.S. Senator from New York, once remarked, "All of us will ultimately be judged on the effort we have contributed to building a New World Order."[19] RFK made this curious statement in 1967, just one year before his assassination. Was he somehow forecasting his own, pending demise?

Newt Gingrich: He's Their Man

The political prospects of men like Newt Gingrich, Robert Dole, Al Gore, and Bill Clinton are heightened to a remarkable degree because of their docile and unquestioning obedience to the agenda and world program of the Illuminati. But their ultimate advancement depends on the competition. The men of the *Inner Circle* are continually on the lookout for fresh talent and can be intense in their active support for proven performers.

Newt Gingrich is, indeed, a proven performer. The man from Georgia has demonstrated over and over again his ability to accomplish the Illuminist agenda. But the best is yet to come as far as Gingrich's value to the controllers is concerned. Next on Gingrich's menu is to oversee in Congress the "Third Wave" revolution. That is the subject of this book's next chapter as we study the hidden, conspiratorial life of Newt Gingrich.

EIGHT

Newt Gingrich and the Illuminati's "Third Wave" Revolution

For nothing is secret, that shall not be made manifest; neither any thing hid, that shall not be made known.

—*Luke 8:17*

As Edgar Allen Poe explained in his short story, "The Imp of the Perverse," criminals have an uncanny urge to confess their crime. Political criminals—Socialists, Communists, Nazis, Republicans, Democrats—have an uncanny urge to confess their crimes in advance. There's a silver lining to this cloud. This self-revelatory compulsion helps us to forecast...

—Franklin Sanders
The Moneychanger

I have an enormous personal ambition. I want to shift the entire planet. And I'm doing it.

—Newt Gingrich
Washington Post

Like serial killers, the most cunning and diabolical of tyrants always have a plan. Coldly, shrewdly, and methodically, they set goals and objectives. Tyrants relentlessly pursue their agenda, they reward allies and punish opponents, stage dramatic propaganda events, and mandate new regulations and laws—all in accordance with "*The Plan.*"

The Illuminati, as a collective association of tyrants, has been engaged in this process of working The Plan for many decades—even centuries. After all, their secret master is Lucifer, a dark and powerful schemer who first conspired with other angelic beings against God untold millennia ago. Through the ages he has inspired innumerable tyrants and caesars to attempt a New World Order. Each, in his turn, failed to bring about global dominion, but The Plan lived on.

Now, this shadowy Plan is coming into greater focus with the revolutionary efforts of Newt Gingrich and other elitist insiders. Their scheme is for a "Third Wave" revolution. Believe me, it's anything but conservative and is designed to radically change America into a fascist "paradise" with citizens stripped of constitutional guarantees. What is promised, in fact, is nothing less than a high tech prison and plantation of global dimensions, superintended by the "masters."

Scripture tells us that, up to now, God has prevented Lucifer's conspiratorial Illuminati agenda from ultimate fulfillment. The final stages of The Plan have long been delayed though God has allowed many dress rehearsals to occur. The French revolution, World War I, the Communist revolution, the Nazi era—Lucifer's Illuminati intended that all these dramatic periods of bloodshed and rebellion would culminate in the end of human history and the ascendance to the throne of world power of their Antichrist. But, it was not to be. The latter phases of the devil's hoary Plan must wait for fulfillment until *God* gives the word:

> And now ye know what withholdeth that he might be revealed in his time. For the mystery of iniquity doth already work: only he who now letteth will let, until he be taken out of the way. And then shall that Wicked be revealed, whom the Lord shall consume with the spirit of his mouth, and shall destroy with the brightness of his coming: Even him, whose coming is after the working of

> Satan with all power and signs and lying wonders. (II Thessalonians 2:6-9)

Moreover, Bible prophecy (II Thessalonians 2; Matthew 24; Revelation, Daniel) reveals the key signs which are to herald the coming of the end. Those signs convincingly point to this generation as that fateful era when human history is to be eclipsed. Therefore, it is imperative that true Christians understand the final increments of Satan's foul agenda. His "Third Wave" Plan, for so long barred by God from implementation, is now about to see its culmination.

The Illuminati Herald Their Criminality in Advance

Do we have evidence—in their own words—that the Illuminati indeed do have a Plan for achieving their corrupt goal of planetary domination and mass murder?

In a recent issue of his excellent publication, *The Moneychanger,* Franklin Sanders points out that criminals—and we can certainly include Illuminati conspirators in this impious category—seem unable to contain a deeply felt compulsion to announce their crimes in advance:

> As Edgar Allen Poe explained in his short story, "The Imp of the Perverse," criminals have an uncanny urge to confess their crimes. Political criminals—Socialists, Communists, Nazis, Republicans, Democrats—have an uncanny urge to confess *their* crimes in advance. There's a silver lining to this cloud. This self-revelatory compulsion helps us forecast...[1]

House Speaker Newt Gingrich is also seemingly possessed of this "uncanny urge" to confess one's crimes in advance. His endorsement of the New Age philosophy of the "Third Wave," detailed in books by radical, liberal theoreticians Alvin and Heidi Toffler, clearly signals Gingrich's criminal intentions to debase American society and establish the new, global order. As we shall see, Newt Gingrich's blueprint for renewing America and for creating a "New Civilization" is the very same Plan pursued throughout the ages by the revolutionary Illuminati.

It is sometimes claimed that Nazi fuhrer Adolf Hitler set forth his own plan for a global, or world, order in his rambling book, *Mein Kampf (My Struggle)*. In the preface, the ambitious, future chancellor of the German Reich writes: "I resolved not only to set forth the object of our movement, but also to draw a picture of its development."[2]

Hitler's blueprint for global domination was strikingly similar in construction to that of today's Illuminati leadership. This is understandable, of course, since the occultic fuhrer received his marching orders from the same "prince of the power of the air" as does today's Illuminati leadership.

This joint blueprint of Hitler and today's elite seeks to build a Fascist Order. A Fascist Order, Webster's Dictionary explains, is "characterized by rigid one-party dictatorship, forcible suppression of the opposition, the retention of ownership of means of production under centralized government control...glorification of war" etc. It is revealing that when Fascist dictator Mussolini was once asked, "What is Fascism?," he bluntly responded: "I'm a Marxist!"

Fascism is always a racist, "my blood is superior to your blood," system as well, and thus we discover that the Illuminati are the ultimate racists, having adopted the satanic doctrine of the god-like, superman bloodline. The Illuminist dogma holds that they are a race of nobility and elitism destined to rule the masses, composed of men and women of perfected god-consciousness.

"The World Plan Includes..."

In order to rule, the Illuminati realize that they must establish an iron grip over all organs of world government and all institutions of society. That is why Vera Stanley Alder, one of the premier theoreticians for the occult world order, has forthrightly stated:

> There is actually a Plan and a purpose behind all creation...World Unity is the goal towards which evolution is moving. The World Plan includes: A World Organization...A World Economy...A World Religion.[3]

Notice that Alder puts The Plan in the context of the entire history of the world since creation. She and other occult conspirators firmly teach that the hidden masters of the advanced spiritual hierarchy have for eons supervised Earth's evolutionary progress, driving mankind ever onward toward a radiant New Age future. Moreover, we are told that this glorious future will see the establishment by enlightened deities (the Illuminati) of a World Order encompassing three vital elements, or pillars, of human endeavor: *political, economic, spiritual.*

By controlling government, money, and religion, The Plan is to achieve success, and the chosen of the Illuminati (the enlightened ones) are to enjoy the fruits of their epic, evolutionary struggle against God and His "inferior" elect. As Manly P. Hall, 33° Mason and one of the 20th century's most acclaimed scholars of secret societies, explains it in his revealing book, *The Phoenix:*

> The real history of mankind is the record of a magnificent struggle for enlightenment...Man has climbed from unfathomable depths, from the very slime and ooze of chaos, impelled by an incomprehensible but irresistible urge. He has raised himself from state to state, from place to place, from world to world, until at last a few in the vanguard of the great procession can now glimpse upon the heights...Only a few are able to define the impulse...For the rest the darkness is still impenetrable.[4]

According to Hall, the occult "Divine Plan" is understood by only a few, though many are dimly aware of its existence and are cooperating with the elite Brotherhood in accomplishing its aims. On that "Great Day" to come, says Hall, humanity will become one and the mysterious "Lord of the World" will openly reign.[5]

But for now, he reveals, those who know "the purpose of the Universal Plan," as he calls it, "must dwell apart from the rest in a universe of their own."[6] They must, he confides, be the keepers of the sacred mysteries, the possessors of the "Secret Doctrine."[7]

Masonry's Invisible Society

In his insightful book, *Lectures on Ancient Philosophy*, Manly P. Hall, 33°, further reveals that the core leadership of the illumined ones—the secret elite knowledgeable of and responsible for The Plan—come from the Masonic lodges.[8] However, he hastens to add that the average member of the Masonic lodge is abominably ignorant of The Plan. Nor is the typical, low-level Masonic initiate aware that inside the secret Masonic fraternity there exists an anonymous, but high-powered, organizational elite bent on global domination and promotion of the cosmic blueprint of their master, Lucifer. Hall explains:

> Freemasonry is a fraternity within a fraternity—an outer organization concealing an inner brotherhood of the elect....It is necessary to establish the existence of these two separate yet independent orders, the one visible and the other invisible.
>
> The *visible society* is a splendid camaraderie of free and accepted men enjoined to devote themselves to ethical, educational, fraternal, patriotic, and humanitarian concerns. The *invisible society* is a secret and most august fraternity whose members are dedicated to the service of a mysterious arcanum acandrum (defined as a secret; a mystery).
>
> In each generation, only a few are accepted into the inner sanctuary of the Work....The great initiate-philosophers of Freemasonry are masters of that secret doctrine which

> forms the invisible foundations of every great theological and rational institution.[9]

What we discover, then, from the poisonous and occultic pen of Manly P. Hall, 33°—the man whom Freemasonry's *Scottish Rite Journal* has acknowledged as the Masonic Lodge's leading scholar of the 20th century—is that: (1) There is a Plan for an Illuminati World Order; (2) The elite leadership, hidden from view, but operating clandestinely as an "invisible society" behind the veil of Freemasonry, know of The Plan and are working for its success; and (3) Their Plan involves the ushering in of the ages-old "Secret Doctrine" of Lucifer—a doctrine designed to bring Antichrist, the son of perdition, to the pinnacle of world power.

My own, in-depth research has uncovered documented proof that only a minuscule percentage of Freemasons know of The Plan. An initiate may progress even up to the 33rd degree and yet be ignorant of the true designs of the hidden elite. They, too, are dupes and victims of a fraudulent and elaborate, cosmic hoax.

Still, regardless of their protests and claims to the contrary, these deluded men are well aware of the anti-Christian, pagan religion of which they have willingly become a part. In the ritual for the 32° they are informed of the Hindu deities whom the Lodge elevates, and they have themselves lain in a coffin and been symbolically "raised" from the dead. Every high-level Mason, including Newt Gingrich and Bill Clinton, is aware that the Lodge accords Jesus Christ no more respect than it does the Zoroastrian god Ahura-Mazda, Buddha, Allah and Mohammed, and Shiva, the Hindu destroyer god.[10]

A Plan to Make All Things New

But the "inner brotherhood"—the "invisible society" whom Manly P. Hall reveals as the "masters of the Secret Doctrine"—*do* know of The Plan. One of them, C. William Smith, a Masonic overlord from New Orleans, Louisiana, wrote extensively of The Plan in the September 1950 edition of *The New Age,* the official journal of the Supreme Mother Council, 33°, of the Scottish Rite, America's largest and most influential Masonic organization. Smith's article was entitled "God's Plan in America," but do not let his mention of "God" throw you off. Smith made it clear that the Masonic "God" is not the Christian God but, instead, is the "Father of Light." This, of course, is the Illuminati's code name for Lucifer, or Satan. Here is some of what C. William Smith had to say in his eye-opening treatise:

> God's plan is dedicated to the unification of all races, religions, and creeds. This plan, dedicated to the new order of things, is to make all things new—a new nation, a new race, a new civilization, and a new religion, a nonsectarian religion that has already been recognized and called the religion of "The Great Light."[11]

Smith went on to reveal that at the time of his article, among the royalty and world leaders working on behalf of The Plan were King Gustaf of Sweden, King Haakon of Norway, and King George of England. These men were said to be illumined men, "Great Lights," who, along with the designated leaders of the United States of America, were destined to lead humanity forward into the "New Age of the world—a Novus Ordo Seclorum." This, he disclosed was The Plan to "unfold the New Order of the world."[12]

A Chosen Race

In tones reminiscent of Hitler's Aryan race theory, Smith suggested that the illumined ones guiding The Plan were the "chosen race:" The founding fathers of America, Smith wrote, such as George Washington, Thomas Jefferson, Benjamin Franklin, John Adams, and Thomas Paine, were of "the highest branch of the fifth Aryan Civilization." But, Smith proudly informed his Masonic audience, the "All-Father" (Lucifer) intends to inspire a new generation of American elite (the

Illuminati) who, in their racial and religious superiority, are fated to be exalted to the heights of godhood:

> The American race will be the sixth Aryan Civilization. This new and great civilization is like an American Beauty rosebud, ready to open and send its wonderful fragrance to all the world.[13]

Do Newt Gingrich, Bill Clinton, and today's fascist American legislators and bureaucrats consider themselves to be superior members of this "sixth Aryan Civilization?"

It is important to understand that the more influential New Age teachers have adopted Helena Blavatsky's strange theory of "Seven Root Races." This teaching holds that reincarnated man progresses through seven race eras. The two highest and most spiritually advanced races are the Aryan and the Aquarian. Aryan man, say the New Agers, is in the final stages of preparation for godhood. In the "Age of Aquarius," the godhood of the illumined elite is realized and a New World Order of peace, love, unity, and harmony encompasses the Earth.

Occult dogma further teaches that overseeing this transformation of Earth and humanity into a New Order, and presiding over The Plan, is a circle of highly developed, racially advanced initiates. These men are claimed to be the most spiritually illumined on the planet. Personally taught by the "Hierarchy" (demon spirits), this tiny circle of elite men sit in council. They constitute the divine Circle of Power. I call them the *Inner Circle*. They are charged with the astonishing task of preparing civilization for the final and last stage—the *Last Day*.

After their preparatory work is finished, then shall come the *One* whom they have long awaited—the occult Master of the Universe, the "One about whom naught be said" at this time. He will be the most exalted and most eminent leader of the Circle of Power. And the *Inner Circle* will slavishly obey him. Together, these ten world rulers will be of "*one mind,* and shall give their power and strength unto the beast." (Revelation 17:13)

Newt Gingrich's Third Wave: "Creating a New Civilization"

This conspiratorial Plan of the invisible elite—the objective, in C. William Smith's phraseology, to "make all things new—a new nation, a new race, a new civilization," should raise a red flag in our minds whenever we hear or read of similar code words expressed. For example, House of Representatives Speaker Newt Gingrich's call for the "renewing of America" and his endorsement of Alvin and Heidi Toffler's Marxist book, *Creating A New Civilization,* should enlighten us as to *who* is pulling puppet Gingrich's strings.

Indeed, Newt Gingrich is a hard-core New Ager. A high-level Mason, the Speaker is a secret establishment clone *par excellence.* Notably, he's a member of both the World Future Society and the Council on Foreign Relations.[14] A devoted globalist and advocate of the New World Order, Gingrich led the Congress in support of the taxpayer giveaway of some $40 billion to the bankers responsible for 1994's astounding collapse of the Mexican peso. The Speaker also slam-dunked the Congress into supporting the so-called "free trade" General Agreement on Tariffs and Taxes (GATT) bill, and he successfully conspired with President Bill Clinton and Rockefeller-Rothschild forces to insure the setting up of the World Trade Organization (WTO), based in Geneva, Switzerland.

In obedience to his Illuminati superiors, errand boy Newt Gingrich has demanded that House members continue to fund and support radical environmental policies. Indeed, Gingrich is a member of the Georgia Conservancy, a prominent pro-Mother Earth group. Gingrich's environmental policies threaten to demolish the constitutional concept of private ownership of lands.

Gingrich is also a chief sponsor of so-called "anti-terrorist" legislation. In reality, these unconstitutional congressional bills are designed to shut the mouths and restrict the First Amendment right of free speech of citizens opposed to Big Brother government. Along these same lines, Mr. Gingrich has long been an ardent supporter of gun control legislation intended to restrict the Second Amendment right of American citizens to "keep and bear arms."

Newt Gingrich is the acknowledged head of the Republican Party, sharing power with his Masonic brother and colleague, Senate Majority Leader Robert Dole, 33°. Regrettably, few Republicans (or Democrats, for that matter!) have the slightest knowledge of Newt Gingrich's unAmerican and radically pro-New World Order views. They would be shocked to discover that Mr. Gingrich is numbered among the most ferocious enemies of American sovereignty. And at least some of Gingrich's admirers from Pat Robertson's Christian Coalition would no doubt find it an eye-opener to discover that the Speaker of the House considers Christian fundamentalist beliefs to be a *dark menace* to society.

However, these facts can easily be gleaned from even the most superficial reading of the Tofflers' sinister new volume, *Creating A New Civilization*, and their earlier works, *The Third Wave* and *Power Shift*.[15] Newt Gingrich admits that he is so enamored of the Tofflers' ideas that *Renewing American Civilization,* the much touted college course Newt personally created and now offers the Republican faithful by video, is based almost exclusively on their philosophies and teachings.

Indeed, Gingrich is so smitten by this revolutionary couple and their New Age, globalist ideas that he personally wrote the foreword for their latest piece of propaganda garbage, *Creating A New Civilization.* Since Mr. Gingrich is so crazy about this book, perhaps it would be a good idea for us to take a closer look at its contents. Here are just a few of the shocking, fascist-oriented proposals and declarations made by the Tofflers:

> The time has come for the next great step forward in American politics. It is not a matter of Democrats versus Republicans, or of left and right...but something more significant...a clear distinction between rear-guard politicians who wish to preserve or restore an unworkable past and those who are ready to transition to what we call a "Third Wave" information-age society...[16]

> A new civilization is emerging in our lives, and blind men everywhere are trying to suppress it. This new civilization brings with it new family styles, changed ways...a new economy, new political conflicts, and...an altered consciousness...Humanity faces a quantum leap forward. This is the meaning of the Third Wave...[17]

> Our argument is based on what we call the "revolutionary premise"...The revolutionary premise liberates our intellect and will.[18]

> Nationalism is...First wave. The globalization of business and finance required by advancing Third Wave economies routinely punctures the national "sovereignty" the nationalists hold so dear...[19]

> As economies are transformed by the Third Wave, they are compelled to surrender part of their sovereignty...Poets and intellectuals of Third Wave states sing the virtues of a "borderless" world and "planetary consciousness."[20]

> The Third Wave...demassifies culture, values, and morality...There are more diverse religious belief systems.[21]

> The Constitution of the United States needs to be reconsidered and altered...to create a whole new structure of government...Building a Third Wave civilization on the wreckage of Second Wave institutions involves the design of new, more appropriate political structures...The system that served us so well must, in its turn, die and be replaced.[22]

The above are just a few of the monstrous anti-Christian, anti-American, and anti-constitutional ideas of the Tofflers expressed in their "Third Wave" book, *Creating A New Civilization*. To say that these proposals mesh with The Plan and Great Work of the Illuminati is a gross understatement. The Tofflers' books provide a blueprint paralleling

Newt Gingrich, Speaker of the U.S. House of Representatives, strongly endorses the book, ***Creating A New Civilization,*** *by Alvin and Heidi Toffler. That notorious book, in turn, parrots the scheme of the Illuminati to destroy the Constitution of the United States and set up a Fascist World Order.*

Significantly, Newt Gingrich is a member of the CFR and also the World Future Society. As shown on one of their publications, the logo of the World Future Society appears strikingly similar to a circular, 6-6-6 configuration.

that of the Illuminati for the destruction of democratic society, the exaltation of a super rich elite, and an all-out assault against Christianity, patriotism, nationalism and the United States Constitution.[23]

Yet, Newt Gingrich not only endorses these crude and unholy ideas and theories, he actually wrote the foreword to the latest Toffler book. Gingrich has also strongly endorsed the Tofflers' debauched *Power Shift*, a book in which the demented couple rant and rave against patriotism, which they denigrate as "the resurgence of flag-waving xenophobia" and as "nationalist demagoguery."[24]

Meanwhile, fundamentalist, biblical Christianity, the Tofflers warn, is "both dangerous and regressive." Beliefs in nationalism, patriotism, and in an exclusive God, say the techno-fascist Tofflers, "give birth to violence or repression."[25] According to the Tofflers, "advanced wealth creation" by the elite can only be achieved when these "Dark Age" menaces are swept away.[26]

Gingrich and Gore: Illuminist Twins

In their fascist, revolutionary book *Creating A New Civilization,* the Tofflers brag profusely about the support their ideas and theories have received both from Vice President Al Gore and House Speaker Newt Gingrich. They write that Gore, as a U.S. Senator from Tennessee, co-chaired the Congressional Clearinghouse on the Future and note that, as Vice President of the United States, he has made their radical agenda a national priority.[27] Of Gingrich, they write:

> Not only does this book *(Creating A New Civilization)* carry a foreword by Gingrich, but it appears on a "reading list" that he recommended to members of Congress and the nation, alongside *The Federalist Papers*...and other classics of political philosophy.[28]

The Tofflers are not overstating things. Both Gingrich and Gore are rabid supporters of the techno-fascist ideals expressed by the Tofflers in their illogical and bizarre books. This should not surprise anyone who knows the record and history of Gingrich and Gore. Newt Gingrich, for example, is a Rockefeller conspiratorial puppet who served as Southeast U.S. Coordinator for Nelson Rockefeller's presidential campaign back in 1968.[29] Now today, Gingrich is so taken with the Tofflers' blueprint for an Illuminist, "Third Wave," one-world structure and their proposal for a global paradigm shift that he was quoted by the *Washington Post* as proclaiming: "I have an enormous ambition. I want to shift the entire planet. And I'm doing it."[30]

Novus Ordo Seclorum: The Happy Utopia

That Newt Gingrich would strongly, even fanatically, endorse such deadly concepts as the ending of American sovereignty, the trashing of the U.S. Constitution, and the classification of Christian fundamentalism as a dangerous and menacing, antiquated "Second Wave" sect that must be suppressed and overthrown, is understandable in light of his loyalty to the Illuminati and its depraved cult of Freemasonry. The esoteric Plan has long decreed that a *universal* World Order be established, to be organized and superintended by men of a higher race consciousness—the men comprising the *Inner Circle* of the Illuminati.

As Masonic authority Carl H. Claudy noted in his book, *Masonic Harvest,* the World Plan consists of "several cornerstones" which, together, are to culminate in the end of human history as we know it. The Plan will result in the founding of *Novus Ordo Seclorum.*[31] When the fiery *Phoenix* rises from the smoldering ashes and cinders of the deconstructed world, then, says Claudy, a Utopia shall result and all men shall be blissful and happy:

> How will it end? If we keep our Masonic philosophy within the framework of Freemasonry—which means within the Fatherhood of God and the brotherhood of man—it will probably round itself out in a vision of a

> *universal religion,* which will embrace all creeds; a *universal government* which will embrace all humanity; a *universal knowledge* which will make all mankind kin, thus outlawing war, eliminating the criminal and bringing about that Utopia in which the search for truth is ended because all truth is evident, and men no more pursue happiness because all men are happy.[32]

You can be sure that the "universal religion" and "universal knowledge" embraced by all in this soon coming Utopia on Earth will *exclude* true, authentic Bible Christianity. And the "universal government" proposed by Claudy will insure this exclusion of true, biblical Christianity. It will be mandatory for the new race to expand its consciousness and to cast off the "evil superstitions" of the Christian religion. The Aquarian forces of "love and goodwill" will seek to replace concepts of a unique God in Heaven, His Son Jesus Christ, and Holy Scripture.

Mankind, according to the Illuminati's spiritual prescription, must be rebuilt on a new foundation of inclusiveness. The principle of diversity *and* unity will be applied. Christianity, of course, absolutely and unequivocally rejects unity with all Luciferian religions, cults, and sects. And since Christianity demands exclusivity and abhors diversity, its practitioners and adherents must be eradicated off the face of planet Earth. They are typecast as a dark menace to society and a roadblock to the universal happiness guaranteed to be the lot of humanity in the soon-coming, radiant and glorious *Novus Ordo Seclorum.*

The Masters to Expand Human Consciousness

These requirements of the coming New Civilization envisioned by Newt Gingrich and his Illuminist superiors, and the tenets of their Plan, were elaborated on in the 24 books of Alice Bailey published by Lucis Trust, a propaganda house that ranks today as a major player in the globalist, end-time conspiracy. Bailey wrote:

> The Plan is concerned with expanding human consciousness...it will reveal to man the true significance of his mind and brain...and will make him therefore omnipresent and eventually open the door to omniscience.
>
> The implementation of this Plan has been the objective of all esoteric training given during the past four hundred years....Humanity needs to realise that there IS a plan, and to recognise its influence in unfolding world events...expansions of consciousness...into which Aquarius is hurrying mankind....
>
> The Plan is concerned with re-building mankind....As human beings begin to take the higher initiations...the true nature of the divine Will will be grasped....[33]

Alice Bailey's many works confirm that the "Masters" are in charge of overseeing the fulfillment of this hellish blueprint for chaos and global order:

> The Masters are working according to a Plan...which will demonstrate a large measure of world unity...marked by universality...that aims at expanding human consciousness...founded in love and...goodwill....[34]

In the many books of Alice Bailey and in other publications of the Lucis Trust and its sister organization, World Goodwill, we find again and again this concept of The Plan which is guiding humanity toward New Age goals of world government and world religion: creating a *New Civilization*.

The Lucis Trust (formerly incorporated in 1924 as Lucifer Publishing!) is a nongovernmental organization (NGO) officially recognized by the United Nations. Indeed, the Lucis Trust has been given responsibility by the UN to maintain that organization's strange and occultic Meditation Room, located in the UN building in New York City.

The membership of Lucis Trust includes some very heavy hitters in the political, economic, and religious arenas, including Sri Chinmoy, Mikhail Gorbachev's Hindu guru who is also the official spiritual advisor for the United Nations;[35] Robert McNamara, former U.S. Secretary of Defense and former President of the Illuminati-controlled World Bank; and Robert Muller, former Assistant Secretary-General of the United Nations and currently head of the Peace University in Costa Rica. Given the prominence of its membership, it would behoove us to pay very close attention to the teachings and activities of the Lucis Trust.

The New Group of World Servers

Interesting is the fact the Lucis Trust openly declares that a secretive group of illumined, New Age notables is now running the planet from behind the scenes. Alice Bailey mysteriously identified this group as the *New Group of World Servers*. In a fascinating booklet published by World Goodwill, we are told that: "Humanity is not following a haphazard or uncharted course—there is a Plan."[36]

Not only is there a Master Plan, but according to World Goodwill's publication, it is the leaders of the New Group of World Servers who are "initiating and carrying forward activities" designed to "implement the Plan." This elitist group of dedicated men is said to "act as a synthesizing factor within humanity laying the foundations for...ultimate world unity:"

> They provide the vision and mould public opinion...The New Group of World Servers has...servers of humanity in every country...They are gathered from all branches of human enterprise...They know exactly what they seek to do. They...emphasize the brotherhood of nations, the unity of faith, and economic interdependence...They can be regarded as the embodiment of the emerging kingdom of God on earth.[37]

If, as we are advised, this elite New Group of World Servers is literally the "embodiment of the emerging Kingdom of God on Earth," then the question is, *which "God" do they represent?* The answer, given by World Goodwill on page four of its mind-boggling publication, is, to use their own words, "very illuminating." This group of world movers and shakers is not acting independently. There are certain, powerful beings in the spirit world directing their activities.

The Lucis Trust's World Goodwill organization confesses that it is this spiritual hierarchy who are in charge of The Plan and are responsible for overseeing its implementation. Alice Bailey reveals: "Behind these (human) leaders and the cooperating men of goodwill are the *Custodians of The Plan,* the inner spiritual Government of the Planet."[38]

We are also informed in the World Goodwill publication that the goal of these other-worldly "Custodians of the Plan" is to train the New Group of World Servers, a human cadre. This group of spiritually advanced human beings will literally become the "embodiment of the Kingdom of God on earth." But, say the authors of the World Goodwill publication, "This kingdom is *not* a Christian kingdom...it is a grouping of all those who—belonging as they do to every world religion and every nation and race and type of political party—are free from the spirit of hatred and separativeness."[39]

In other words, the coming "Kingdom of God" is to incorporate the principles of unity and one-worldism. This is the same set of ideas proposed by Newt Gingrich and the Tofflers as put forth in their books, *Power Shift, The Third Wave* and *Creating A New Civilization.*

According to the World Goodwill organization, "The immediate world problem is...overpopulation, trade barriers...the uneven distribution of wealth, and our uncoordinated higher education."[40]

Sounds like a wish list of the Communist Internationale, the Trilateral Commission, the Bilderbergers, and the Council on Foreign Relations, doesn't it?

Fortunately, say the authors, the "Enlightened Ones whose destiny it is to watch over human evolution and to guide the destinies of men" are right now, even as you read this, working to fulfill The Plan and solve these problems. These enlightened men are said to have "no mental limitations" and no religious biases. They are the servants of humanity and of the planetary hierarchy, chosen to usher in world government and "to build the new world of tomorrow."[41]

Newt Gingrich's enthusiastic acceptance of the "Third Wave" agenda stamps him as one of these Enlightened Ones. If he truly has been chosen to "bring order out of chaos," Mr. Gingrich deserves to be watched very closely in the coming months and years. After all, he himself declared his intention to "shift the planet."

NINE

The Meteoric Rise of Wicked Bill Clinton: A Classic Case Study of Illuminati Influence

But as it is written, eye hath not seen nor ear heard, neither have entered into the heart of man, the things which God hath prepared for them that love him.

—*I Corinthians 2:9*

As the Scripture says, our eyes have not yet seen, nor our ears heard, nor our minds imagined what we *can build...We can do it.*

—Bill Clinton
Democrat Party National Convention,
New York City

Nature, in its fullest, is God.

—Al Gore
Earth in the Balance

The Illuminati is a group which, like an oversized and malevolent octopus, extends its claw-like tentacles out into every nook and cranny of society and government. The symbol of the all seeing eye on our one dollar bill masterfully pictures the omnipresent and vile character of the Illuminati. The grotesque eye of Lucifer atop the pyramid stares at every American each time a man or woman takes a dollar bill out of a wallet or purse, yet few people pay attention to the image. Even fewer know its dark meaning. But the strange and mysterious image *does exist;* the Illuminati who designed it and placed the eye and pyramid on the U.S. currency *do exist.* Their existence, in fact, is amply proven by the fascinating story of Bill Clinton's meteoric rise to the pinnacle of political power as President of the United States.

In September, 1992, in my *Flashpoint* international newsletter, the intriguing feature article was entitled, "Bill Clinton and the Bilderberger Conspiracy." Here's part of what I said in that timely piece:

> Bill Clinton could well become the next president of the United States of America. How did he do it? How did this unknown governor of a small, mostly rural state suddenly vault to the top even though his past is clouded with *proven* allegations of adultery, military draft dodging, and other counts of moral turpitude? Is someone—or some group—now lurking in the shadows, pulling his strings?

My answer to this question was powerful and direct. "Yes," I revealed, "Bill Clinton is owned lock, stock, and barrel by the Secret Brotherhood, the powerful world elite known as the Illuminati." I then went on to detail Clinton's Illuminati background and the reasons why this flawed and wicked man was chosen by the *Inner Circle* to be one of their chief instruments to bring chaos and bloodshed to the world and to build a Gestapo police state in America. Bill Clinton's election paves the way for the final stage of the Great Work that is the goal of the conspirators.

An Impressive Performance

Bill Clinton's pedigree and résumé is important because his career and life provide convincing documentation of the Illuminati's ability to recruit, cultivate, and install in the highest political office on Planet Earth twisted and perverse men who do the bidding of the elitists. Certainly, Mr. Clinton has performed extremely well in a brief time period for his unseen superiors.

With the assistance of Masonic brothers, House Speaker Newt Gingrich and Senate Majority Leader Robert Dole, Clinton has successively rammed through Congress gun control legislation, United Nations and World Bank funding, and massive foreign aid spending. He has crammed NAFTA, GATT, and the World Trade Organization (WTO) down our throats and thumbed his nose at the citizenry by giving billions of dollars to Wall Street bankers to bail them out in the debacle of the Mexican peso collapse.

President Clinton has also encouraged a national hatred of patriotic, Christian, and constitutionalist groups and organizations. Clinton's Presidential Decision Directive (PDD) 25, issued by his National Security Agency, ordered the U.S. military to be merged with United Nations forces and gives UN commanders direct authority over U.S. officers.[1]

All of these feats by President Bill Clinton—and many more not mentioned—have caused the Illuminati to heap praises and rewards on their loyal acolyte. He is a shining light for all aspiring politicians—a role model, and a prime example of what can be done by a man with pliant flesh and a willingness to please his masters.

Slick Willie, Bilderberg Bill, and Professor Quigley

The seduction and indoctrination of Bill Clinton began as a boy, when he was first chosen by Masonic recruiters because of his blood and family ties to certain conspiratorial figures. They gave rising young Bill Clinton a job out of high school as an intern to Arkansas' reprobate U.S. Senator J. William Fulbright and educated their recruit at Georgetown University, a Catholic Jesuit school where Clinton's Illuminati mentor was the late Professor Carroll J. Quigley.

Next, Clinton was off to Oxford University in England where, as a Rhodes Scholar, he was introduced to the finer points of The Plan of the world conspiracy. After that, his elitist superiors shuffled their promising, new servant-in-training to Yale University, the home of George Bush's Skull & Bones Society.

A law degree from Yale in hand, Clinton returned to Arkansas, a state that has been totally controlled for decades by the Rockefeller banking family. Indeed, it was Arkansas Governor Winthrop Rockefeller, reputedly a homosexual, who helped guide young Bill's career. At the record age of just 29, Clinton became the state's attorney general. Soon, the Secret Brotherhood would reward their promising and faithful servant with the coveted political post of Governor of Arkansas, a position which Clinton would eventually use as a launching pad for the presidency.

The press back in Little Rock first tagged Bill Clinton "Slick Willie" because of his talent for political trickery, shrewdness, and deception. But I propose yet another nickname for the man who has so successfully served the Illuminati as president: *"Bilderberg Bill."* You see, it was the Bilderbergers who, in 1991 at their secretive meeting in Baden Baden, Germany, put the final stamp of approval on Clinton's try for the oval office.[2]

In his acceptance speech in New York at the Democratic Party National Convention, Bill Clinton acknowledged his debt to a man who was greatly responsible for his initiation into the ranks of the world's secret elite: Professor Carroll J. Quigley.

When Bill Clinton uttered the following words that night in Madison Square Garden, every syllable was addressed to the hidden men who intend to rule over us, the monied czars and potentates of the Secret Brotherhood:

> As the Scripture says, our eyes have not yet seen, nor our ears heard, nor our minds imagined what *we* can build...We can do it.
>
> As a teenager I heard John Kennedy's summons to citizenship. And then, as a student at Georgetown, *I heard that call clarified by a professor named Carroll Quigley...*[3]

There are two esoteric secrets that were hidden in these passages. First, twisting the Scriptures, Clinton affirmed the goal of the Secret Brotherhood to *build* a New World Order. In contrast, the Scriptures refer to what *God,* not man, has *already built* and prepared for those who love Him. The actual wording of the Scriptures is found in I Corinthians 2:9:

> Eye hath not seen, nor ear heard, neither have entered into the heart of man, *the things which God hath prepared* for them that love Him.

Second, Clinton briefly mentioned John Kennedy's "summons to citizenship" and then quickly followed that up by assuring his secret society listeners that, at Georgetown University, this call was "clarified" for him by Professor Carroll Quigley.

What is the crucial difference between President John F. Kennedy's summons and Quigley's clarification? Simply this: JFK's famed patriotic speech was addressed to Americans, not world citizens!: "Ask not what your *country* can do for you, but what you can do for your *country.*"

But the late Carroll Quigley, like all globalist members of the Illuminati's Secret Brotherhood, detested and reviled the very thought of country and nationalism. Quigley actively conspired for World Government, and it was he who first brought Bill Clinton in on The Plan for global domination by the elitists. How Quigley "clarified" Kennedy's words can therefore be stated as follows:

> Ask not what your planet and its masters can do for you, but what you can do for your planet and its masters.

The Aim of the Conspirators

Professor Quigley admitted his involvement in the world conspiracy in his astonishing 1,300 page book, *Tragedy and Hope,* published in 1966. Quigley wrote of his fellow conspirators: *"Their aim is nothing less than to create a world system of financial control in private hands able to dominate the political system of each country and the economy of the world as a whole."*[4]

Bill Clinton's praise of his mentor, Carroll Quigley, was proof that he is a puppet of the Illuminati and its powerful, financial front group, the Bilderbergers. He signalled to them in his New York address that, after his election as president, he would do their bidding by ushering America into the New World Order.

Clinton's use of the word "clarified" was therefore no accident. World Goodwill, the globalist organization founded by occultist Alice Bailey of the Lucis Trust, has said that The Plan to usher in the New Age Kingdom on Planet Earth needed to be *clarified,* or explained, to the masses through propaganda.[5]

Other New Age globalists frequently spout the same type of propaganda. For example, in her illuminating article in the World Goodwill bulletin, entitled "The Earth Charter and the Clarification of the Plan," Angela Harkavy stated:

> The message...should be concise, short, and clear to help us articulate the framework for behavior and action in the New Age...In the next nine months all the government, organizations, institutions and peoples involved in this process will be envisioning and articulating the *clarification* of The Plan...[6]

World Goodwill has explained that *world synthesis,* including a unified world government and economy, was at the core of this "clarification" process. "The momentum to unity is unstoppable," the organization has announced.[7]

The Fast Track to the New World Order

Bill Clinton was charged by his superiors in the *Inner Circle* with the responsibility of seeing to it that America continues on the fast track to the New World Order. To accomplish this, he has worked at presenting *their vision* of the future to the citizenry—and has earnestly sought to convince Americans that it is in their best interest to cooperate with the hidden Plan of the conspirators. His objective has been to "clarify" John Kennedy's call for service to country by arousing in the masses an overwhelming desire to serve the United Nations and, indeed, the whole world. Sentiments such as patriotism and love of country must be eliminated.

In his acceptance speech in New York, Clinton quoted the scripture, *"Where there is no vision, the people perish."* This, too, was by design. The occult conspirators have long emphasized the necessity for their agents to *clarify* and impart to the populace their *vision* of what the world is to become.

For example, Tom Carney, leader of the occult group, *Arcana Workshops,* based in Manhattan Beach, California, told his organization's members that, because "The Plan" is prospering, the veil of secrecy is being removed. Carney also revealed that the main task of the occult hierarchy—which he and others identify as the New Group of World Servers—is to *clarify the vision* for the masses:

> Everyone has heard the quotation, "Where there is no vision, the people perish"...That is the role the New Group of World Servers plays in relation to humanity... It is precisely this effort—to move the outlines of the Plan into the range of the planetary intelligentsia—that is the work of the New Group of World Servers.[8]

Onward to the New Millennium

According to Arcana Workshops' Tom Carney, the seven-year period 1993-2000 is crucial if the New Age Plan is to succeed. Humanity, he says, is "pregnant with new life," and he exhorts fellow disciples to go forth and exploit this fantastic time of opportunity.

"The place is here, the time is now," trumpets Carney.[9]

Yes, Bill Clinton has been given a mission by the brotherhood of the Illuminati, the evil and calculating men whom I called the Secret Brotherhood in my book, *Dark Majesty*. His job is to be the chief propagandist and principal mover to implement the New World Order. His task is to convince the American people that he is for the common man, that he supports the everyday working man and woman. But in fact, Bill Clinton and his Vice President, Al Gore are tools of the super rich. Both men represent the masters of high finance. This is why Clinton's campaign funding comes from men connected to such Wall Street and foreign investment firms as Lehman Brothers, Nikko Securities, and Goldman Sachs.

It is also why Clinton's lawyer-wife, Hillary Rodham, is on the board of directors of the socialist, anti-family group which masks itself under the name of the Children's Defense Fund. This organization undermines families by creating divisiveness between children and parents. Reportedly, it is funded in part by a Communist front group, the New World Foundation, which has a record of supporting Communist activists like Angela Davis and sponsoring chaos through the funding of Marxist guerilla groups in Central America. Hillary Clinton once served as chairperson for the New World Foundation.[10]

A Member of Three Conspiratorial Fronts

Bill Clinton is an active member of three, key, conspiratorial front groups: the Trilateral Commission, the Council on Foreign Relations, and the Bilderbergers. He is also a supporter of a super-secret, new CIA spy organization that is sweetly but deceptively called the "National Endowment for Democracy." As president, Clinton has rapidly prepared America for the coming *Great Initiation* of the world.

Al Gore: Spiritual Guru of the Illuminati

That coming Great Initiation will be much more than a political and economic, watershed event. It will be the penultimate extravaganza in a spiritual drama that has coagulated and gathered steam now for some 2,000 years. If Bill Clinton has played a key part in the elaborate political and economic preparations for this earth-changing event, then we would have to give his vice president, Al Gore, credit for helping to develop the *spiritual* climate necessary to implement the coming, mind-boggling changes.

In June, 1992 in Milwaukee, at the annual convention of the liberal-oriented Presbyterian Church USA denomination, the pastors and other delegates participated in a Native American Indian ritual. The ritual ceremony involved walking through smoking sage and was intended to expel unwanted spirits and attract favorable ones.

This was a demonic, pagan ritual of which then U.S. Senator Al Gore, a self-proclaimed Southern Baptist, would have been proud. In his bestselling book, *Earth in the Balance: Ecology and the Human Spirit,* Gore claims there is a spiritual dimension involved in the ecology of the Earth. He roundly denounces fundamentalist Christianity while he applauds Hinduism, Buddhism, and other Eastern religions. Gore also endorses the Mother Goddess revival, Native American shamanism, and Earth spirit worship.[11]

In his book, Al Gore glowingly writes of "Vast Earth the Mother of all...fondling all creation in her lap." He also recites an Indian prayer addressed to "O Great Spirit" and insists that "Native American religions...offer a rich tapestry of ideas."[12]

As for his own religious ideas, it's plain that Senator Gore is *New Age all the way.* All of us—born again or not, he stresses, already have "God within." He criticizes those Christians who believe it is "heretical...to suppose that God is in us."[13] For Gore, God is not a personal being somewhere "out there" in a place called heaven; instead, every man is God and thus, every man has God within. We are all part of God because, Gore believes, *the creation itself is God!* "By gathering in the mind's eye all of creation," writes Gore, "one can perceive the image of the creator vividly."[14]

"Nature, in its fullest," he adds, "is God."[15]

The perfect religion for man, according to Gore, is

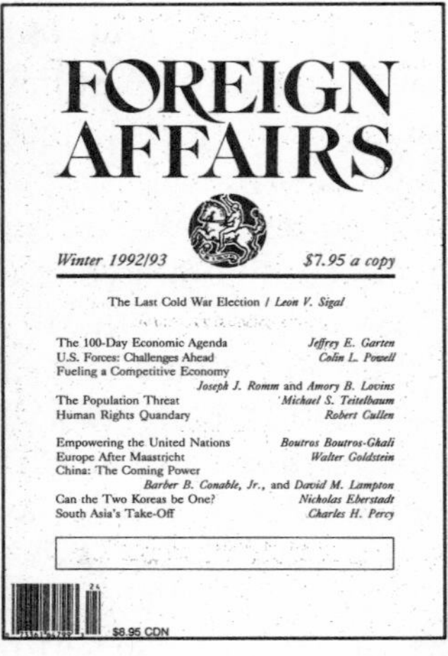

FOREIGN AFFAIRS

Winter 1992/93 *$7.95 a copy*

The Last Cold War Election / *Leon V. Sigal*

The 100-Day Economic Agenda *Jeffrey E. Garten*
U.S. Forces: Challenges Ahead *Colin L. Powell*
Fueling a Competitive Economy *Joseph J. Romm* and *Amory B. Lovins*
The Population Threat *Michael S. Teitelbaum*
Human Rights Quandary *Robert Cullen*

Empowering the United Nations *Boutros Boutros-Ghali*
Europe After Maastricht *Walter Goldstein*
China: The Coming Power *Barber B. Conable, Jr.*, and *David M. Lampton*
Can the Two Koreas be One? *Nicholas Eberstadt*
South Asia's Take-Off *Charles H. Percy*

$8.95 CDN

Above left: *President Bill Clinton, an Illuminati clone, is a member of the CFR, the Trilateral Commission,* ***and*** *the Bilderbergers.*

Right: *Upon Bill Clinton's election the CFR used its journal,* ***Foreign Affairs****, to outline the exact program the* ***Inner Circle*** *required of their servant Bill Clinton. Included in that issue were articles by General Colin Powell and United Nations Secretary-General Boutros Boutros-Ghali.*

Lower left: *Vice President Al Gore and Massachusetts U.S. Senator John Kerry, a member of the Skull & Bones Society, are seen here preaching their New Age doctrines at Rio de Janeiro's* ***Earth Summit*** *in June 1992.*

therefore the New Age, Mother Earth religion as taught by the late philosopher Teilhard de Chardin. De Chardin, a Jesuit priest whose New Age occultism was so vile that the Vatican itself was once forced to reprimand him, taught that man and the planet are both evolving toward godhood, toward the "Omega Point." There is no personal God in heaven said de Chardin; man and the cosmos are all there is. Together, they are one and they are divine.[16]

Al Gore endorses this pagan Earth religion of Teilhard de Chardin as a "new faith" that is much needed by the masses. "The fate of mankind," he writes "depends upon the emergence of a *new faith in the future*. Armed with such a faith, we might find it possible to *resanctify the earth*."[17]

Al Gore's remedy for society's ills would lead us straight into the fires of hell. History records that in the era before Christ when the pagan religions flourished, their "sanctification of the Earth" meant untold misery, suffering, and death for the inhabitants of the planet. Child sacrifice, ritual mutilation of bodies, cannibalism, and inhumane savagery on a colossal scale were commonplace. Now the Vice President of the United States wants to restore these same conditions to humanity today.

In that blood-soaked, past era, strong men ruled over the weak as kings and princes, pretending to be gods and supermen. The beast world system over which they presided was, in time, thankfully overthrown as God's truth steadily prevailed. Now, the strong men and the twisted disciples of "Mother Earth" are back, and their fanatical, insane Plan is to reinaugurate the whole world into their bloody, occult paradigm. Their Plan calls for a fiery and awful Great Initiation.

In my book *Mystery Mark of the New Age,* I describe just what is to occur during this ominous event the Satanists glowingly call the "Great Initiation."[18] If you have not yet read this eye-opening book, please, I urge you—obtain and read it at once. It is essential that we who love America and who know God prepare for the wickedly dangerous hard times that are almost upon us:

For then shall be great tribulation, such as was not since the beginning of the world to this time, no, nor ever shall be. (Matthew 24:21)

TEN

The One-Eyed Infidel and The Naked Man on a White Horse

Lee Harvey Oswald was reported to have feared "Devilmen" who were in "key positions within each world government."

—Neal Wilgus
The Illuminoids

Nor is Antichrist unknown to Mohammedan theology in which he is called Masth al Dajjal, the false or lying Christ...He is to be one-eyed and marked on the forehead with the letters C.F.R., i.e. Cafir or Infidel.

—*Encyclopaedia Britannica* (1904)

To fully understand the dangerous and evil conspiracy of the Illuminati and its *Inner Circle,* we must investigate and be able to ascertain, "what are their *goals?*...what is it they seek to achieve?" I believe the answer can be stated as follows:

(1) A Greedy Desire for Power

(2) Service to Their Master, Satan

(3) A Dictatorial World Order

First, we must realize that the *Inner Circle* and its associates conspire together for the sake of *personal power*. It is a heady and exhilarating experience to sit at the pinnacle of world authority—to issue orders and directives to trembling underlings and to watch smugly as your commands—up to and including murder and genocide—are precisely carried out.

The fact is that lower-level subordinates confer god-like status on their Illuminati masters. Italian Prime Minister Silvio Berlusconi, although a fiercely loyal Roman Catholic devoted to the Virgin Mary, was quoted in *The European* newspaper as exclaiming: "Instead of a picture of the Virgin I have for years kept on my bedside table a photograph of Giovanni Agnelli."[1]

Agnelli, the billionaire owner of a fortune created by his Fiat Motor Corporation, is a high-level Illuminati chieftain and a member of the uppity fraternity of super rich known formally as *The Alliance* and informally as the *Bilderbergers*.

One can understand Berlusconi's sentiment better by realizing that membership in the Bilderbergers is one of the most coveted objectives of lower-level Illuminati subordinates. Many no doubt point to the success of Bill Clinton as a prime example of the wonderful things that can accrue to a lower-level servant given access to the extraordinary men who attend the annual conferences of the Bilderbergers.

Clinton's ascendancy escalated when he was elected to the very selective Trilateral Commission in September of 1988. The ambitious Georgetown University graduate was made a member of the Council on Foreign Relations in July of 1989. But it was not until he attended his first Bilderbergers conference in 1991 in Baden Baden, Germany that Bill Clinton's political fortunes took an upward lunge. It was decided there at Baden Baden that Clinton, then the unknown governor of the rural, backwaters state of Arkansas, would be given all the money and media attention necessary for electoral success. Only a year and a few months later, William Jefferson Clinton was sworn in as President of the United States of America.

Shockingly, one of the new President's first satanic acts in office was issuance of an executive order permitting aborted babies to be dismembered and their vital body fluids, flesh and organs to be sold for profit.

Devilmen in Government?

My research proves that covetous men like Bill Clinton must demonstrate something more than mere ambition to win acceptance to the ranks of the elite. They must acquiesce to blatant occultism and reject the absolutes of biblical Christianity. Since these men are energized by the insane desire for power, *they have literally sold their souls to Satan.* The Adversary promises to deliver to them awesome powers and wealth which they may exercise for their personal pleasure and enjoyment. The men of the *Inner Circle* are guided and owned by material passions, i.e. *mammon,* or money. That is why they became devilmen.

It is reported that Lee Harvey Oswald, framed by the government and fingered as the lone assassin in the JFK assassination, feared "Devilmen" who were in "key positions within each world government."[2] Was Oswald referring to the unseen men of the Illuminati?

Hitler, too, feared the occult powers of his adversaries. The fuhrer knew of the Illuminati because he, himself, was an initiate of satanic groups such as the Vril Society and the Thule Society, groups which professed a belief in the ancient wisdom and the powers of darkness.[3]

To protect himself and his regime against what he felt to be the satanic, magical powers of the Illuminati, Hitler adopted the swastika, an occultic sun sign, as the symbol for his Third Reich. At the time he did so, the swastika had long been used as a magical talisman by Masons and in Eastern religions. It is doubtful that the average German at the time had any idea of the occult meaning and sinister implications of their own, national emblem.

The sun sign is universally a symbol of Lucifer, who was called by New Age psychic Edgar Cayce the "Solar Angel."[4] The Lucis Trust, a major globalist organization, identifies Lucifer as the "Solar Logos" (Logos in Greek means divine "Spirit"). Hitler's swastika may, in fact, see a revival and comeback in future years. Meanwhile, however, let us focus our attention on other curious symbols now used by Illuminati front groups.

The symbol of the Swastika, adopted by the Nazis, is a sign of Lucifer, the sun deity, and has very ancient origins. The Swastika also takes different forms. Far left, is the "left path" sun sign of Hitler; second is the "right path" Swastika, signifying white magic as opposed to Hitler's black magic design. Third is the Gamma Cross version, used by the ancient Cathars of France and Spain; and far right is the sun wheel Swastika, used by the Nazis but also found on ancient Greek coins. (Source: ***The Twisted Cross****, by Joseph Carr)*

Secrets of the Trilateral Commission Symbol

Two of the most sinister organizations on planet Earth are the *Trilateral Commission* and the *Council on Foreign Relations*. The logos of both of these organizations speak louder than words. The Trilateral logo is an interlocking system of three arrows, each designed to suggest the number "6." Thus: 6-6-6. The shape and projectory of these arrows causes a triangle of three parts to be formed. In occult paganism, this represents the unholy trinity of deities worshipped in the ancient Mystery Religions.

Note, also, that the arrows are shaped like a triangular circle and point to the "One," symbolically meaning that *all things* are to come under the domination and control of the Illuminati and, eventually, its Antichrist leader. The world is to become as one. The global mission of the Trilateral Commission to make all things one is expressly stated in the organization's own literature. We are informed that the Trilateral Commission seeks to foster free trade and cement political and economic ties between the world's three, most important global regions: America, Asia, and Europe. Thus, the meaning of the term "trilateral" in the organization's name.

The logo, or symbol, of the Trilateral Commission.

That the 6-6-6 shaped Trilateral logo has deep globalist significance is also revealed in the occult teachings of Alice Bailey, founder of the Lucis Trust and World Goodwill. In her works, we discover references to a *triangle of powers*—three major centers (in Britain, "centres") of spiritual and physical influence—being set up on Earth in the last days by "Sanat Kumara"—an occultic code name for Satan. Could this be a reference to the mission of the Trilateral Commission?

> Only in the final root-race of men upon our planet will the essential central Triangle make its appearance and function openly...The areas of conscious creative activity, out of which this triangle of functioning embodied energies will emerge, is already in preparation. One point of this future triangle will emerge out of the field of *world governments,* of politics and of statesmanship; another will appear out of the *world religions,* and a third out of the general field of *world economics and finance.*[5]

Read again Bailey's forecast of a *triangle* of energies—"three major Centres." This triangle is said to consist of "world governments," "world religions," and "world economics and finance." Again we see the three objectives of the Illuminati—a New World Order, the unification of all sects to result in a diverse, yet cooperative, World Religion, and a global financial colossus. Bailey further tells us that, "at the close of the age, the three major Centres will be in complete, unified, and synchronized activity."[6]

The coordination of the three major world centers, she adds, will be accomplished by "a star with nine points." Sir John Sinclair, in his commentary on the legacy of Alice Bailey, remarks that these nine points represent nine different groups of New Age workers—financiers, clergymen, psychologists, etc. But, adds Sinclair, occult theology teaches that in the last days, as the Aquarian Age approaches, a *tenth* group will emerge. There will be a star of *ten* points.[7] Could this be a veiled reference to the ten men of the *Inner Circle* and the separate Illuminati groups of workers these ten men supervise?

Bible Prophecy and Illuminati Symbolism

An astounding passage in Revelation 16:14-16 also causes prophecy students to take notice of the tri-fold message contained in the Trilateral Commission symbol. There we read that from the mouth of the dragon, or Satan, issue *three* frogs. These three frogs symbolize satanic powers affecting the whole globe.

> For they are the spirits of devils, working miracles, which go forth unto the kings of the earth and of the whole world, to gather them to the battle of that great day of God Almighty...And he gathered them together into a place called in the Hebrew tongue Armageddon. (Revelation 16:14, 16)

These three frogs (the three arrows of the Trilateral logo?) are under the command of the Antichrist, also known as the beast: "And I saw the beast, and the kings of the earth, and their armies, gathered together to make war against Him (Jesus Christ)"...(Revelation 19:19)

Is this reference in Revelation to the "kings of the earth" the key to our understanding the identity of the ten men who comprise the *Inner Circle* of the Illuminati? I believe that is exactly the case. In Revelation 17, we are told that in the last days, there will be *ten kings,* or world rulers. They will command many people and nations encompassing the entire globe. Moreover, these ten men will be of "one mind" and will "give their power and strength unto the beast."

Turning again to Bible prophecy, it is possible to uncover more startling revelations about this fascinating, yet ominous, symbol of the Trilateral Commission.

In II Thessalonians 2, Ezekiel 38, and elsewhere in Bible prophecy, we are told that the Antichrist will seek to conquer the city of Jerusalem. He will even rebuild the Jewish temple and enter therein, declaring himself the supreme deity of planet Earth. The city of Jerusalem will become the world's capitol. It is from this city that the Antichrist will preside over a global empire.

It would do us well to remember that the city of Jerusalem in the last days is prophesied to be a place of great abominations and blasphemy. The rejection of Christ by most of today's Jewish inhabitants of that city and the involvement of Israel's present-day leaders in Masonic intrigue make this once, great city a veritable den of iniquity. Just see how God describes Jerusalem in the end-times. Revelation 11:8, for example, strongly denounces this city and its inhabitants, comparing Jerusalem to the wicked "Sodom and Egypt."

It is from this city, Jerusalem, spiritually identified in God's Word as a last days "Sodom and Egypt," that the Illuminati's Antichrist leader will make his last, desperate bid to unite the Earth. To do so, he knows he will have to appear a man for all religions. For centuries, Jerusalem has been the boiling point of conflict between three, great world religions—Christianity, Islam, and Judaism. How will the Illuminati's Antichrist seek to resolve this ages-old crisis?

Significantly, Revelation 16:19 states: "And the great city was divided into *three parts.*" Already we see indications that, by the year 2000, the city of Jerusalem will be divided into Christian, Moslem, and Jewish sectors; i.e., *three parts*. The plan is to internationalize the city and give the United Nations control over its administration. Yet, Jerusalem will be a world center for all three major religions. This helps us to understand the New Age religious doctrine of a synthesized "unity-in-diversity."

Star of David Conceals a Mystery

A key to this important mystery regarding the part Jerusalem is destined to play in the unfolding, end-times drama may well be the symbol of the *Star of David.* This six-pointed star is the national emblem of today's Israel and is found on that country's flag. But the Star of David is not now, nor has it ever been, a holy symbol. It is an ancient, magical sign of immense evil. In fact, the six-pointed star conceals and incorporates within its design the very same principles of the occultic Secret Doctrine which are to be discovered in the swastika!

Sadly, the Jewish people and the vast majority of the citizens of Israel have no idea whatsoever of the diabolical, hidden meaning concealed in the six-pointed star. The Star of David, is in reality a, "graven image" which God finds abominable. Is it any wonder that the second of the Ten Commandments given by God to Israel through Moses carries a stiff warning to violaters:

> Thou shalt not make unto thee any graven image, or any likeness of any thing that is in heaven above, or that is in the earth beneath, or that is in the water under the earth. Thou shalt not bow down thyself to them, nor serve them: for I the Lord thy God am a jealous God, visiting the iniquity of the fathers upon the children unto the third and fourth generation of them that hate me; And shewing mercy unto thousands of them that love me, and keep my commandments. (Exodus 20:4-6)

The awful truth is that the misnamed Star of David, made up of two, joined triangles, represents none other than the Sun God of the ancients, known as Baal, Remphan, Horus, and by other names. We know that these deities are merely stand-ins for Lucifer, or Satan, for all idols, graven images, and occult symbols represent the devil.

The Scriptures identify the devil as the "beast that rises up out of the sea" (Revelation 13:1) and as "the great dragon...that old serpent" (Revelation 12:9). Whether the occult world uses a five-pointed star (pentagram) or a six-pointed star (hexagram or "Star of David") is irrelevant. Both of these symbols, and many more besides, clearly represent the forces of darkness.

The six-pointed, two triangle, Star of David, adopted by the nation of Israel for its flag (top left), has long been recognized by occultists as a sign of white and black magic.

Top right: *This is the original emblem of Helena Blavatsky's Theosophy Society. Notice the crowned, circular serpent, Ouroboros, and the Swastika inside the circle.*

Bottom row: *Shown here are talismans, or charms, used by occultists which employ versions of the six-pointed star.*

The Naked Man Riding a White Horse

Meanwhile, another conspiratorial Illuminati organization, the Council on Foreign Relations, employs a logo of a *rider on a white horse*. To understand the horrendous meaning of this curious logo, we need only turn to Revelation 6 of our Bible. There, we discover that the first of the dreadful and bloody "Four Horsemen of the Apocalypse" is the rider on the white horse!

> And I saw when the Lamb opened one of the seals, and I heard, as it were the noise of thunder, one of the four beasts saying, Come and see. And I saw, and behold a white horse: and he that sat on him had a bow; and a crown was given unto him: and he went forth conquering, and to conquer. (Revelation 6:1-2)

The CFR logo, as pictured in the organization's official journal, *Foreign Affairs,* depicts a strong, virulent, and naked rider astride a magnificent white steed. He aggressively stretches upward his right arm in a defiant demonstration of victory and triumph. But look at the mysterious hand gesture. Are the man's fingers symbolizing the occultic sign of the horned devil, *el diablo,* or is this a mere illusion?

Observe also that the naked man on the white charger is pictured against the background of a totally black circle. I believe this represents the *Inner Circle* of the Illuminati, while the naked man on the white horse represents the

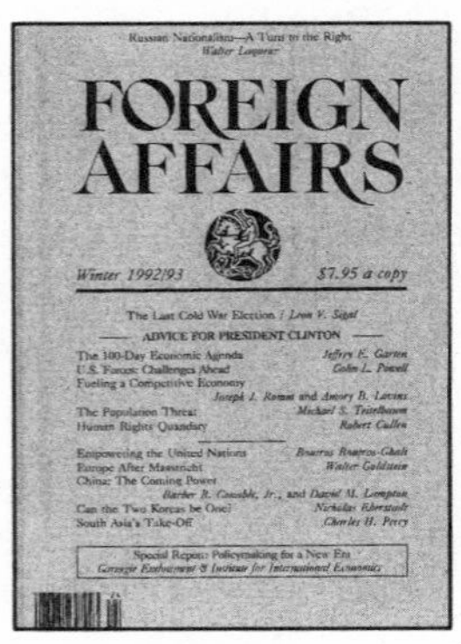

*This revealing logo is found on the front cover of each issue of **Foreign Affairs**, the official journal of the Council on Foreign Relations.*

Antichrist to come, the leader who will preside over the *Council of the Inner Circle* and, indeed, over the whole world.

The False Christ to be a One-Eyed Infidel?

While we cannot place our faith in their theology, it is nevertheless interesting that Moslem teachers long ago warned of an Antichrist to come. Amazingly, they predicted that when he appears, this evil leader can be identified by the letters C.F.R.! Moreover, they warned he would have "one eye." Is this a reference to the Illuminati's all seeing eye of Horus, printed on our U.S. one dollar bills? In the 1904 edition, volume two of the *Encyclopaedia Britannica* we find this fascinating passage:

> Nor is Antichrist unknown to Mohammedan theology in which he is called Masth al Dajjal, the false or lying Christ...*He is to be one-eyed and marked on the forehead with the letters C.F.R., i.e. Cafir or infidel.*

By 1919, the year that the CFR, the Council on Foreign Relations, was spawned by President Woodrow Wilson, his aide, Colonel House, and European co-conspirators, other agents of the Illuminati had bought the rights to the *Encyclopaedia Britannica* and had expunged this material, which was originally found on page 126 of the 1904 edition. Thankfully, I have an authenticated copy of this reference stored safely away in my files, lest it someday go down some Orwellian "black hole," courtesy of Big Brother's Gestapo.

A Dictatorial World Order: The United Nations Plot

What we do know for certain is that when this Antichrist infidel does emerge on the world scene, he will put the finishing touches on a New World Order. To please their master,

Satan, the men of the Illuminati must furiously and continuously work to establish a global political, economic, and religious order. These are the three legs of the beast—government, money, and unholy religion. Their goal is to create a dictatorial New World Order, which will delight their hellish master and bequeath to these men fabulous raw powers of control over the masses. To complete their ambitious quest, the men of the *Inner Circle* are more than willing to lie, kill, steal, and destroy society as we know it to bring in this New World Order.

The *United Nations* is the vehicle chosen to establish over the face of the whole Earth the authority of these ten wicked men. Up to now the UN has been weak and it has needed the armed might of the United States to execute its declarations and threats. But the goal is to make the United Nations a supreme power in its own right. A plot has been hatched to transfer to the UN the bulk of all the world's armed forces.

To comply with this new plot, faithful Illuminist, President Bill Clinton, has issued executive orders implementing *Presidential Decision Directive (PDD) 25*. PDD 25 is a National Security Council memorandum requiring United States military officers to follow the orders of foreign military officers under the authority of the UN. This is the first time in American history U.S. troops have been placed under the command of foreigners, and it is a direct violation of the U.S. Constitution. The Constitution assigns to the President of the United States alone the privilege and responsibility of acting as Commander-in-Chief of the U.S. Armed Forces.

The UN, as the command center of the New World Order, is now being empowered to suppress internal rebellions in every country on Earth and to launch invasions against and violate the sovereignty of nations which refuse to kowtow to the New World Order. If a president or a prime minister of an independent sovereign nation anywhere in the world defies the secret directives of the *Inner Circle* of the Illuminati, his or her nation will be attacked and conquered, just as the U.S.A. invaded Panama, a sovereign nation, and arrested its leader, Manuel Noriega.

This war-like, imperialist character of the New World Order was prophesied in the Bible:

> And they worshipped the dragon which gave power unto the beast: and they worshipped the beast, saying, Who is like unto the beast? who is able to make war with him?...and power was given him over all kindreds, and tongues, and nations. (Revelation 13:4, 7)

Will American Patriots Revolt?

Evidently, the *Inner Circle* believe that in the near future, as the people of the United States and perhaps a few other democratic countries begin to understand the desperate situation of the citizenry under despotic Illuminati rule, they might revolt. The greatest fear of the Illuminists is that patriots and Christians in the U.S.A. will rise up and cast off America's despicable, totalitarian overseers. That is why, in their Newt Gingrich-endorsed books *Power Shift* and *Creating A New Civilization,* Alvin and Heidi Toffler badmouth fundamentalist Christians and nationalist patriots as relics of the "Dark Ages" and as dangerous menaces to the rising Third Wave global civilization.

To forestall such rebellion by patriots and fundamentalist Christians, in a recent issue of the CFR's authoritative journal, *Foreign Affairs,* a frightening warning was given by Arthur Schlesinger, formerly a presidential advisor to Roosevelt and Kennedy. Angrily denouncing the "isolationist impulse" and railing against the perceived dangers of nationalism, Schlesinger declared that certain people in America were creating real problems for the United Nations. The UN, he cautioned, "will not shrink from establishing its will against the evil-doer or evil-planner."[8] In other words: "Watch out, America First patriots—you evil nationalists are gonna get it!"

Strongly endorsing a United Nations global army, complete with its own international S.W.A.T. team—a "rapid deployment force," Schlesinger threatened: "We are not going to achieve a New World Order without paying for it in blood as well as in words and money."[9]

Blood and Chaos to Bring Forth New Order

What Schlesinger is alluding to is the *Inner Circle's* dictum that only through *chaos* and bloodshed can global *order* be established. Their slogan is *Ordo Ab Chao,* which, in Latin, means Order Out of Chaos.

The capstone of the New World Order will be installed on the global pyramid by both flattery and force. As a World Goodwill publication explained it in 1980, the New International Economic Order can only come about by the *destruction* of the old order. Through chaos will emerge a "new creation:"

> In the destruction of the old world order and in the chaos of these modern times, the work of the new creation is going forward; the task of reconstruction, leading to a complete reorganization of human living, and to a fresh, real orientation of human thinking, is taking place.[10]

A Great Leader is Needed

Naturally, a strengthened United Nations, being structured as a World Government, will need a *leader,* a great leader, a man eminently qualified to head up a global army, a planetary IRS, an international environmental police force, and a United Nations intelligence agency combining all the insidious talents of Israel's murderous *Mossad* spy agency, America's infamous CIA, and Russia's notorious KGB. These are the *three* intelligence legs of the beast. The Antichrist, moreover, will have to be a man who is authoritative and occultly empowered to reign over a *Council of Wise Men.*

Believe me, the elitists at the highest echelon of the *Illuminati* have just the right man in mind for this new, all-powerful position of *World Fuhrer*. Isn't that why their own in-house agency, the Council on Foreign Relations, has adopted its strange but revealing logo: *A man riding a white horse?*

A quarter of a century ago, European leader Henri Spaak, then the Secretary-General of NATO, in a moment of frustration and despair, blurted out, "We are tired of piecemeal solutions to our problems. Give us a man—whether he be devil or god—and we will follow him."

Now today, in these last fateful months before the seventh millennium, as we draw near to the year 2000 AD, Mr. Spaak's wish is about to come true. The rider is about to mount the white horse. He will lead a strengthened and vigilant world army and he will preside over an organization, the United Nations, which shall cast a piercing stare from its all seeing eye throughout the four corners of the globe. The one-eyed infidel will sit at the helm of World Government.

The U.S. Constitution, our standard for more than two centuries, is fast being set aside, and the masses make not a murmur of protest. The One World Government which the Illuminati has worked for and dreamed of is now in sight. The grand scheme of the CFR, the Trilateralists, the Bilderbergers, and other conspiratorial groups is being crowned with success.

Listen closely: Can you hear it?—the echo of that tremendous voice that came to the Apostle John on the Isle of Patmos so very long ago. The voice that once revealed a great, great mystery: *"Come and see...behold a white horse: and he that sat on him had a bow; and a crown was given unto him: and he went forth conquering, and to conquer."* (Revelation 6:1-2)

ELEVEN

Circle of Intrigue: The Colossal Plot of the Solar Serpent

And there was war in heaven...and the great dragon was cast out, that old serpent, called the Devil, and Satan, which deceiveth the whole world: he was cast out into the earth, and his angels were cast out with him...woe to the inhabiters of the earth and of the sea! for the devil is come down unto you, having great wrath, because he knoweth that he hath but a short time.

—*Revelation 12:7, 9, 12*

In the mythology of the primitive world, the serpent is universally the symbol of the sun...The serpent was universally represented by the sun symbol, the circle or disk.

—Bishop Alexander Hislop
The Two Babylons

God is a circle...

—Hermes Trismegistus
Dictionary of Symbolism

Satan and his legion of demon spirits seem to have an unusual fondness for the geometric image we call the *circle*. In occult literature and throughout the ages in pagan teachings and rituals, the circle is given preeminent stature. The same is true for the secret societies and for Luciferian globalist organizations. Whether in the Rosicrucian Order, the Skull & Bones Society, or the Trilateral Commission and Council on Foreign Relations, the circle holds an exalted status. Indeed, the circle is one of the supreme symbols, marks, and emblems of the historical satanic establishment, ancient and modern.

In my study and investigation of the origins and development of the Illuminati and its World Conspiracy, I have often been struck at the degree of homage and reverence paid to the circle. My conclusion is that there is a veiled and profoundly evil significance to this mysterious circular symbol.

I believe it is most appropriate for this book to be titled, *Circle of Intrigue*. What is unmasked and laid bare to scrutiny here is an exclusive group—a small band—of ruthless and perverse elitists. In their vacuous diabolism, these men specialize in intrigue and deception on a planetary scale. In league with like-minded women, these men form a *Circle of Conspiracy*.

By its very nature, of course, conspiracies are founded, managed, and diligently pursued on the basis of *intrigue*. Machiavellian plots are hatched in secret, extraordinary events are orchestrated clandestinely, and masks, ruses, and treachery are continuously made the order of the day.

It is important that before we move into the meat of this book and expose the covenant of death entered into by the Illuminati, we first analyze the hidden meaning of the symbol which so uniquely represents their monstrous Plan. As we shall see, though the shape of the circle appears to be benign and its curvature of innocent, geometrical proportions, nevertheless, as interpreted by the occult theocracy which now controls so much of this planet, the circle is a potentially deadly emblem. The circle combines within its form both an overpowering lust for power and a slavish devotion to Satan incarnate by deceived, yet reprobate, men.

The Circle Represents Satanic Deity

In one of the most honored of scholarly Masonic volumes, *An Encyclopedia of Freemasonry*, Dr. Albert Mackey, 33°, explains the esoteric meaning of the circle as follows:

> *Circle.* The circle being a figure which returns into itself, and having therefore neither beginning nor end, has been adopted in the symbology of all countries and times as a symbol sometimes of the universe and sometimes of eternity. With this idea in the Zoroastrian mysteries of Persia, and frequently in the Celtic mysteries of Druidism, the temple of initiation was circular. In the obsolete lectures of the old English system, it was said that "the circle has ever been considered symbolical of the Deity; for as a circle appears to have neither beginning nor end, it may be justly considered a type of God, without either beginning of days or ending of years. It also reminds us of a future state, where we hope to enjoy everlasting happiness and joy."[1]

Note that, above, Mackey informs us that, "the circle has ever been considered symbolical of the Deity." Now since, in its ignorance and superstition the Masonic Lodge worships Lucifer, also known as Satan, we can thus infer that the Deity, or god, of Freemasonry is none other than the devil himself. Of course, the infernal devil is not particular about which name is used by man in worship of him. As Mackey indicates, the deity was symbolized by the circle in "the Zoroastrian mysteries of Persia, and frequently in the Celtic mysteries of Druidism." The Zoroastrians called their deity "Ahura Mazda," while the Druids worshipped "Hu." Both were recognized as the "Sun God," and thus the circle or disc of the sun was an appropriate symbol of veneration. But, in the Christian Scriptures, all gods except *the* one God of the universe are devils.

The irrefutable fact that it is the devil who is symbolized by the circle is reinforced by countless other teachings of occultists and secret society hierophants over the years. Hermes Trismegistus, the "Thrice Greatest Magician" who was worshipped in ancient Alexandria, Egypt, as the gnostic equivalent of Satan, was said to have taught that, "God is a circle whose centre is everywhere and circumference is nowhere."[2]

Symbol of a Promised Utopia

Observe, too, that Mackey optimistically tells his readers that the symbol of the circle "reminds us of a future state, where we hope to enjoy everlasting happiness and joy." This has always been Satan's great lie—that man can attain peace, love, happiness, and fulfillment through his Plan. That is the false hope and illusion the Illuminati and its Secret Brotherhood hold out to the world today. Since the Garden of Eden, the Serpent has promised man a utopia, a glorious paradise on Earth, if only he would reject God's commandments and focus on man himself.

The Tower of Babel was but one of the tragic instances of vainglorious kingdom-building by Satanic-inspired rulers. Remarkably, we find that the most common artist depiction of the architecture of the infamous Tower of Babel is that of an ascending edifice made up of concentric *circles* in the form of a ziggurat. Indeed, all of the bloodiest dictators and tyrants throughout history have been kingdom-builders, seeking to persuade their subjects that a heaven on Earth is within man's grasp—within his "upward reach."

The symbol of the circle is of serpentine origins. Manly P. Hall, 33°, in *Secret Teachings of All Ages* writes: "All symbols having serpentine forms of motion signify the solar energy in one of its many forms."[3] What better reason, therefore, for the Illuminati to adopt as one of its most revealing emblems the circular image of *ouroboros,* the serpent and dragon biting and feeding on its own tail. In *Alchemy: The Secret Art,* Stanislas de Rola notes that ouroboros is "an emblem of the eternal, cyclic nature of the universe ('from the One to the One')."[4]

In his book we find a picture of the serpentine dragon, ouroboros, vividly painted in the colors of green and red. Again, we discover a hidden message which, in this instance, is deciphered by the author: "Here," comments de Rola, "as in all alchemical art the colouring is part of the message: green is the colour of the beginning; red is associated with the goal of the Great Work."[5]

Just as de Rola intimates, to the Illuminati, colors are

deeply significant. Green is the color of the fertility goddess, nurturer of Earth and nature. Through the revolutionary environmental movement, the Fascist Illuminati intend to globalize humanity and plunder private property from individuals. In Greece, Rome, Sumeria, and Britain, the ancient predecessors of today's Illuminists worshipped the great, green Earth goddess.

Red, meanwhile, is the color of the great red dragon: Satan, or Lucifer. The fiery, red sun is his image. Thus, in Revelation 12:3 we read of this astonishing, symbolic image of evil which is to appear in the last days and come down to Earth: "And there appeared another wonder in heaven; and behold a great red dragon." We also find in Revelation 17 that Satan's wicked, last days religious system—the worldwide church of the devil—is depicted as a prostitute and harlot sitting upon a beast that is the color of scarlet, or red:

> So he carried me away in the spirit into the wilderness: and I saw a woman sit upon a scarlet coloured beast, full of names of blasphemy, having seven heads and ten horns. And the woman was arrayed in purple and scarlet colour, and decked with gold and precious stones and pearls, having a golden cup in her hand full of abominations and filthiness of her fornication: And upon her forehead was a name written, MYSTERY, BABYLON THE GREAT, THE MOTHER OF HARLOTS AND ABOMINATIONS OF THE EARTH. (Revelation 17:3-5)

The Cosmic Pair: God and Goddess

Green, then, is the color of the green Earth goddess, representing the world and its kingdoms who are the consort and prostitute for Satan. He, in turn, is the red dragon or red beast, also known in deep occultism as the fiery orb of the sun. He is depicted by occultists as "god of light."

J.C. Cooper, author of numerous books on occult philosophy such as *Yin and Yang* and *Taoism: The Way of the Mystic,* remarks of the circle: "As the Sun it is the masculine power, but as the soul or psyche and as the encircling waters (of the Age of Aquarius) it is the feminine, maternal principle."[6]

The Cosmic Pair is formed by the combining of the masculine (the Sun) and the feminine (the Earth) principles. This is the transformative process of alchemy—the *Great Work*—which the higher-level Masons and the masters of other secret orders call *"Squaring the Circle."* The symbol of a circle within a square represents this process. In reality, this symbol represents the conquering of the four corners of the Earth by Satan, whom the Illuminati revere as the great Sun God who shows them the way to their own divine nature.

Though occult concepts like this are complex and difficult for laymen to understand, the top echelons of the Illuminati are expected to study and interpret the symbols, colors, numbers, and codes of their occult craft. They also know the Secret Doctrine, which involves the alchemical, dialectic process of the synthesizing of opposites. Thus, in the Great Work, the masculine (Satan, the Sun God) will have succeeded in his quest for the Holy Grail (i.e. for leadership of the universe) when he totally conquers the Earth (the feminine) *and* wholly extinguishes the Christian Church, which he despises and fears. The Bible tells us that Satan's quest is in vain, that shortly after the Evil One celebrates his greatest future victory, the crowning of his Antichrist on Earth, the Lord will destroy him.

In Hegelian dialectical terminology, the Great Work will be accomplished when Satan and his Antichrist (Thesis), having done battle for eons with the people of God on Earth (Antithesis), overcomes them and their God and reconciles all things unto himself (Synthesis). This is the core teaching of the Secret Doctrine and is most revealing, for what it means is that Satan cannot succeed in his grotesque mission *unless* he is able to subdue and destroy Christianity. Satan may vainly declare, as did one character in a Shakespearean drama, "The world is mine oyster," but his idle boast cannot be accomplished—the Great Work of the Illuminati can never be realized—until the Holy Spirit power of every Christian believer is removed and eradicated from the world. No wonder the Illuminati and its leadership detest and despise true Christian patriots!

The occult teaching is that when The Plan, with its goal of the Great Work, is accomplished, the circle will be complete. The red and green colors of the Serpent, the masculine and the feminine, will be integrated and become "One." Satan will be Lord of all! The circle of the Serpent, ouroboros, will end with the head and the tail joined in unholy matrimony.

Profane Architecture Carries Hidden Messages

This is the symbolic meaning of much of the pagan and even the modern, New Age architecture in vogue today. As Hans Biedermann states in his *Dictionary of Symbolism,* in the pagan, mystery religions, "The circle is the ultimate, the perfect form." Biedermann also writes:

> The legendary Hyperborean Temple of Apollo is described as circular and the capital of Plato's "island of Atlantis" as a system of concentric rings of land and water.[7]

According to Biedermann, the prehistoric Stonehenge monument of Druidic England has parallels with the ancient temples dedicated to the great goddess. Biedermann also points to the mystical teaching that, "the canopy of the heavens is represented as a round dome...because of the circular trajectory of the stars around the celestial pole."[8] The round dome is a popular style of architecture found in Washington, D.C., Rome, and capitals around the globe.

Biedermann, like every other scholarly occultist, mentions the snake biting its own tail (*Ouroboros,* which, translated, means "Fiery King of the Underworld"), as a symbol for the eternal reign of the (satanic) deity. Meanwhile, "Squaring the Circle," he says, is involved with creating perfect, divine man."[9] That, of course, is Illuminist language referring to their belief that they are a god race worthy of beneficent

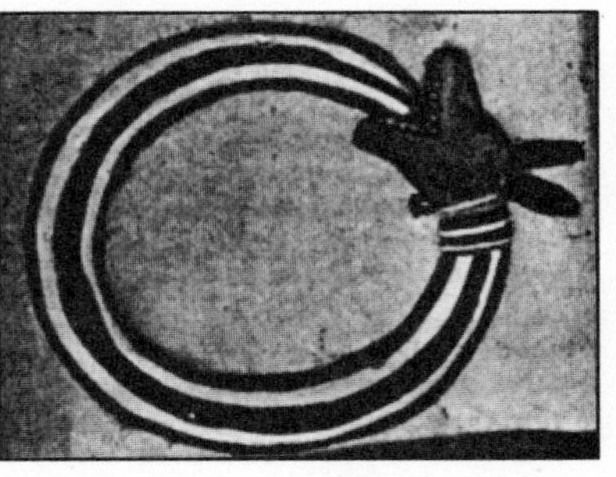

Three versions of ***Ouroboros****, the circular serpent biting its own tail.*

Above left: *This version is from* ***Atlanta Fugiens****, by Michael Maier, 1618.*

Above right: *This version of Ouroboros is from Dahomey, West Africa.*

Bottom: *An early, hand-painted Masonic apron depicts many occult symbols, including the serpent Ouroboros, the skull and bones, the X, and the goddess in the sun.*

Top: *The famous painting of the Tower of Babel by 16th century artist Bruegel. Observe the concentric circles.*

Bottom: *The all seeing eye and pyramid inside the circle is a prominent feature of the United States one dollar bill. The phrase* ***Novus Ordo Seclorum*** *is translated: "New (Secular) World Order." Does the all seeing eye reveal the Illuminati Plan to rebuild the Babylonian civilization and restore its unholy tower of unity?*

rule over the inferior and less conscious races of planet Earth.

Continuing his relating the circle with the "Deity," the Sun God, Biedermann also accurately reports that "various Native American peoples" employ the circle as a spiritual symbol of overriding importance. That is why, he says, their camp and tepee were in the form of a circle and why the tribal chiefs and elders sat in council in a circle. Circular dances are yet another indication of the supernatural values attributed by Native American tribes to the circle.

A Supernatural Message to the Initiated

In all of the Eastern religions, occult societies, and secret orders we find the circle conveying a hidden but supernatural and magical message to the initiated. British writer J. R. R. Tolkien, a blatant occultist who, nevertheless, is exalted in some misguided Christian evangelical and Catholic communities, gave us his *Lord of the Rings*. The symbol of the Olympic Games is a series of interconnected rings, understandable since the tradition of an olympic sporting event came from the Greeks, and the very term, "olympic," comes from the name of the Greek goddess, Olympia.

Deluded Americans attracted to Zen Buddhism are taught that the circle stands for enlightenment, while Sufi Moslem devotees practice ritual dervish dancing—in circles, naturally.

Still others, especially those in the martial arts, unwittingly pay homage to the oriental *Yin/Yang*. This symbol is the very epitome of the dialectic, alchemical process, combining the dark and the light, the masculine and the feminine, inside a circle with its satanic "S" shooting through its

The Yin/Yang is a dialectical symbol signifying the ungodly synthesis of light and darkness.

diameter. In the so-called art or practice of *t'ai-chi,* the gullible student is informed that the circular, and yet dualistic, yin/yang symbolizes the "One." Indeed, it does represent the one—the *one* bloodthirsty devil, who, in his ferocity and stupidity, seeks to torment the righteous and who successfully enslaves his carnal and overly ambitious Illuminati puppets.

"In India," writes Manly P. Hall, "the God Prana—the personification of the universal life force—is sometime shown surrounded by a *circle* of bees. Because of its importance in pollinating flowers, the bee is the accepted symbol of the generating power."[10]

Both in the Hindu and in the Buddhist religions, the gods and man-deities are often pictured with a circular halo around their heads, with the sun rays of the halo radiating outward. In his classic 19th century text, *The Two Babylons,* Anglican Bishop Alexander Hislop noted that in all the pagan religions, the "nimbus peculiar circle of light" was depicted encompassing the head of the gods and goddesses:

> The disk, and particularly the *circle*, were the well-known symbols of the Sun-divinity, and figured largely in the symbolism of the East. With the circle or the disk the head of the Sun-divinity was encompassed. The same was the case in Pagan Rome. Apollo, as the child of the Sun, was often thus represented. The goddesses that claimed kindred with the Sun were equally entitled to be adorned with the nimbus or luminary circle.[11]

Circe, Daughter of the Sun

Hislop was the greatest archaeological and pagan religious expert of his day; indeed, he remains the greatest of *any* era. Among his research discoveries was the excessive honor and devotion paid by Romans to the goddess *Circe.* She was said to be the "Daughter of the Sun" and was pictured with her head surrounded by a circle. Much of the art and many of the statues of antiquity portray Circe in this fashion.

Hislop also unmasks the fact that the Roman Catholic pontiffs and their underlings adopted the circle of light, the sun disk, and the halo of pagan goddesses such as Circe, for their unbiblical version of Mary—the Madonna. The medieval and renaissance painters followed this example in their religious works of art. "Let anyone compare the nimbus around the head of Circe," writes Hislop, "with the head of the Popish Virgin, and he will see how exactly they correspond."[12]

Hislop also revealed the fascinating fact that the Roman Emperors believed that they, too, on notable occasions, were surrounded around their heads with "the luminous fluid which encircles the heads of Circe and the gods."[13]

"It was assumed by them," he explains, to be "the mark of their divinity."[14]

In his prophetic book, *The Angels Laughed,* Samuel Marrs writes of Circe's astonishing and continuing influence on Christianity and the world today:

> *Circe* is comparable in legend to the Isis of Egypt, Ishtar of Babylon, and Ashtarte, the national deity of the Phoenicians. It is also where the words "Circle" and "Circus" are derived. The circle is the first step a witch or sorceress takes before casting a spell; and the circus is where our flesh is entertained.
>
> *Circe* was the daughter of Helias the sun god, and Perse the sea-nymph. She was found guilty of murdering her own husband and as punishment was banished to the island of Aeaea.
>
> *Circe* was an enchantress and sorceress who was said to occupy a great hall atop a high, mist-shrouded hill, nestled within a woodland grove where she wove a giant web. Her servants were wolves, lions, and other wild beasts who once were men. She enticed...men to feast with her and gave them a mixed-drugged drink that changed them into swine...Sailors were lured to the Island of Aeaea by Circe's beautiful music.[15]

Echoing Marrs' findings, Milton wrote that Circe, "the daughter of the sun," gave unto men her "charmed cup" and that whoever tasted of it "downward fell into grovelling swine."[16] Sounds like a mythical representation and metaphor for today's Illuminati and its Circle of Intrigue, doesn't it? Consider that Circe was involved in: sorcery... murder... weaving a giant web... wild beasts who were once men...drugs, seduction and destruction...and the turning of men into swine!

Piggish Men Made Perfect?

A fascinating fact is that the lovers of Circe *enjoyed* being swine. They reveled in their debased lust and gluttony. Indeed, in the myth of Circe we discover that her followers are "perfect" in their self-seeking desires. Amazingly, Circe was said to be the "purifier" who brought men to a state of purification and perfection so that, in their newly divine state, they could be as piggish, evil, and selfish as they wished. After all, they were deities!

As Adolf Hitler once taught, such men are not subject to the ordinary morals of inferior civilization. Being gods, they are beyond good and evil. Hitler's twisted theology led he and his minions to commit the most heinous of crimes, yet they believed themselves to be immune from common standards of decency and righteousness. The SS initiate was said to be "perfect" in his nobility and racial characteristics.

Such unholy concepts are not unknown in Freemasonry, for we read in Albert Pike's works frequent mention of the "Lodge of perfection."[17]

The New Age movement holds similar beliefs, teaching that man can achieve *samadhi*, or *enlightenment*—that is, perfection and divinity. Many in the New Age pay homage to Buddha, the late India guru whom devotees call the "enlightened one." Many New Agers say that Buddha and the Lord Maitreya are the same divine being. Eye-opening is the fact that the Masons, too, hold Buddha in great awe. Pike, in *Morals and Dogma*, writes: "The Hindus held that Buddha descended on Earth to raise all human beings to the *perfect* state."[18]

Full circle, then, we find: *Circe.* The same, lying spirit of Circe which inspired the emperors, senators, priests and priestesses, and merchants of Rome is with us today. She is a myth, but the demonic spirits who conceived her in the minds of men are *alive!* They have possessed a new generation of emperors (presidents and prime ministers), senators (politicians), priests and priestesses (clergy), and merchants (corporate chairmen/bankers). The spirit of Circe still whispers in the ear of the Illuminati the "flattery" that the prophet Daniel forecast would be the chief spiritual and psychological weapon of the Antichrist-beast at the end-time:

> And in his estate shall stand up a vile person...he shall come in peaceably, and obtain the kingdom by *flatteries.* (Daniel 11:21)

What greater flattery than to tell a chosen elite that they are perfect and like gods! This, in fact, *is* being taught to a select group of men, as evidenced by the following:

> As Humanity is the crown of the animal kingdom, so is the "Perfect Man" the crown of humanity. It is to this stage of the Perfect Man, who by contemplation and by virtue can enter into the pure thought of the First Intelligence...This journey is called the Circle of Existence.[19]

Translated, this means that the Illuminati, in their black lodges, teach initiates of the superiority and higher consciousness of man made "perfect" by *contemplation* (religious ritual and spiritual exercises) and by *virtue* (nobility of purpose). They further teach that perfection is made possible by numerous lessons learned during divine man's *Circle of Existence* (i.e., through successive reincarnations). Having become perfect, the Illuminatus supposedly becomes a "pure thought" being: a god who is One with the First Intelligence (the hazily defined, energy force "God" of the Illuminati—i.e. Lucifer!)

It is ironic that while the Illuminati claim to be "Perfect

Man, the crown of humanity," the environmental movement, which they fund and control, accuses man of being inferior or, at best, only co-equal with animals, birds, and insects. The clear lesson here is that the Illuminati lay claim to being gods while ordinarily mortals are fit only for servitude...or for extinction.

Perfect Man to Perish

Though they lay claim to deity, the fate of the Illuminati is to perish like men. Their revered Circe is, in fact, the daughter of the Sun God. She represents the last days, religious system on Earth during the reign of the Illuminati. Samuel Marrs affirms this, noting that in the myth of *Circe* we clearly have a picture of the last days on Earth under the Antichrist. Circe, he says, is the daughter of Babylon (Revelation 17), the world system of the last days on which the prophet Isaiah pronounced God's judgment:

> Stand now with thine enchantments, and with the multitude of thy sorceries, wherein thou has labored from thy youth...Thou art wearied in the multitude of thy counsels. Let now the astrologers, and the stargazers, the monthly prognosticators, stand up, and save thee from these things that shall come upon thee.
>
> Behold, they shall be as stubble; the fire shall burn them; they shall not deliver themselves from the power of the flame. (Isaiah 47:12-13)

From these prophecies we can discern the eventual fate of the Illuminati and their New World Order. Their great powers will fail them. Their money shall be worthless. Their sorcery will be of no help.

Moreover, Aleister Crowley, Helena Blavatsky, Hitler, Churchill, Reagan, Brezhnev—all these powerful men and many like them have availed themselves of the use of astrologers and stargazers. But in the last days, the Illuminati will be overcome with worry, fear, and anxiety because their magicians and astrologers will prove incompetent and ineffective. Finally, they will meet a pitiful end—being thrown into the fiery pit of hell where they will burn forever. This is their destiny because they rejected the Truth that could save them.

Light of the Solar Serpent

The fact that the satanic religions of antiquity claimed a circle of light around the heads of their deities was an especially blasphemous and criminal act against God. Jesus our Lord is indisputably the Great Light of the World, the Sun of Righteousness. His Holy Spirit is described in Acts 2 as "tongues like as of fire." Thus, Hislop warns, "Sun-worship and the worship of the host of heaven (through necromancy and spiritualism) was a sin against the Light—a presumptuous, heaven-daring sin."[20]

Only the serpent, the devil, could be so audacious and grotesque in lack of character that he could falsely claim that title and trait representative of God alone—the Light of the World, the Holy Fire. In the pagan religions, "Along with the sun, as the great fire-god and...identified with him was the serpent worshipped."[21]

"In the mythology of the primitive world," Hislop states, "the serpent is universally the symbol of the sun."[22] The serpent, then, was universally represented by the sun symbol, the *circle* or disk. Moreover, this serpent was said to be "the great *enlightener* of the physical world...and to have been the *great enlightener* of the spiritual by giving mankind the knowledge of good and evil."[23]

In ancient Babylon, Hislop recounted, the King, Nimrod, was worshipped as a deity. A type of Antichrist, he was acclaimed to be "the Sun-god, who was regarded not only as the *illuminator* of the material world, but as the *enlightener* of the souls of men, for he was recognized as the revealer of goodness and truth."[24]

The Antichrist soon to come, the final member of the Illuminati's *Inner Circle* of intrigue, will also be universally acclaimed as "God." In Revelation 13, we are told that the false prophet will cause *fire* to come down from heaven in the sight of men, so that, through this miracle, the masses will believe that the beast is the "God of Light and Revealer of the Holy Fire," the worthy successor to and very incarnation of Nimrod, the King of Babylon.

Now we must bring into consideration the loathsome role of the Illuminati. They, too, claim to be the *enlightener,* or illuminator, of mankind. They, too, proclaim that they, being the super race, are divinely endowed with the knowledge of good and evil. They further declare that, being gods, they need no external God to tell them what is right and what is wrong. Their goal of the Great Work proposes to illuminate, or *enlighten,* all of mankind. They shall show all who are fit how to become divine Aquarians and shall initiate the world into an Age of Enlightenment. Those of inferior consciousness who are unfit will be removed from the Earth. They are impediments to the radiant dawning of the New Solar Age of Aquarius.

What utter blasphemy! Hislop perhaps said it best when he commented of their boast of being the god-men who shall enlighten the world: "This, of course," said Hislop, "implies tremendous depravity on the part of the ringleaders in such a system."[25]

The Serpent and Freemasonry

The identification of the serpent as the enlightener of the world finds even greater understanding when we investigate the esteemed status of the serpent within the highest levels of Freemasonry!

This idolatrous worship of the unholy serpent by international Freemasonry, indisputably a symbol of Satan, brings to mind the decisive and inspired statement of the Apostle Paul. Such men, he wrote, dishonor God, changing the glory of God into an image and likeness of "creeping things," that is, of *serpents* (Romans 1:23). Worse, if that were possible, the Masons and the pagan religionists alike pay homage to the *phoenix* serpent, with its crown on its head signifying "king." The occultists esteem this reptile to be the most *spiritual* in nature, being long-lived and having the quality of renewing its youth.[26] In all the sacred rites and mysteries, therefore, the phoenix was introduced, just as he is today inside the darkened walls of Masonic temples and the secret orders of the Illuminati.

And so it is, that throughout the centuries, in every generation, evil men and women who organized themselves into *circles of intrigue* vainly believed that, in worshipping at the altar of the phoenix serpent, they were *renewed* and made immortal. That is why the men of the Illuminati and its satanic, ancestor organizations and religions have been patient in their ages-old quest for global dominion. They are instructed that the Great Work cannot necessarily be accomplished in one or two generations. The dialectical conflict between opposites must continue until, someday, in the last day appointed, a final *synthesis* is achieved—and God is overthrown. In the interim, the Illuminati are led to believe that, being divine, illuminated beings, they shall not die but live. Through successive incarnations (reincarnation), they believe that they will lead the world ever onward, gloriously toward a New Age dawn.

Camelot and the Arthurian Legend

The lie spawned by the Illuminati is that when they, the god-men, finally ascend to the throne of *total* world power, all resisters will be overthrown and eradicated and the masses will applaud their demise. Humanity will then enter the Golden Age, an unparalleled era of peace and prosperity. The coming Golden Age is represented by many in the *Inner Circle* as reminiscent of *Camelot,* the paradisiacal kingdom presided over by the legendary King Arthur and his royal court. According to this Illuminati legend, King Arthur (in reality a type of Antichrist) will draw around him the bravest and noblest knights in the realm. They and their monarch will comprise the *Circle of the Round Table.*[27]

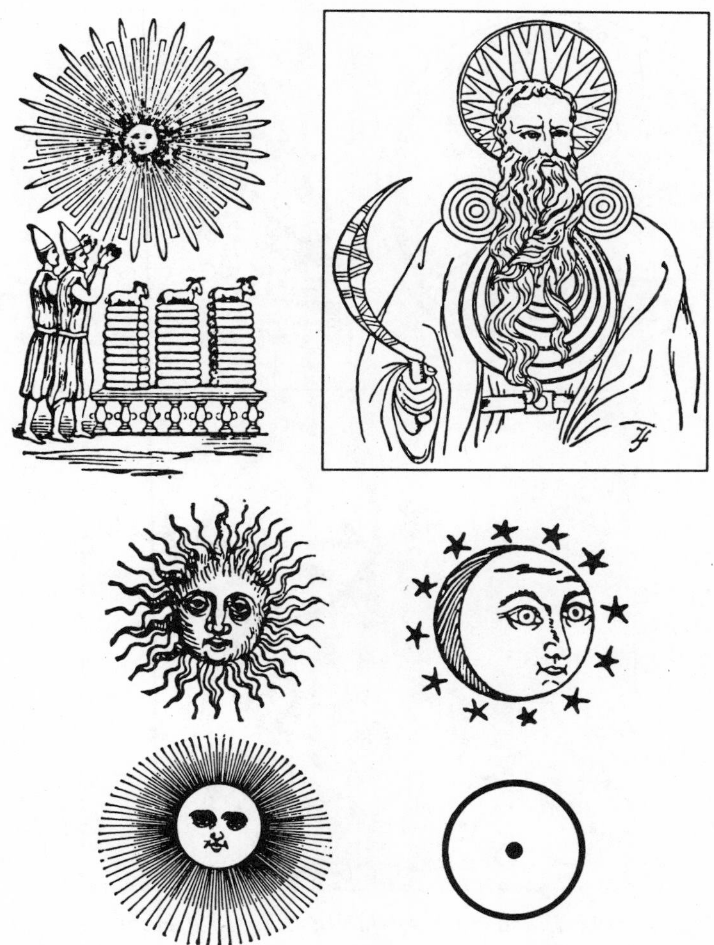

Top left: *The Sun God was worshipped in Babylon, Egypt, Peru, and among many of the ancients. This drawing is from Hislop's* ***The Two Babylons****.*

Top right: *An Arch-Druid from pagan Great Britain in his ceremonial robes (from Wellcome's* ***Ancient Cymric Medicine****).*

Bottom: *These four symbols of the Sun God all came from* ***recent*** *New Age publications. The point within the circle is well-known as a Masonic symbol.*

Top left: *The Illumined Serpent. In* ***The Two Babylons,*** *Hislop writes: "In the mythology of the primitive world, the serpent is universally the symbol of the sun.... As the sun was the enlightener of the world, so the serpent was held to have been the great enlightener of the spiritual, by giving mankind the knowledge of good and evil."*

Top right: *The regenerated Phoenix Bird rises from the flames and ashes.*

Bottom: *In this 17th century alchemical drawing, the Antichrist King and his unholy trinity (three crowns over Earth) worship the transforming fire from their sun deity, symbolized by the triangle within a circle.*

King Arthur and the Round Table. In this Gothic miniature, an apparition of the Holy Grail is conjured up.

In Great Britain today, certain members of the Illuminati, including Prince Charles and Prince Philip, take part in the rituals and symbols of an odd secret society called the *Order of the Garter*. This Order, with its ceremonial magic, is thought to be a precursor to the coming establishment of the *Circle of the Round Table*. So demented are the leaders of the Illuminati that they fancy themselves to be the modern-day inheritors of the Arthurian legend. Upon the appearance, expected soon, of their great and divine king, or ruler, they would be knights of the Circle of the Round Table, noble and exalted co-rulers of Camelot.

The Branch Davidians and the Satanic Ritual Calendar

Earlier, I quoted Stanislas de Rola, who referred to the "goal of the Great Work." By this the conspirators make reference to the Luciferian Plan of the Illuminati, the occult theocracy which today seeks a New World Order and a global spirituality wrested from the hands of God. The Great Work involves the elimination and the purging and "cleansing" from the Earth of all resisters to the New Order.

Aleister Crowley, 33° Mason and Grand Master of the satanic O. T. O., taught that the Great Work, the "transformation of humanity," will be accomplished in the last decade of the 20th Century. In de Rola's *Alchemy: The Secret Art* we find an Illuminist-coded message of what will be the fate of Christians and other rebels during the latter stages of the Great Work. First, we are told that the Great Work "may only be begun in the spring, under the signs of Aries, Taurus, and Gemini."[28] This is the reason, of course, why the Branch Davidians were assaulted and burned with fire on April 19, 1993 and why the federal building in Oklahoma City was firebombed on April 19, 1995.

What's more, exactly 50 years prior to the Waco holocaust (the word holocaust means a "burned sacrifice"), on April 19, 1943, Hitler's storm troopers used flame throwers to incinerate the brave Jewish resisters fighting from the sewers in the Warsaw, Poland ghetto.

According to the Satanic Calendar of High Holy Days, April 19 inaugurates a period of blood sacrifice to the Beast, culminating in the Grand Climax on May 1st each year. May 1st (May Day), of course, is celebrated in Red Square (note the color, red) in Moscow each year by a huge parade and spectacle. It was also on May 1, 1776 in Bavaria that Adam Weishaupt founded the Order of the Illuminati, and it was May 1st when the ancient Druids honored their great Sun God and Goddess with an uninhibited festival complete with initiations, sex orgies, drunken revelry, and human sacrifice.

The May pole and the *circle* ritual conducted around it symbolized the male phallus, the regenerative organ of the Sun God. Meanwhile, the ceremonial site used for worship of this solar deity was traditionally a circular arrangement of large rocks and boulders. At Stonehenge, England are the remains of one such site. It is significant that the arrangement of tables and chairs in the room where the United Nations Security Council meets is patterned after Stonehenge.

Humanity to be Purged and Cleansed

In *Alchemy: The Secret Art,* Stanislas de Rola further informs us: "As a preliminary to the Great Work itself, the subject (humanity) must be purified, rid of its attle."

"This," he explains, "is done by a means well known to metallurgists, which does, however, we are told, require great ingenuity, patience, and labour."[29]

The veiled message here is clear: humanity is to be purged and cleansed of the dangerous elements—that is, of Christians and patriots and other enemies—which inhibit the "pure race" of enlightened man from assuming its role as man's divine rulers. But the Illuminati brotherhood is cautioned that this is *not* an easy task. It requires "great ingenuity, patience, and labour."

Thus, the reason for the arcane and mysterious language and the veiled, coded messages of the Illuminati we so often discover imbedded in many of today's most popular publications and writings becomes clear. As de Rola divulges:

> Though full of promise, these texts invariably contain elaborate devices to deter the unworthy. They are couched in a language often...obscure and impenetrable. For secrecy is inextricably woven into the fabric of alchemy, and is still invoked by modern alchemists.[30]

By "alchemy," the Illuminati refer to what has become popularly known as the Hegelian dialectic, the scientific process now being used by the elite and their collaborators to program the mass mind and to drive man willingly ever closer to his own enslavement. The alchemical processing of humanity, achieved by the continual, induced *conflict of opposites,* is at the very essence of what the occultists, in hushed tones, tout as their Secret Doctrine.

This so-called Secret Doctrine is no longer secret to you if you have read and studied the documentation and explanations found here in *Circle of Intrigue.*

TWELVE

A "Code of Hell"—The Lawless Quest for Global Dominion

For you see your calling, brethren, how that not many wise men after the flesh, not many mighty, not many noble, are called: But God hath chosen the foolish things of the world to confound the wise...

—I Corinthians 1:26-27

Oh! men, of what cannot you be persuaded? I never thought that I should become the founder of a new religion.

—Adam Weishaupt, founder of
the Order of the Illuminati

It is veritably the code of hell.

—Mirabeau, during the
French Revolution

The unlearned and the ignorant scoff and doubt the existence of evil cliques of men bent on global dominion. Filled with self-deceit and pompous arrogance, they far too quickly dismiss as "ridiculous" the massive proofs that there is, indeed, an *Inner Circle* of the Illuminati, a magical sect of power-wielding, ruthless men devoted both to self-aggrandizement and to the common goal of World Empire. However, Carroll J. Quigley, the Professor of International Affairs who mentored Bill

Clinton at Georgetown University in Washington, D.C. and introduced the ambitious, future president to the conspiratorial agenda, was one who carefully and meticulously investigated the privileged "inner core" of Illuminati initiates. In his book, *The Anglo-American Establishment,* Quigley stated flatly that there *is* such a group:

> There is...an *inner core* of intimate associates who unquestionably knew that they were members of a group devoted to a common purpose and an *outer circle* of a larger number on whom the inner circle acted by personal persuasion, patronage distribution, and social pressure. It is probable that most members of the outer circle were not conscious that they were being used by a secret society.[1]

World history, if studied diligently and without prejudice, shows the indelible marks of the ambitious men of the Illuminati, and it illustrates their perennial quest for global dominion. History further records that this cabalistic group has been active both in Europe and in the United States. Since World War II, they have also manipulated events in Japan and Asia.

A Power to Fear

On July 14, 1856, British Prime Minister Disraeli, a brilliant statesman at the time, delivered a startling address in the House of Commons. He stated:

> There is...a power which we seldom mention in this House...I mean the secret societies....It is useless to deny, because it is impossible to conceal, that a great part of Europe—the whole of Italy and France and a great portion of Germany, to say nothing of other countries—is covered with a network of these secret societies, just as the superficies of the earth is now being covered with railroads. And what are their objects? They do not attempt to conceal them. They do not want constitutional

> government; they do not want ameliorated institutions... they want to change the tenure of land, to drive out the present owners of the soil and to put an end to ecclesiastical establishments. Some of them may go further....[2]

At almost this same exact time, the secret societies of which Disraeli warned Britain about launched a despicable campaign to subvert and conquer the United States of America. Their efforts resulted in one of the most bloody and brutal eras in the annals of American history as brother fought against brother in the Civil War, 1860-1865. Their sign, the X of the Egyptian Sun God, Osiris, was prominently displayed on the Confederate flag. Angered and frustrated over their failure to establish an Illuminati-controlled republic in North America, they had their agents, John Wilkes Booth and co-conspirators, assassinate President Abraham Lincoln. His successor, Vice President Andrew Johnson, was a Mason and one of them.

In 1913, in his book *The New Freedom,* Woodrow Wilson intimated the awesome and pervasive power of these hidden men when he revealed:

> Since I entered politics, I have chiefly had men's views confided to me privately. Some of the biggest men in the United States, in the field of commerce and manufacture, are afraid of somebody, are afraid of something. They know that there is a power somewhere so organized, so subtle, so watchful, so interlocked, so complete, so pervasive, that they had better not speak above their breath when they speak in condemnation of it.[3]

Unfortunately, Wilson's ambitions got the best of him, and later, as President of the United States, he served the Illuminati with keen devotion, paying rapt attention to their fond goal of World Government. Though Wilson's treacherous plot for U.S. membership in the League of Nations failed to win in the U.S. Senate, the secret elite's puppet chief executive was able to obtain passage and implementation of two key objectives of the Illuminati. In 1913, the Federal Reserve Act was passed, giving incredible unconstitutional powers to the bankers as well as insuring that untold billions of taxpayer dollars would go into their bulging coffers in future years.

That same year, Woodrow Wilson and his mentors claimed that the 16th Amendment to the U.S. Constitution had passed the constitutionally required approval of two-thirds of the state legislatures. The 16th Amendment authorizes the federal government to levy and collect an income tax, something our nation's founding fathers had never dreamed would ever occur. In fact, as recent research proves, only a handful of state legislatures had actually approved the income tax amendment. It was a dismal failure, but the newspapers of that era, weak and easily misled, bought the lie and dutifully reported to their readers the false results Wilson fed to them.[4]

How shocked the citizens of the United States must have been to have a constitutional amendment which they abhorred and considered an abomination stuffed down their throats. Still, how many knew that this foul deed was committed by an unseen group of greedy elitists, the same men whom President Wilson himself had once described as "a power...so organized, so subtle, so watchful, so interlocked, so complete, so pervasive, that they had better not speak above their breath when they speak in condemnation of it."

Foundations of Power

But, *who* are these terrible, fear-inspiring men? How did they come to possess their awesome, breathtaking power? Sir Winston Churchill, the famed Prime Minister who bravely led the hardy British to victory over the Nazis in World War II, once wrote that the origins of this despicable group can be traced back to "Spartacus." He was referring, of course, to Adam Weishaupt, the Bavarian, Jesuit professor who, on May 1, 1776, founded in Europe the revolutionary *Order of the Illuminati.*

It was Weishaupt who established the modern principles

upon which the Illuminati would carry out its perennial mission—its Great Work. One of his cardinal principles was the almost paranoid maintenance of secrecy and covert action. "It is the unvarying rule of secret societies," he cautioned, "that the real authors never show themselves."[5]

In reality, Churchills' estimation of the origins of this group of world conspirators is inaccurate. The Illuminati can be traced all the way back to the *Knights Templar* and the disgustingly occult brotherhood which came to its peak in Europe with the election of Jacques de Molay as its Grand Master.[6]

Jacques de Molay was burned at the stake by France's King Philip the Fair in 1314, having been arrested, tried, and found guilty of blasphemy, of plots to overthrow governments, and of sacrilegious homosexual acts. His fellow, persecuted Templars then went into hiding, creating a number of secret societies and front groups in France, Italy, Germany, Russia, Belgium, Spain, Scotland, Ireland, Poland, and England. By the 18th century, they again came out of the closet, openly establishing the *United Lodge* of Freemasonry in London in 1717 and also the occultic *Grand Orient Lodge* in Paris. Their notorious efforts spread to America, and many of the founding fathers of the United States were either Masons, Jacobins, or Rosicrucians—or all three.[7]

Today, the power of this odious group and its many secret societies and organizations is immense. If it were not for the grace and mercy of God and His hand at work supporting biblical Christianity and American patriotism, the fires of freedom and liberty would have long since been completely extinguished.

The Objectives

The modern-day Illuminati counterparts of Adam Weishaupt are, however, convinced that their time has come. They believe that, at last, final victory is within their grasp. Their forebearer, Adam Weishaupt, aptly code named "Spartacus," meaning the warrior for Satan, long ago had proposed the objects of their ages-old campaign to undermine, suppress, and capture society. The French historian Henri Martin, in his epic *History of France, Volume XVI,* summed up these objectives. He explained that Weishaupt:

> ...proposed as the end of Illuminism the abolition of property, social authority, of nationality, and the return of the human race to the happy state in which it formed only a single family without artificial needs...every father being priest and magistrate.[8]

We can see in these objectives the utter wickedness of the Illuminati's Master Plan for global domination. No private property would be allowed—except, of course, the vast holdings of the Illuminati themselves. Nationality, too, would be abolished so that all men would form "a single family." Finally, the Christian church would be eradicated so that every man would be his own "priest," his own judge (or magistrate) of what is right and what is wrong.

A Conspiracy Against God and Heaven

This last objective is the key to understanding the phenomenal grip the Illuminati has had on its membership. It is the diabolical glue that binds them together even across the generations. *Theirs is, in fact, a massively evil, single-minded conspiracy against God and against His Word!*

It is a supreme and deadly mistake to consider the scheme of the Illuminati merely a greedy conspiracy of the super rich to gain more riches. True, the Bible says that "the love of money is the root of all evil." But these men's inordinate passion for wealth and possessions—and the power such riches bring—is not the *first cause* of their plot and conspiracy. The first cause is their hatred and utter disregard for the most High God in heaven and His Son Jesus Christ.

This is why the Illuminati are hell-bent on deifying themselves as gods. Having rejected and spit on God's Truth, they proclaim themselves "Priests and Kings." Priests of *which* religion, though—that is the question. Just *whom* do they serve? Historian Martin's comments are most revealing: "Priest of we know not what religion, for in spite of their frequent invocations of the God of Nature, many indications lead us to conclude that Weishaupt had...no other religion than Nature herself."[9]

By "Nature herself," we must conclude that Weishaupt and his Illuminati worshipped none other than Lucifer, or Satan, for such euphemisms as the "God of Nature" are cleverly designed to disguise the true character of Illuminism. Its Lord is the devil and His church is indeed "Mother Nature herself"—Mystery, Babylon the Great, the *Mother of Harlots*. (Revelation 17)

Yet, the Illuminati find significant value in claiming to be "Christian." Weishaupt himself revealed to higher initiates that his secret society was a "hidden Christianity" which made use of the ancient "Mysteries."[10]

A New Christianity for Gullible Priests and Ministers

The Illuminati have never rejected the clergy outright. Indeed, from the days of "Spartacus," they have favored and sought to recruit such men of the cloth as would agree to their definition of what is true, yet hidden, "Christianity."

The German aristocrat Baron von Knigge, an illuminist who went by the code name "Philo," wrote a letter to a fellow conspirator in which he explained the "new Jesus" and new, "hidden Christianity." His letter revealed that the Illuminati had devised its campaign to deceive and recruit ignorant and gullible members of the clergy:

> We say then: Jesus wished to introduce no new religion, but only to restore natural religion and reason to their old rights. Thereby he wished to unite men in a great universal association, and through the spread of a wiser morality, enlightenment, and the combating of all prejudices to make them capable of governing themselves; so the secret meaning of his teaching was to lead men

> without revolution to universal liberty and equality. There are many passages in the Bible which can be made use of and explained, and so all quarrelling between the sects ceases if one can find a reasonable meaning in the teaching of Jesus—be it true or not. As, however, this simple religion was afterwards distorted, so were these teachings imparted to us through *Disciplinam Arcani* and finally through Freemasonry, and all masonic hieroglyphics can be explained with this object. Spartacus has collected very good data for this and I have myself added to them,...and so I have got both degrees ready....
>
> Now therefore that people see that we are the only real and true Christians, we can say a word more against priests and princes, but I have so managed that after previous tests I can receive pontiffs and kings in this degree. In the higher Mysteries we must then *(a)* disclose the pious (Christian) fraud and *(b)* reveal from all writings the origin of all religious lies and their connexion....[11]

Weishaupt himself was thrilled to discover that ungodly, pompous and arrogant priests, pastors, and other church leaders flocked to his secret society. To inspire their choice, he even invented an advanced "Priest's degree." In one revealing correspondence he wrote to a friend expressing his amusement over the stupidity of these supposed "men of God:"

> You cannot imagine what consideration and sensation our Priest's degree is arousing. The most wonderful thing is that great Protestant and Reformed theologians who belong to Illuminism still believe that the religious teaching imparted in it contains the true and genuine spirit of the Christian religion. Oh! men, of what cannot you be persuaded? I never thought that I should become the founder of a new religion.[12]

Destined for Greatness

"Soon," Wieshaupt excitedly told fellow illuminists in his inner circle, "we will be able to provide priests and clergy for all of Bavaria." They will, he proclaimed, be given the choice assignments in seminaries and universities. Eventually, he predicted, their teachings of "Reason" (a cryptic code word meaning the worship of Lucifer through self-deification) will spread. The teaching of the "new Jesus" will also spread throughout the globe as the "universal brotherhood" grows unchecked. He further inspired his colleagues by triumphantly prophesying that they were destined for greatness:

> Do you realize sufficiently what it means to rule—to rule in a secret society? Not only over the lesser or more important of the populace, but over the best men, over men of all ranks, nations, and religions, to rule without external force, to unite them indissolubly, to breathe one spirit and soul into them, men distributed over all parts of the world?[13]

To achieve such lofty, and glorious ambitions, "Spartacus" (Weishaupt) warned, will require the uttermost level of deceit and concealment:

> We must consider how we can begin to work under another form. If only the aim is achieved, it does not matter under what cover it takes place, and a cover is always necessary. For in concealment lies a great part of our strength. For this reason we must always cover ourselves with the name of another society. The lodges that are under Freemasonry are in the meantime the most suitable cloak for our high purpose, because the world is already accustomed to expect nothing great from them which merits attention....As in the spiritual Orders of the Roman Church, religion was alas! only a pretence, so must our Order also in a nobler way try to conceal itself behind a learned society or something of the kind....A society concealed in this manner cannot be worked

> against. In case of a prosecution or of treason the superiors cannot be discovered....We shall be shrouded in impenetrable darkness from spies and emissaries of other societies.[14]

A "Code of Hell"

The diabolical plot of Weishaupt had opposition among the kings and royalty of Europe. Yet, ultimately, few could stand in the way of this great, satanic plague on society. The illuminists everywhere infiltrated the lodges of Freemasonry. They established other secret brotherhoods and orders as well, such as the Jacobins. They succeeded in overthrowing the government of France, one of the strongest nations on Earth at the time, and sent its King and Queen—as well as hundreds of thousands of other innocent citizens—to the guillotine.

Mirabeau, one of the leaders of the French Revolution, was reported as crying out in joy and ecstasy, during one, particularly decadent orgy of sex and bloodshed. The (Illuminist) sect, he declared, has succeeded in seizing the gold and using the populace as revolutionary fodder. This is not democracy, he laughed, "It is veritably the code of hell."[15]

The Plot Against America

It is important to know that the Illuminati also invaded the United States through their subversive activities. Indeed, they found America a fertile territory for their heinous Plan. Some of the richest men of the 13 original states were Masons. In their Masonic orders they had already willingly become accomplices to the devil's sick and ancient plot against God. Their blood oaths had bound them to the Evil One, and so Illuminism was able to take hold of their hearts, their brains, their lives.

The proposed U.S. Constitution of 1787 masterfully reflected the illuminist scheme. It was craftily designed by the rich conspirators to grab power away from the individual states and the people and to eventually concentrate all governmental power at the federal level—which was to be under the control of a new aristocracy: the Illumined Ones. But the Illuminati were outmaneuvered by a force they had not fully reckoned with: *the "little people" of America.*[16]

The wealthy men who were covert illuminists sought to convince the ordinary, middle-class citizens of the United States that the drafted Constitution would be of great benefit to them. The press, then as now under the thumb of the rich, was used to convey the necessary propaganda thought capable of persuading the masses to accept the conspirators' document. But the "little people" unexpectedly rose up as one, pointing out that the Constitution, as offered, was a hoax and a rich man's sham. It is, the people grumbled, the result of a conspiracy of the super rich!

Several famous patriots joined—and even led—the people in their righteous and indignant rebellion against the Illuminati's proposed Constitution. One was Patrick Henry, the brave man who had once proclaimed, "Give me liberty or give me death." Now, Henry once again took the side of the "little people," the ordinary, hard-working *Christian* American. We do not need this new Constitution, he cried out, the present *Articles of Confederation* is more than sufficient to preserve our liberties and secure our prosperity.[17]

The people forthrightly agreed, pointing out to their state legislators that the proposed Constitution failed to provide guarantees to insure that the inalienable rights of the people would be protected from the potentially capricious and dastardly acts of a marauder federal government. There is no *Bill of Rights,* they accurately noted.

Keep in mind that, in the late 1700s, the common people were *more analytical, literate, and well-read* than today's dumbed-down citizenry. Frenchman Alexis de Tocqueville, who came to the United States during this period, wrote that of the humble pioneer homes he visited, every single family owned a few volumes of Shakespeare.[18]

Sensing defeat and unable to win over the minds and hearts of an angry and aroused citizenry, the Illuminati finally conceded. Their politicians agreed that if the people would allow their state legislators to approve the Constitution, the first order of business in the newly constituted Congress would be passage of a *Bill of Rights*.

Only this concession could please the citizenry. Even though the vast majority knew little about the Illuminati and the evil schemes of the men behind the plot to create a New World Order *(Novus Ordo Seclorum)*, nevertheless, they *well knew* the end result of the tyranny that would quickly ensue if a Bill of Rights was not guaranteed to them.

Thanks to the "Little People"

And so, it is not the George Washingtons, the James Madisons, and the John Adamses to whom Americans owe gracious thanks for the liberties and freedoms we have enjoyed now for over 200 years. Instead, it is the deserving "little people" who go unrecognized. We owe the many unnamed, unknown, and unheralded Christians and patriots who said "No!" to the Illuminati's front men back in the 1780s a heavy debt of undying gratitude.

The perceptive American novelist Taylor Caldwell once wrote of this fabulous and unexpected success of the "little people," whom she categorized as the social body known as the Middle Class. "The middle class," she observed, "made the dream of liberty a possibility, set limits on the government, fought for its constitutions, removed much of governmental privilege and tyranny (and) demanded that rulers obey the just laws as closely as the people."

Taylor Caldwell made the point that the elite are angered and outraged that the ordinary masses have risen up and are determined to make war against the "rebels." The elite she says, gathered themselves together and grumbled, "Are we not by birth and money entitled to rule a nation of docile slaves? Do the people not understand that they are truly inferior dogs who need a strong hand to rule over them?"

The elitists, said Caldwell, hate the people with a purple passion, and have resolved to subvert and abolish their restrictive Bill of Rights and put the middle class once again under subjection:

> Little wonder that the elite hated the middle class which challenged them in the name of God-given liberty. And little wonder that this hatred grew deeper as the middle class became stronger and imposed restrictions through which all the people, including the most humble, had the right to rule their own lives and keep the greater part of what they earned for themselves.
>
> Clearly, if the elite were to rule again, the middle class had to be destroyed. It had to be destroyed so despotism and the system of tribute could be returned, and grandeur and honor and immense riches for the elite—assuring their monopoly rule of all the world.[19]

Caldwell's analysis was both astute and prophetic. The Illuminati have carried out a systematic campaign for decades now to undermine the Bill of Rights and to set up a feudal, if high tech, police state. Through NAFTA, GATT, the WTO, and the intrigue of international finance, they have defrauded the working man and woman. So much so that according to a recent study, "Inequality between rich and poor in the United States is far worse than even its harshest critics have charged."[20]

James Smith, economist with the Rand think tank, finds that, "wealth inequality in America is simply enormous." "This disparity in wealth," he notes, "comes as the pension system is in steep decline and the promises of Social Security programs seem impossible to keep."[21]

The Rich are in Big Trouble

It is an inspirational fact, recorded in the Bible, that God dearly loves those whom the world demeans as the "little people." Indeed, the Scriptures caution that it is the rich who are most in peril of God's judgment. Jesus told the young rich man, "go and sell all thou hast, and give to the poor, and thou shalt have treasure in heaven: and come and follow me." But the young man refused, for he had great possessions.

> Then said Jesus unto his disciples, Verily I say unto you, That a rich man shall hardly enter into the kingdom of heaven. And again I say unto you, It is easier for a camel to go through the eye of a needle, than for a rich man to enter into the kingdom of God. (Matthew 19: 23-24)

In I Corinthians 1:19, 26-27 we discover that the Illuminati, who pridefully call themselves "The Wise Men," and who would be kings and rulers—the nobility of this world—are in big, big trouble with God:

> For it is written, I will destroy the wisdom of the wise, and will bring to nothing the understanding of the prudent. For ye see your calling, brethren, how that not many wise men after the flesh, not many mighty, not many noble, are called: But God hath chosen the foolish things of the world to confound the wise; and God hath chosen the weak things of the world to confound the things which are mighty.

If this were not warning enough for the arrogant and blasphemous super rich of the Illuminati to cause them to change their ways and repent of their wicked schemes, they may well consider the startling, end-times prophecy recorded in James 5:1-6:

> Go to now, *ye* rich men, weep and howl for your miseries that shall come upon *you*. Your riches are corrupted, and your garments are motheaten. Your gold and silver is cankered; and the rust of them shall be a witness against you, and shall eat your flesh as it were fire. Ye have heaped treasure together for the last days. Behold, the hire of the labourers who have reaped down your fields, which is of you kept back by fraud, crieth: and the cries of them

> which have reaped are entered into the ears of the Lord of sabaoth. Ye have lived in pleasure on the earth, and been wanton; ye have nourished your hearts, as in a day of slaughter. Ye have condemned *and* killed the just; *and* he doth not resist you.

The Bible has very harsh words for the Illuminati and their henchmen. But to those who trust in God, there is the promise that the Lord will come again and have mercy on the afflicted and the downtrodden:

> Be patient therefore, brethren, unto the coming of the Lord. Behold, the husbandman waiteth for the precious fruit of the earth, and hath long patience for it, until he receive the early and latter rain. Be ye also patient; stablish your hearts: for the coming of the Lord draweth nigh. Behold, we count them happy which endure. Ye have heard of the patience of Job, and have seen the end of the Lord; that the Lord is very pitiful, and of tender mercy. (James 5:7-8, 11)

THIRTEEN

Mind Control and the Gruesome Reality of the World Conspiracy

And all that dwell upon the earth shall worship him, whose names are not written in the book of life of the Lamb slain from the foundation of the world.

—*Revelation 13:8*

I claim...the existence of a conspiracy for the destruction of the Western world as the prelude for shepherding mankind into a sheep's pen as a prelude to One World tyranny.

—A. K. Chesterton
The New Unhappy Lords

Those who manipulate this unseen mechanism of society constitute an invisible government which is the true ruling power of our country. Our minds are molded...largely by men we have never heard of.

—Walter Bernays
Propaganda

They meet and conspire in secret. They plot against God and His people. They manipulate the financial markets and enrich themselves while causing misery for working men and women everywhere. They stage revolutions and invent revolutionary political and religious doctrine. They use the mass media to propagate doctrines and oppress their opposition by unrighteous means. They bring sickness and death to entire populations, merely to please their strange god. Yet, they hate and despise the One, True God.

They believe themselves a superior race imagining that they can trace their bloodline back to a pure heritage of height consciousness. They conceive their destiny to be that of divine kings ruling over an impotent, inferior, and deceived peasantry. They amuse themselves by magick, secret signs and handshakes, and occult symbology. They conduct rituals in black lodges, sacrificing the blood of the innocent, as they pay homage to their dark prince: *Lucifer!*

They are the Illuminati.

Do Conspiracies Really Exist?

The ignorant and the ill-informed do not believe that the Illuminati even exist. *"I do not believe in conspiracies,"* these foolish people say. Some, with a smirk creasing their face, claim that, *"Conspiracies are not possible; that's not the way the world works."*

Really? Conspiracies are not possible? How intellectually lacking a statement! The scoffers and doubters are in a dangerous state of denial. The facts are simply *not* on their side. Even though our history books are, today, drastically incomplete, having been horribly rewritten to reflect the prevailing, politically correct ideology, the truth about conspiracy is found in every single epoch of history.

In ancient Rome, a conspiracy resulted in Caesar's untimely demise. Rome's citizenry was shocked to discover that Caesar's best friend, Brutus, was involved in the deadly scheme. Jesus Christ, the Son of God, died by His own choice, and yet, a conspiracy was involved. Judas, one of Christ's twelve disciples, treacherously sold out His Lord for 30 pieces of silver.

Throughout the middle ages, we are told, kings conspired together to assert the "divine right" of monarchs. The Vatican and the monarchies conspired together to suppress true science and to keep the peasants in bondage. The Catholic hierarchy also conspired with the crusaders to reconquer the Holy Lands from the Moslems, sending hundreds of thousands into battle and death.

Martin Luther conspired with German princes and disgruntled Catholic priests in a movement we now call the Protestant Reformation. Striking back, the Pope used the brutal Ignatius of Loyola, a Spanish general, and his Society of Jesus (the *Jesuits*) to launch a Counter-Reformation.

Conspiratorial intrigue among and between the Houses of Royalty in England, continental Europe, and Russia was bountiful for hundreds of years, up to the World War I era and since.

In 1917, a conspiracy was hatched by world revolutionaries in the United States and Europe to capture Russia through subversion. Their goal: to transform the vast Russian empire into a Socialist state. A small band of wicked men, calling themselves Bolsheviks and preaching the liberation of the working man through Marxism, seized the reigns of power in Moscow. Their plot was financed by foreign banking and corporate interests. After executing Czar Alexander and his entire family, the co-conspirators, led by Vladimir Lenin, Trotsky, Stalin, and others, began their bloody regime under the banner of World Communism.[1]

Millions of innocent men, women, and children were butchered by the Communists; countless others suffered and perished in Russian gulags—all because of a conspiracy by a relatively small group of determined thugs.

Before two more decades were out, yet another tiny band of men had ascended to power in neighboring Germany. They were the Nazis. A few years earlier their ideological counterparts, the Fascists, had overthrown the constitutional government in Rome, Italy. Hitler and Mussolini gained their high positions by political intrigue and by Machiavellian deception. Their method was conspiracy, and their strategy called for social engineering, military warfare, and the enslavement and death of millions.

While battering the Hitler/Mussolini axis powers into oblivion, the allied forces unfortunately gave birth to two, even more wicked coalitions. First, the world witnessed the Soviet encirclement of Eastern Europe. Second, there was the rise to power of Mao Tse Tung in Red China.

In countries like Hungary, Yugoslavia, Poland, Rumania, and in East Germany, local Communist agents, conspiring with Moscow, grabbed for power. Over the succeeding decades such dictatorial brutes as Yugoslavia's Tito, East Germany's Honecker, and Romania's Caecescu brought misery and death to their captive citizens. Conspiracies had catapulted such men to power—conspiracies aided or backed by Soviet armed might.

In Red China, Mao Tse Tung and his small group of insurgents conspired together in a "Long March" to unseat General Chiang Kai Shek, the nationalist leader. Inspiring the peasantry and clandestinely supported by both the Soviet Union and the United States, the Red Communist revolt succeeded. Up to 25 million people were massacred immediately following Mao's assumption of power. Another 50 million died in other purges over the years. In one infamous purge, the youthful "Red Guards," egged on by Mao, tortured, humiliated, and even cannibalized millions of victims.

Mao's murderous reign was engineered by conspiracy. During his era, he gave money, weapons, and political support to conspiratorial revolutions in other Asian countries—in Vietnam, for example, and in Cambodia. In Vietnam, Communist conspirator Ho Chi Minh and his followers uprooted the French colonialists and then fought off and eventually killed 50,000 American servicemen who were sent in vain to that oriental land from across the Pacific Ocean. The American people went along with this vicious war mainly because their leaders conspired to prevent them from knowing the truth about the causes of the conflict.

In Cambodia, a puny numerical force under the savage *Khmer Rouge* (Red Cambodian) madman, Pol Pot, conspired, first, to overthrow the country's monarch, Prince Sihanouk and then, later, to topple from power Sihanouk's pro-American successor, General Lon Nol. By 1973, their bloody conspiracy had succeeded. Within a few short years, almost two million Cambodians were sent to concentration camps, tortured, and then slain. Many of these innocent victims suffered incredible atrocities and mutilations. Their heads were decapitated and their skulls were heaped into piles of ghastly human pyramids. Some of these hideous monuments are still in evidence today, kept as unholy testimonials to the gruesome toll of an evil conspiracy.

Considering this massive array of evidence to be found in the annals of human history, how strange, how very moronic and vacuous, is that idiotic statement by the unthinking fool of modern-day society: "I do not believe in conspiracies. The world doesn't work that way." As Santayana once wrote, "Those who do not learn from history are doomed to repeat it."

Conspirators Founded the U.S.A.

Are these men and women so abominably ignorant and unlearned that they are unaware of the American experience, let alone the history of conspiracy in the world at large? Our founding fathers—Washington, Henry, Jefferson, Madison, *et al.* were conspirators! They conspired against the legally constituted authority. I am not debating the morality of their cause, simply stating the obvious nature of their audacious—and successful—conspiratorial endeavor.

As citizens of a nation born out of conspiratorial intrigue and today enjoying the fruits of that conspiracy, it is strange—even a bit bizarre—to hear many modern-day Americans proclaim, "I do not believe in conspiracies. The world doesn't work that way."

Of course, it is undeniable that the world *does* work that way. Conspiracy is the meat of history. It is one thing that does work in politics, in finance, and in many other areas of human activity. Conspiracies have been known to bring great rewards to its secret membership. A successful conspiracy can bring material prosperity, as well as influence and authority (translated: *power!*) to its perpetrators. Men who would be rich and who would exercise authority and dominion, of necessity, regularly foment and join themselves in conspiracies.

If There Is No Conspiracy, Why Not?

In his insightful book, *America's Secret Establishment,* Antony Sutton, discusses conspiracy. He notes, for example, that business conspiracies were so prevalent—and so damaging to the U.S. economy—that early this century, Congress passed the *Sherman-Antitrust Act.* That legislation, vigorously enforced to break up AT&T and other monopolies and combinations, operates on the reasonable and historically demonstrated belief that conspiracies do exist and that they are harmful and inimical to the peoples' interests. Sutton asks:

> If there can be a conspiracy in the market place, then why not in the political arena? Are politicians any purer than businessmen?[2]

In the February 8, 1920 issue of London's *The Illustrated Sunday Herald,* Sir Winston Churchill, destined to become the voice and inspiration of the English people as their Prime Minister during the dark days of World War II, wrote that from the days of Illuminati founder Adam Weishaupt (1776), a "worldwide conspiracy has been growing." According to Churchill, the hidden leaders of this centuries-old world conspiracy:

> ...played a definitely recognizable role in the tragedy of the French Revolution. It has been the mainspring of every subversive movement during the 19th century; and now at last, this band of extraordinary personalities...have gripped the Russian people by the hair of their heads, and have become the undisputed masters of that enormous empire.[3]

In my pivotal book, *Dark Majesty,* I mention the work of yet another Englishman, A. K. Chesterton, who wrote the revealing book, *The New Unhappy Lords: An Exposure of Power Politics.* After fully investigating the reality of world conspiracy for a quarter of a century, Chesterton declared:

> I claim... the existence of a conspiracy for the destruction of the Western world as the prelude for shepherding mankind into a sheep's pen run as a prelude to One World tyranny.[4]

Chesterton further stated that if the idea of so large a conspiracy seems preposterous, then consider the absurdity of belief in a world innocent of design. Noting the natural tendency of men to associate themselves for gain and to favor their own lot to assure profit, Chesterton goes on to assert:

> In brief, if there is no conspiracy, *why* is there no conspiracy? Why should nature abhor all power vacuums except this particular vacuum? If the means of controlling the lives and destinies of mankind exists, as undoubtedly they do exist, why should use of them go by default? It is not as though there was any shortage of unscrupulous manipulators.[5]

History is Planned...in Advance

R. E. McMaster, Jr., in his excellently researched volume, *The Power of Total Perspective,* states:

> There are two views of history: (1) History happens by accident or (2) It is planned. The general public is taught that history happens by accident. However, the upper echelons...know that history is planned.[6]

Why do the elitists plot to keep from us the knowledge that history is planned in advance? McMasters explains that:

> If future planning is not in the best interest of the vast majority of the people, then it is kept hidden. Otherwise, the enlightened public would see to it that the plan was scrapped. The definition of a hidden plan contrary to the general interests is a "conspiracy." But "conspiracy" is not

> a word which Americans like to use, because we have been conditioned...[7]

The deluded masses, McMasters reports, haven't the vaguest understanding of how the world is controlled and how events are staged for the benefit of conspiratorial overlords. "We, the people," he writes, "are pawns in the money game."[8]

Remarkably, McMasters exclaims, there is a movie that tells the truth about this conspiracy. That movie is the thought-provoking *Network,* starring Faye Dunaway and Peter Finch. "*Network,*" says McMasters, "focused on how television is used to program and control the masses for the benefit of the multinational corporations. The television networks condition the masses to react emotionally, without thinking, contrary to their own interests."[9]

In the most brilliant monologue of the entire movie, a multinational corporate chairman who heads the TV network, Mr. Jensen, lashes out at an idealistic newsman who wants to positively change the public's perceptions:

> "You are an old man who thinks in terms of nations and peoples. There are no Russians. There are no nations. There are no peoples... There is only one holistic system of systems, one vast, interwoven, interacting, multivariant, multinational dominion of dollars... That is the atomic, subatomic and galactic structure of things today... you get up on your little 21-inch screen and howl about America and democracy... There is no America, there is no democracy. There is only IBM and ITT and AT&T and DuPont and Dow and Union Carbide and Exxon. Those are the nations of the world today. What do you think the Russians talk about in their counsels of state? Karl Marx? They get out their linear programming charts, statistical decision theories, mini-max solutions, and compute the price/cost probabilities of their transactions and investments just like we do. We no longer live in a world of nations and ideologies... The world is a collage of corporations, inexorably determined by the immutable

> bylaws of business. The world is a business... and it has been so since man crawled out of the slime..."
>
> "Our children will live... to see that perfect world... one vast ecumenical holding company for whom all men will work to serve a common profit, in which all men will hold a share of stock, all necessities provided, all anxieties tranquilized, all boredom amused. And I have chosen you... to preach this evangel."

In other words, McMasters concludes, *Network* forecast the victory of money and megabusiness—i.e. Fascism—over the human spirit.

However, as accurate as this may be, *Network* failed to tell the whole story. First, though money and corporate power are certainly primary objects of the Illuminati, this is not their *only* motivation. As we have seen, these evil men are demonically possessed. They have sold their very souls to Satan and they must dance to his tune. That is their destiny—and their shame.

But Western civilization as a whole must share the blame for our current state of depravity and our inordinate desire for materialism and gain. We must also share the blame for the coming, great tragedy, for we have allowed the once, great Christian Church to be assaulted and worn down, until it is only a shell of its former self. Now, mankind suffers a savage destiny unless we turn to God and conditions can be reversed. Jean Raspail, author of *Camp of the Saints,* alludes to the current state of despondency and moral delusion when she comments:

> For the West is empty, even if it has not yet become really aware of it. An extraordinarily inventive civilization, surely the only one capable of meeting the challenges of the third millennium, the West has no soul left. At every level—nations, races, cultures, as well as individuals—it is always the soul that wins the decisive battles. It is only the soul that forms the weave of gold

> and brass from which the shields that save the strong are fashioned. I can hardly discern any soul in us.[10]

The Conspiracy Enjoys Success

The fact that so many people in America and the Western nations are so stupefyingly ignorant of The Plan and design of the Illuminati is *prima facie* evidence that, until now, the conspiracy has been incredibly successful in harboring its intentions and schemes. After all, a conspiracy that has been exposed and "outed" loses much of its power base. The secrecy factor—the abundant ability to manipulate and delude gullible and unsuspecting victims who have no idea whatsoever that they are being taken—lends maximum power and influence to the perpetrators of the conspiracy. *They,* the insiders, hold the hidden hand, while the unwitting are made to pay dearly for their immature denial and their trusting naivete.

If, for example, the American people were to awaken from their slumber and rise from their lethargic state to realize that *both* major political parties—Democrat *and* Republican—are controlled by the same, invisible cabal, they would be so outraged they would demand an immediate end to the ridiculous deception.

If the media were not owned by this cabal and the citizenry were told the truth about the banking and money system and the fraud of the so-called Federal Reserve Board, the elite who comprise this cabal would be forced to forfeit the billions of dollars they now accrue, thanks to a purposely dumbed-down electorate.

If the American people were to discover the shocking truth that wars are—in the words of one famous warrior, the late General Smedley, U.S.M.C., "a racket"—and that wars are artificially created to take advantage of the resulting chaos, they would become furiously angry and indignant. So much so that they might well revolt and rise up *en masse* to overthrow and demolish their tormentors: the Illuminati.[11]

Occult Technologies Used to Control Minds

It is to the benefit of our overseers, the conspirators, to work diligently to insure that the truth is never fully told, and if it is, to never be fully understood by the masses. Thus, the devil and his disciples have, over the centuries and especially in the 20th century, developed sophisticated technologies to control peoples' minds. This is accomplished through the agency and assistance of demon spirits and with the full cooperation of the self-appointed cultural elite and the debauched masters of the mass media (TV, movies, newspapers, magazines, music, art, religion, and entertainment).

The process used by the Illuminati conspirators and their willing agents to cloud and persuade the minds of men is that of *propaganda*. In 1928, Walter Bernays published a book entitled *Propaganda*. In it, he explained how the public mind is manipulated and controlled. Bernays wrote:

> Those who manipulate this unseen mechanism of society constitute an invisible government which is the true ruling power of our country. Our minds are molded, our tastes are formed, our ideas suggested, largely by men we have never heard of.[12]

Satan, that great magician of the mind, and his Illuminati disciples use mass hypnosis, illusion, pageantry, magick, and alchemy to keep the masses in an intoxicated state of brain drunkenness. Men and women in a state of stupor and trance have no protection from this latter-day assault on the mind.

Try as they may, they fall under a strong delusion just as was prophesied to occur by God's Word (II Thessalonians 2). Russia's Mikhail Gorbachev, trained in the Illuminist doctrine of the "conflict of opposites," speaks of introducing the masses to a *"A New Way of Thinking."*[13] This is a process whereby the masses experience a clouding and perversion of the mind. Through the magick of induced *contradictions,* man becomes double-minded and thus robotized and compliant. New Agers describe this as: a *transformation of consciousness,* and as a *paradigm shift.*

The doctrinaire, esoteric theologists of the Illuminati know and employ the medieval secrets of alchemy. A form of mental sorcery, they practice the transmutation of matter to spirit, melding the deluded into a contradictory, yet magical, *oneness* frame of mind: *Unity-in-diversity.*

This, in fact, is the Great Work of the Illuminati—their ages-old plan to illuminate mankind, to transform the world. They realize that once this campaign is successful, men shall willingly and eagerly accept that black is white and white is black, light is dark and vice versa, that masculine equals feminine, and that God is whatever or whoever the controllers say He is. No more and no less. As George Orwell expressed it in his frightening prophetic novel, *1984,* a deluded people come to fervently believe that "Freedom is Slavery" and "Ignorance is Strength," and they hate and despise anyone who denies this "New Truth," this "New Paradigm."

This, then, is a key element of the Secret Doctrine, the philosophy which so fascinated and enthralled men like Sweden mystic Emmanuel Swedenborg and German dictator Adolf Hitler—and which continues today to captivate the sick minds of the Illuminati. At its essence, this doctrine produces a global mind-link and a society of slaves—slaves unable to distinguish between Communism and Capitalism or Christianity and the New Age religions.

The chilling, awful thing is that the man of tomorrow, whose malleable and flexible mind is purposely designed and alchemically honed to perceive a New Way of Thinking by *alchemists* in the employ of the Illuminati, will not recognize even the all-crucial difference between God and His adversary, the devil. Already we are seeing this happen. The moral decay of our society has become a monumental tragedy. No one is safe because of the failure of callous men and women to feel guilt and to acknowledge the pain and suffering they inflict on others. This failure of discernment shall inevitably lead to the greatest moral breakdown of all time: the staggering inability to distinguish between *life and death.*

This plague of undeveloped conscience shall soon result

in a ruthless crackdown against Christians, patriots, and other dissidents targeted by the controllers as scapegoats. It will then happen just as Jesus Christ our Lord warned: *...whosoever killeth you will think that he doeth God service.* (John 16:2)

FOURTEEN

Pain, Death, and the Armageddon Script

And when he had opened the fourth seal, I heard the voice of the fourth beast say, Come and see. And I looked, and behold, a pale horse: and his name that sat on him was Death, and Hell followed with them.

—*Revelation 6:7-8*

We're in charge of God's selection process for planet Earth. He selects, we destroy. We are the riders of the pale horse "Death." We come to bring death to those who are unable to know God.[9]

—Barbara Marx Hubbard
The Book of Co-Creation

Let Light and Love and Power and Death
Fulfill the purpose of the Coming One.

—*The Great Invocation of the Lucis Trust*

It is simply amazing how successful the Illuminati has been in molding the minds of the unwitting and controlled masses. This brainwashing operation has been so staggeringly successful that a good part of the American populace is ready, even eager, to persecute and perhaps kill to help the Secret Brotherhood achieve its aims.

The bizarre scheme of the Illuminati to brainwash the multitudes was exemplified when José Arguelles, the mastermind of the New Age's World Harmonic Convergence Day, was able to persuade millions of people throughout the world to meet together on August 16-17, 1987. On that day, masses of New Agers, whom some in the media idolized as "visionaries," met to invoke the New Age kingdom and to meditate and visualize in hopes that a quantum-leap could be made into a universal state of new consciousness.

A Long Range Plan for A New World

Most of these people, were not "space cadets" and zanies, though they appeared to be radical and far-out to logical-thinking Christians. Arguelles, for example, is a highly acclaimed professor of art from a university in New Mexico. Through an extensive interview with the well-known New Age magazine *Meditation*, Arguelles explained that World Harmonic Convergence Day actually kicked-off a five-year plan during which the Earth would be purified and prepared for a coming New Age kingdom.[1]

He stated that it would take at least 20 years from 1987 to "regenerate heaven." To accomplish this regeneration, Arguelles said that civilization must be *destructured* so that an energy wave will sweep the earth. "Helping to bring about the new day on earth," he explained, "would be the establishment of an international "mediarchy."[2] The new consciousness would be promoted by globalist activists in the news media—on TV, radio, newspapers, magazines, electronics communications and computer networks on a worldwide basis. Indeed, Arguelles remarked, this mediarchy is already in place and is swelling with numbers each day.

Surrendering to the Higher Intelligence

Interestingly, José Arguelles said that it was mankind's destiny to "surrender to the higher intelligence that rules the planet."[3]

And who is this higher intelligence? On that point, Mr. Arguelles was somewhat mute. But in his book, *The Crystal Earth Papers*, Arguelles explains that there is a "Council of Geomants" set up on a global basis. These men are pagan ritualists and it is their duty to "coordinate all earth rituals worldwide."[4]

Before we scoff at Arguelles, we might consider the fact that we do have instances of people like Francois Mitterand, former President of France, one of the world's most powerful and rich nations, conducting earth rituals on top of a sacred mountain in France. Meanwhile, we have former President George Bush, who was leader of the most powerful military nation on the face of the earth, being exposed as a member of the occultic Skull & Bones Society and possessing a history of initiation through certain pagan rituals involving human bones and coffins.

Also in the *Crystal Earth Papers*, Arguelles writes that chaotic events will soon result in the *replacement of current governmental and political structures*. New values will be instituted for mankind, to include cooperation, collaboration, and unification on behalf of the "Spirit of the Earth."

Then, during the five-year period, 1997-2002, we will all see a timespan to become known as the "Era of Reseeding." Ominously, Arguelles explains that during this Era of Reseeding, major population areas will be thinned-out.

"The human population will be resettled," he explains, "while the care of the planet will be entrusted to shamanic (sorcery and magic) exercises."[5]

Finally, during the glorious era 2007-2012 will come the "Era of the New Harmony." And on December 21, 2012 (winter solstice) the Crystal Kingdom of the earth will be set up.[6] Evidently, this is Arguelles' version of the final victory of the Illuminati and their total conquest of humanity.

Arguelles also says that our present industrial civilization will be phased out. United Nations personnel will develop plans for economic battalions to redistribute the wealth equally to make sure that the poor receive some of what the more affluent now have.

"Change or Die!"

Now for those who may discount the writings of Professor José Arguelles as the incoherent ramblings of some kind of New Age crazy, I can simply refer you to those of Barbara Marx Hubbard. Hubbard is widely regarded in the world peace and environmental communities. Indeed, she and Cable News Network (CNN) TV czar Ted Turner have worked closely together in the past to develop news programs with an environmental and world peace flavor.[7] Hubbard was actually on Walter Mondale's list of ten women whom he considered in 1980 to be his running mate on the Democrat Party's ticket for President and Vice President. Geraldine Ferraro got the job, but Hubbard seemed to have the support of many delegates, and in fact she was nominated and received some 300 of the votes cast at the nominating convention.

Barbara Marx Hubbard, like Jose Arguelles, worries that if the New World Order *doesn't* come into being, then advanced humans like her cannot evolve into gods. Now keep in mind that Hubbard claims to be a Christian who believes in Jesus. She comes from the wealthy class: Her family was so influential that in one of her books, *The Hunger of Eve*, she casually mentions the fact that as a young person she was frequently a visitor to the oval office during the administration of her father's friend, President Dwight D. Eisenhower. So this is a woman of some influence and, according to her supporters, much substance. So when Hubbard remarks that "no worldly peace can prevail until the self-centered members of the planetary body *either change or die*, that is the choice," perhaps we should listen up.[8]

Hubbard wrote those words in her book titled, *The Book of Co-Creation: An Evolutionary Interpretation of The New Testament*. Hubbard also went on to say:

> We, the elders have been patiently waiting until the very last moment before the quantum transformation, to take action to cut out this corrupted and corrupting element in the body of humanity. It is like watching a cancer grow.

> Something must be done before the whole body is destroyed...
>
> We're in charge of God's selection process for planet Earth. He selects, we destroy. We are the riders of the pale horse "Death." We come to bring death to those who are unable to know God.[9]

In this remarkable passage, then, we find that according to the writings of Barbara Marx Hubbard, there are certain of us who are unevolved and therefore negative and destructive. There can be no world peace until we are dealt with. We are either going to have to change or die, that is our choice. What a choice!

Amazingly, there are few in the media who are willing to criticize Barbara Marx Hubbard's very strange ideas. Hubbard has worked very closely with the Esalen Institute of California to promote their Soviet-American friendship projects. The Esalen Institute, a major New Age think tank, is the group that sponsored recent visits to the United States by former Soviet President Mikhail Gorbachev as well as a visit to the United States by Gorbachev's successor, Boris Yeltsin. Does all this not give you some indication that mankind has entered a twilight zone of unspeakable proportions?

Pain on the Horizon?

What Hubbard is suggesting is that we're going to see *pain* on planet Earth. This is the same thing that two occult organizations sponsored by the Secret Brotherhood are also saying. Those organizations, World Goodwill and Lucis Trust, both of which were founded by theosophist and Freemasonry advocate Alice A. Bailey, have a membership which includes some of the world's most powerful men. For example one of the members of Lucis Trust is Robert McNamara, former U.S. Secretary of Defense and former President of the World Bank.

In its propaganda leaflet titled *The Challenge of*

International Unity, Lucis Trust carefully explains that the United Nations must be supported in its efforts to unify all the nations and erase existing forms of nationalism. Internationalism and world unity, says the leaflet, must be instituted at once. On the back cover of the leaflet is a prayer, or affirmation, of "unification." Here is some of the wording from that prayer:

> The sons of men are one and I am one with them.
> I seek to love, not hate;
> I seek to serve and not exact due service;
> I seek to heal, not hurt.
>
> Let pain bring due reward of light and love.
> Let the soul control the outer form,
> And life, and all events,
> And bring to light the Love.

I assume that your eye was fastened on that unusual line *"Let pain bring due reward of light and love."* This was not the first time that the Lucis Trust, and its sister unit, World Goodwill, have suggested that pain will be necessary to bring in the New World Order designed by the men of the Secret Brotherhood. In the 1940s, the Lucis Trust came up with a prayer that it propagated as useful for summoning the New Age Christ to appear on Earth. That prayer was called *The Great Invocation*. In every book published by the Lucis Trust Publishing Company—and at least 30 books have been published so far—is inserted a detachable copy of *The Great Invocation*. Hundreds of thousands of copies have by now been distributed around the United States, and many churches, especially liberal Protestant and some apostate Catholic groups, begin their worship services by reading aloud *The Great Invocation.*

The Great Invocation is without question of satanic origins. Read for yourself the arcane, yet scary, words of this prayer from Hell:

> Let the Lords of Liberation issue forth
> Let the Rider from the Secret Place come forth

And coming, save.
Come forth, O Mighty One

Let Light and Love and Power and Death
Fulfill the purpose of the Coming One.
From the center where the Will of God is known
Let purpose guide the little wills of men
The purpose which the Masters know and serve.

Let the Plan of Love and Light work out
And may it seal the door where evil dwells.

Let Light and Love and Power restore the Plan on Earth.

The Plan

What "Plan" is *The Great Invocation* referring to? Could it be the Plan of the Secret Brotherhood? Vera Stanley Alder, who almost 30 years ago heralded a coming New World Order, flatly proclaimed, "There is actually a Plan." Its aims, she said, include establishment of "a World Organization . . . a World Economy . . . a World Religion."[10]

John Randolph Price, president of a Texas-based group called the Planetary Commission, also has had much to say about this Plan. On one occasion Price trumpeted this clarion call: "The New Age *will be* . . . a new heaven on earth *will be* . . . the revolution has begun."[11]

A Magical Formula

Again, we might well pose the question: So what if there is such a thing as *The Great Invocation*? Surely, no one in world authority would echo the words of this horrid little prayer of meditation. And surely, it must have been designed by some demented mind or as some kind of a joke. Sorry, but that is simply not true.

The Great Invocation is considered so powerful a magical

formula to conjure up a New World Order and a New Age Kingdom on Earth that the Lucis Trust and World Goodwill bought up full-page ads in the *Reader's Digest* magazine on at least two occasions, the last being in late 1991, in hopes that the readers' minds would become conditioned to the emergence of the New World Order.

But the most astonishing use of *The Great Invocation* was at the Earth Summit in Rio de Janeiro in 1992. It was at this gala festival, the Earth Summit, sponsored by the United Nations Environmental Program, that President Bush and 130 other major world political leaders, ranging from Germany's Chancellor Helmut Kohl to France's President Francois Mitterrand and Britain's Prime Minister John Major, that a document called *The Earth Charter* was signed and sealed. That document called for world governments to take positive steps to protect Mother Earth.

On the first day of the proceedings of the Earth Summit, the delegates did not see anything wrong at all with the reading from the podium of *The Great Invocation.*

The conspiracy gets thicker and the fog and smoke seem to envelop us completely when we consider the fact that the mastermind of the Earth Summit conference happened to be a man named Maurice Strong—a prominent New Age, Hindu cultist. When we consider who Maurice Strong is and what he stands for, we can more easily comprehend the reason why *The Great Invocation* was used in place of a Christian or other prayer at the assemblage of international representatives in Rio de Janeiro, Brazil.

The Armageddon Script

All of this is proof that ours is a magical fantasy world, by design. The global theater is now in the final stages, the grand finale of a marvelous 6,000-year long play. Peter Lemesurier said as much in his thought-provoking book, *The Armageddon Script.*[12] Lemesurier, a dedicated New Age intellectual, proposes that a Great World Leader will soon enter the stage of this fantastic human production of the last days. He will reign from the Holy City of Jerusalem. That leader, whom Lemesurier said could be "the New David," a messiah-type, will be accompanied by associates. It would be their task to bring the great drama of human activity through to a staggering and climatic ending. And this, he suggests, is exactly what has been occurring for so many centuries and is now about to reach the pinnacle of action.

Therefore, Lemesurier tells us that the time is ripe for everything to be brought to a head:

> Their script is now written, subject only to last-minute editing and stage-directions. The stage itself, albeit as yet in darkness, is almost ready. Down in the pit, the subterranean orchestra is already tuning up. The last minute, walk on parts are even now being filled. Most of the main actors, one suspects, have already taken up their roles. Soon it will be time for them to come on stage, ready for the curtain to rise.
>
> The time for action will have come.[13]

If Lemesurier is correct, then the whole world has been cast into a spell. We, the peoples of the Earth, have been mesmerized by the magicians. We now find ourself in a hypnotic, trance-like state. Most of us have had our consciousness altered. We are in an immobile condition, unable to act or even to think logically. What is even more frightening is that we are totally oblivious to what is really, truly going on around us.

It is important to understand that just as individuals can suffer lapses of consciousness and sink into psychological states of nothingness, entire nations can likewise experience psychological breakdown. Such was the case in Nazi Germany in the 1930s and 1940s and in Japan during the same era. As you will recall, historians love to talk about Hitler's hypnotic speeches. They regale us with stories about those piercing hypnotic eyes that so captivated the masses. We're led to believe that the entire German nation was cast into a spell of illusion. And that it was only with the lifting of that spell by the allied forces of General Dwight Eisenhower that the people of Germany were able to cast their shackles off, to pull the blinders off their eyes, and to suddenly understand the repugnant and revolting spectacle that lay all around them.

They Didn't Want to Know

Recently, I read portions of the 1945 report by the Office of Strategic Services—the precursor of the CIA—regarding the liberation of Dachau, a concentration camp in Germany. The most shocking portion of the report was what it had to say about the townspeople of Dachau. It seems that the citizens of this little German town did not complain and did not attempt to overthrow their oppressors but continued to cooperate in deception even though they lost their freedom in the process.

The report tells us that the people of Dachau had to have known what was going on in their midst, yet they chose to remain apathetic. Most amazing, they refused to admit that they had ever known or had the opportunity to know of the atrocities and butchering that were occurring 24 hours a day amongst them. Here's a portion of that 1945 report:

> These words crop up again and again . . ."We were lied to in every respect," but they admit they knew the camp existed. But they saw the work detail of the inmates passing through the streets under guard, and in some instances the SS behaved brutally even towards the townspeople.
>
> When asked if they realized that within the last three months before the liberation 18,000 men lost their lives within a stones-throw of where the people live, they claimed they were shocked and surprised.
>
> When asked if they never saw transports of dead and dying pass through the streets along the railway, they referred only to the last one. They insist that most of the

> trains came in at night and they were sealed cars. However, it was established that anyone who stated that he saw only one train come in the daytime was telling a flat lie. There are quite a few such people in Dachau.
>
> Did they never ask what was in the endless procession of cars that came in and always went out empty?
>
> The analysis of the anti-Nazi element of the town: 1) The people knew what was going on in the camp, even 10 years prior to liberation; 2) The town did a thriving business from the concentration camp guards; 3) 90 percent are guilty and have dabbed themselves with the blood of innocent human beings; 4) The people are to blame for their cowardice—they were all too cowardly. They didn't want to risk anything. And that was the way it was in all of Germany.

The Fearsome Shadow Hanging Over Us

Does this same conclusion apply to America today? Do Americans really, deep down in their hearts, know what is going on, but they are too apathetic to care? If Americans do understand what is going on, that a terrible conspiracy exists to take away their freedoms and subvert our democratic processes and terrorize us all, who has the responsibility of determining the facts—and, what's more, exposing them?

If we do nothing, can we be accused of complicity in allowing the most heinous of crimes to occur, right in our midst, just a stone's throw away? Do we really want to see the fearsome shadow that now hangs over each one of us in this grand country that was established by patriots who were willing to give up every last drop of blood in their bodies to fight tyranny? Or is it just that people do not really see? Have they not discovered that, though the lights are dazzling and would blind us, somewhere down in the pit, the orchestra is tuning up? Meanwhile, back behind the curtains, a shadowy group of men is getting ready to bound on stage and perform the ultimate, tragic act whereby all of mankind will be either murdered or enslaved.

We are reminded of the words of Winston, the character in George Orwell's strangely prophetic novel, *1984*. Winston attempted to fight the system and to discover the truth. What he found was so unbelievable that the whole tragic affair overwhelmed him. Seeing what the world was becoming, and realizing that it was by design of the hidden elite led by Big Brother behind the scenes, Winston told his oppressors that *he* would never become part of that system.

The answer came back: "In the end you will do more than understand it. You will accept it, welcome it, become part of it."

But Winston continued to protest that the drama must end, that perhaps it was not even real.

"Do you want to know what kind of world it's going to be?" O'Brien taunted his prisoner, Winston. "I'll tell you," he said. "Picture a jack boot stomping on the face of man—forever!"

Have we not reached the conclusion of the drama in which the world is now entering the last moments of the final and concluding act? I present in the pages of *Circle of Intrigue* convincing evidence that this is, indeed, the situation which now confronts us. If the world has not been turned into a vast theater of illusion and magic by a Secret Brotherhood, known as the *Inner Circle* of the Illuminati, then what explanation do we have for today's inexplicable events?

A Way of Escape—and Victory!

There is, in fact, only one way to escape the strong delusion and trap constructed by the Illuminati on instructions from their satanic master. To defeat the Lie, one must possess the Truth. And the Truth is found only in Christ Jesus. He who willingly shed His blood on the cross for our sins offers mankind eternal victory through Him. Only believe, and repent, and you will be saved. That is the promise of God. In this promise is found hope, and victory, and destiny.

APPENDIX

The World Conspiracy—An Insider Membership List

After years of investigating the Illuminati and its powerful cabal of ten hidden masters, I believe there is ample documentation proving that the names of the following individuals deserve to be included in the ranks of either the *Inner Circle* of the Illuminati or of its servants. Not all these men fully understand the dark designs of the *Inner Circle*. Some may be unaware of even the existence of the *Inner Circle*. Certainly, not all are cognizant of the Luciferian nature of the conspiracy. But through their membership in Illuminati fronts and organizations sponsoring a New World Order and globalist aims, and based on their financial associations and other factors, each of these men demonstrate their loyalty to the conspiracy.[1]

This is by no means a complete list, but its breadth provides dramatic proof of the monstrous influence the Illuminati has on society. Examine this list and see how many names of corporate chairmen and presidents, and how many names of politicians and bankers, appear. Obviously, Fascism lives!

Listed with each person's name is their current position and nationality, along with information regarding their membership, if known, in the Council on Foreign Relations *(CFR)*, Trilateral Commission *(TLC)*, or the Bilderbergers *(B)*. I have also notated with *(M)* those who are known to be affiliated with a Masonic order. Of course, though significant, these are only a few of the organizations connected with the Illuminati's *Inner Circle*. There is also the Skull & Bones Society, Aspen Institute, Knights of Malta, *Opus Dei*, Club of Rome, Bohemian Grove, World Economic Forum, World Federalists, and many others.

Please keep in mind that the CFR, TLC, the Bilderbergers, and Masonic orders also have a *confidential* list of members who do not wish their affiliation made known to the public. I have reason to believe, for example, that billionaires Ross Perot and Vice President Al Gore are, in fact, members of the Council on Foreign Relations, although their names do not show up on current membership lists or directories. In addition, foreign political leaders have their own, indigenous equivalent of the CFR.

Giovanni Agnelli	Industrialist (Fiat Motors), Italy	B
Madeline Albright	U.S. Ambassador to United Nations	CFR/TLC
Lamar Alexander	Former Secretary of Education, U.S.A	M
Paul Allaire	Chairman and CEO, Xerox Corp., U.S.A.	TLC
Otto Wolff von Amerongen	Chairman and CEO, Otto Wolff, Gmbh, Germany	B
Dwayne Andreas	Chairman, Archer Daniels Midland, Inc., U.S.A.	B/CFR TLC
Les Aspin	Former Secretary of Defense, U.S.A.	CFR
Bruce Babbitt	Secretary of Interior, U.S.A.	CFR/TLC
Lloyd Bentsen	Former Secretary of Treasury, U.S.A.	B/CFR TLC
Prince Bernhard	Monarch, The Netherlands	B
James H. Billington	Librarian of Congress, U.S.A.	B/CFR
Conrad Black	Chairman, Hollinger, Inc., Great Britain	B/CFR

David Boren	President, University of Oklahoma, U.S.A.	CFR/M
Boutros Boutros-Ghali	Secretary-General, United Nations, Egypt	
Mike R. Bowlin	President, Atlantic Richfield Co., U.S.A.	CFR
Ernest Boyer	President, Carnegie Foundation, U.S.A.	CFR
Stephen G. Breyer	Supreme Court Justice, U.S.A.	CFR
Tom Brokaw	NBC-TV News Anchor, U.S.A.	CFR
Edgar M. Bronfman, Sr.	Chairman, Seagrams, Inc., Canada	CFR
Lester Brown	President, Worldwatch Institute, U.S.A.	CFR
Zbigniew Brzezinski	Former National Security Advisor, U.S.A.	CFR/TLC
William F. Buckley	Publisher and Columnist, U.S.A.	B/CFR
M. Anthony Burns	Chairman, Ryder Systems, Inc., U.S.A.	TLC
George Bush	Former President, U.S.A.	CFR/M TLC
Robert E. Callado	Chairman, AT&T, U.S.A.	TLC
Gen. John R. Calvin	Supreme Allied Commander, SHAPE, U.S.A.	B
King Juan Carlos	Monarch, Spain	M
Lord Peter Carrington	Former Secretary-General, NATO; director of Hambros Bank, Great Britain	B
Robert Carswell	Chairman, Carnegie Endowment for International Peace, U.S.A.	CFR
Jimmy Carter	Former President, U.S.A.	CFR/TLC
John Chafee	U.S. Senator (R-RI)	B/CFR
John Chancellor	NBC-TV News, U.S.A.	CFR

Elaine Chao	President, United Way, U.S.A.	CFR/TLC
Dick Cheney	Former Secretary of Defense, U.S.A.	CFR
Jacques Chirac	President, France	M
Jean Chrétien	Prime Minister, Canada	
Warren Christopher	Secretary of State, U.S.A.	CFR/TLC
Bill Clinton	President of U.S.A.	B/CFR M/TLC
Hillary Clinton	Co-President of U.S.A.	
Jon Corzine	Chairman, Goldman, Sachs & Co., U.S.A.	B
William J. Crowe, Jr.	Chairman, Foreign Intelligence Advisory Committee, U.S.A.	CFR
Etienne Davignon	Executive Chairman, Societe Generale de Belgique, Belgium	B
John M. Deutsch	Director of CIA, U.S.A.	CFR/TLC
Christopher Dodd	U.S. Senator (D-CT), U.S.A.	CFR
Robert Dole	Senate Majority Leader, U.S.A.	M
William T. Esrey	Chairman, Sprint Corp., U.S.A.	B
Dianne Feinstein	U.S. Senator (D-CA), U.S.A.	TLC
George Fisher	Chairman and CEO, Eastman Kodak, U.S.A.	TLC
Thomas Foley	Former Speaker of the House of Representatives, U.S.A.	B/CFR
Gerald Ford	Former President, U.S.A.	CFR/M
Louis Freeh	Director of FBI, U.S.A.	
Walter Frehner	Chairman, Swiss Bank Corp., Switzerland	B
Kathryn Fuller	President, World Wildlife Fund, U.S.A.	CFR
Richard L. Gelb	President, Bristol-Myers Squibb Co., U.S.A.	CFR

Richard Gephardt	Minority Leader (Democrat), U.S. House of Representatives, U.S.A.	CFR
Fritz Gerber	Chairman and CEO, F. Hoffman-LaRoche & Co., A. G., Germany	B
David Gergen	Former Presidential Advisor, U.S.A.	B/CFR TLC
Newt Gingrich	Speaker of the House, U.S.A.	CFR/M
Ruth Bader Ginsburg	Supreme Court Justice, U.S.A.	CFR
Peter Goldmark	President, Rockefeller Foundation, U.S.A.	CFR
Jack Goldsmith	Chairman, Federated Department Stores, Inc., U.S.A.	CFR
Mikhail Gorbachev	New World Order Evangelist, Russia	M
Al Gore	Vice President, U.S.A.	M
Katharine Graham	Publisher, *The Washington Post,* U.S.A.	B/CFR
Hanna H. Gray	President, University of Chicago, U.S.A.	CFR
Alan Greenspan	Chairman, Federal Reserve Board, U.S.A.	CFR/TLC
Robert D. Haas	Chairman and CEO, Levi Strauss, Inc., U.S.A.	CFR/TLC
Karl Von Habsburg	Heir to Habsburg Throne and Dynasty, Austria	
Otto Von Habsburg	Member, European Parliament	B
Henry Hamill	General Partner, Goldman, Sachs & Co., U.S.A.	CFR
Cor A. J. Herkstrotrer	Chairman, Royal Dutch Shell Petroleum, The Netherlands	B
Robert Hormats	Vice Chairman, Goldman, Sachs & Co., U.S.A.	TLC
King Hussein	Monarch of Jordan	M

Jesse Jackson	Afro-American Politician, U.S.A.	CFR/M
Phillippe Jaffre	Chairman, Elf Aquataine Co., France	B
Peter Jennings	ABC-TV News Anchor, U.S.A.	B/CFR
Samuel Curtis Johnson	Chairman, S.C. Johnson & Son, Inc., U.S.A.	TLC
Peter R. Kann	Chairman, Dow Jones & Co.; Publisher, *Wall Street Journal,* U.S.A.	CFR
Donald Kendall	Former Chairman, Pepsico, Inc., U.S.A.	B
John Kerry	U.S. Senator (D-MA)	CFR/M
Henry Kissinger	Former Secretary of State, U.S.A.	B/CFR TLC
Yotaro Kobayshi	Chairman, Fuji Xerox Co., Ltd., Japan	TLC
Helmut Kohl	Chancellor, Germany	B
Hilmar Kopper	Spokesman of Board, Deutsche Bank, A. G., Germany	B
William Kristol	Chairman, Project for the Republican Future, U.S.A.	B
Thomas Labrecque	Chairman, Chase Manhattan Bank, U.S.A.	CFR/TLC
Anthony Lake	National Security Advisor, U.S.A.	CFR
Count Otto Lambsdorff	Member, German Parliament	B/TLC
Alexandre Lamfalussy	General Manager, Bank for International Settlements, Switzerland	B
Norman Lamont	Director of N. M. Rothschild, Great Britain	B
Gerald Levin	Chairman and CEO, Time-Warner, U.S.A.	TLC
Joseph Lieberman	U.S. Senator (D-CT)	CFR

Rush Limbaugh	Talk Show Host, Republican Party, U.S.A.	
Winston Lord	Department of State, U.S.A.	B/CFR TLC
Joseph Luns	Secretary-General, NATO	B
John Major	Prime Minister, Great Britain	
Nelson Mandela	Prime Minister, South Africa	
Helmut Maucher	Chairman, Nestle, Ltd., Switzerland	B
Hugh L. McCall, Jr.	Chairman and CEO, Nationsbank, U.S.A.	TLC
David McLaughlin	President, Aspen Institute, U.S.A	B/CFR
Robert McNamara	Former President, World Bank, U.S.A.	B/CFR TLC
Francois Mitterand	Former President, France	M
Walter Mondale	Former Vice President, U.S.A.	CFR
Akio Morita	Chairman, Sony, Japan	TLC
Daniel P. Moynihan	U.S. Senator (D-NY)	CFR
Hosni Mubarak	President, Egypt	
Rupert Murdoch	Publisher, Harper & Row and others, Australia	
Allen E. Murray	Chairman, Mobil Oil, U.S.A.	CFR/TLC
Sandra D. O'Connor	Supreme Court Justice, U.S.A.	CFR
Harry Oppenheimer	Chairman, Anglo American Co., Ltd., South Africa	
Claiborne Pell	U.S. Senator (D-RI)	CFR
Ross Perot	Corporate Owner; Politician, U.S.A.	M
Peter G. Peterson	Chairman, Blackstone Gp., U.S.A.	CFR
Rudolph A. Peterson	Chairman, Bank America Corp., U.S.A.	B/CFR

John J. Phelan, Jr.	Chairman, New York Stock Exchange, U.S.A.	CFR
Heinrich von Piere	Chairman, Siemen's Gmbh, Germany	TLC
Frank Popoff	Chairman, Dow Chemical, U.S.A.	CFR
Colin Powell	Former Chairman JCS, U.S.A.	CFR
Prince Philip	Monarch, Great Britain	M
Dan Quayle	Former Vice President, U.S.A	B
Yitzhak Rabin	Prime Minister, Israel	M
Dan Rather	CBS-TV News Anchor, U.S.A.	CFR
Robert Reich	Secretary of Labor, U.S.A.	
Charles Robb	U.S. Senator (D-VA)	TLC
John D. Rockefeller	U.S. Senator (D-WV)	CFR/M TLC
David Rockefeller, Jr.	Chairman, Rockefeller Financial Services, U.S.A.	CFR/M
David Rockefeller, Sr.	Former Chairman, Chase Manhattan Bank, U.S.A.	B/CFR M/TLC
Lord Eric Roll	President, S. G. Warburg Group, Great Britain	CFR
William V. Roth	U.S. Senator (R-DE)	TLC
Baron Guy de Rothschild	President, Compagnie du Nord, Paris, France	B
Lord J. Rothschild	N. M. Rothschild & Sons (Bank), Great Britain	B
Emma Rothschild	Director, Centre for History and Economics, Cambridge Univ., Great Britain	B
Robert Rubin	Secretary of the Treasury, U.S.A.	
Renato Ruggiero	Secretary-General, WTO, Switzerland	B
Jurgen Schrempp	Chairman, Daimler-Benz A. G., Germany	B

George Schultz	Former Secretary of State, U.S.A.	CFR/TLC
Klaus Schwab	President, World Economic Forum, International	B
Donna Shalala	Secretary of Health and Human Services, U.S.A.	CFR/TLC
John Shalikashvali	Chairman, JCS, U.S.A.	CFR
Albert Shanker	President, American Federation of Teachers (Union), U.S.A.	TLC
Olympia Snowe	U.S. Senator (D-ME)	CFR
Richard Snyder	Chairman, Paramount Pictures, U.S.A.	CFR
George Soros	International Investor, Great Britain	
J. Paul Sticht	Chairman, RJR Nabisco, U.S.A.	CFR
Peter Sutherland	Former Director-General, GATT and World Trade Organization, Ireland	B
Strobe Talbott	Former Secretary of State, U.S.A.	CFR/TLC
J. Martin Taylor	Chief Executive, Barclays Bank, Ltd., Great Britain	B
Margaret Thatcher	Former Prime Minister, Great Britain	
Dick Thornburgh	Former Attorney General, U.S.A.	CFR
Lawrence Tisch	Chairman, CBS-TV, U.S.A.	CFR
Russell Train	Chairman, World Wildlife Fund, U.S.A.	CFR
Ted Turner	Chairman, Cable News Network, U.S.A.	M
Laura Tyson	Chairman, Council of Economic Advisors, U.S.A.	CFR
Paul A. Volcker	Former Chairman, Federal Reserve Board, U.S.A.	CFR/TLC
Kurt Waldheim	President, Austria	B

Lynn R. Williams	International President, United Steel Workers of America (Union), U.S.A.	B
James D. Wolfensohn	President, World Bank, U.S.A.	B/CFR
Walter Wriston	CEO, Citibank, U.S.A.	CFR
Boris Yeltsin	President of Russia	
Vladimir Zhirinovsky	Russian Politician	
Mort Zuckerman	Publisher, *U.S. News & World Report,* U.S.A.	B/CFR

FOOTNOTES AND REFERENCES

Chapter 1: *The Astonishing Global Power and Influence of the Inner Circle*

1. See Texe Marrs, *Millennium: Peace, Promises, and the Day They Take Our Money Away* (Austin, Texas: Living Truth Publishers, 1990); and Texe Marrs, *Dark Majesty: The Secret Brotherhood and the Magic of A Thousand Points of Light* (Austin, Texas: Living Truth Publishers, 1992).
2. Tim Castle, "Big Names Team Up for Merger Windfall," *The European,* March 5-11, 1992, p. 22; David Warsh, "Volcker: Fighting Inflation in Russia?," Knight-Ridder Tribune News Service, article in the *Austin American-Statesman,* February 16, 1992, p. J-1.
3. Thierry Navolin, "World Bank Finds Its Renaissance Man," *The European,* June 9-15, 1995, p. 19.
4. William F. Jasper, *Global Tyranny: Step By Step* (Appleton, Wisconsin: Western Islands, 1992).
5. Texe Marrs, *Dark Majesty, op. cit.,* pp. 35-38.
6. See Helmut Schmidt, *Men and Powers: A Political Retrospective* (New York: Random House, 1989), pp. 221-228. Also see: *Newsletter From A Christian Ministry,* published by Fritz Springmeier, Portland, Oregon; "Another Disgusting Look at the Bohemian Grove," *Contact,* August 6, 1995; *World Magazine,* September 4, 1982; and "Wild and Crazy V.I.P.'s," *Spy* magazine, November 1989.
7. H. R. Haldeman, *Haldeman's Diaries* (New York: G. P. Putnam's, 1994).
8. Interview With David Rockefeller, Jr., *New York Times,* October 16, 1992.
9. Texe Marrs, *Dark Majesty, op. cit.,* pp. 62-63.
10. Andrew Pollack, "Bush to Speak at Conference Linked to Rev. Moon's Church," New York Times News Service, article in the *Austin American-Statesman,* September 4, 1995, p. A4.

11. John J. Robinson, *Born in Blood: The Lost Secrets of Masonry* (New York: M. Evans & Co., 1989); Michael Baigent and Richard Leigh, *The Temple and the Lodge* (New York: Arcade Publishing/Little, Brown, & Co., 1989).
12. *Ibid.*
13. Carl Blumay, *The Dark Side of Power: The Real Armand Hammer* (New York: Simon & Schuster, 1992). Also: Texe Marrs, "Al Gore and the Communist Bagman: A Sordid Family Affair," *Flashpoint* newsletter, March 1993, p. 2.
14. Michael Collins Piper, "Quayle Gets Nod From *Post,*" *Spotlight* newspaper, January 27, 1992, p. 1.
15. Dan Quayle: *Standing Firm* (New York: HarperCollins, 1994).
16. See Texe Marrs, *The Parliament of the World's Religions: An Insider's Report* and *Phoenix Rising: Satan's One World Religion Takes Flight* (Audiotape reports, Living Truth Publishers, Austin, Texas).
17. Bhushan Bahree, "Ruggiero is Named WTO Head in Move That May Spur Rivalries for Other Posts," *Wall Street Journal,* March 24, 1995, p. A5A.
18. *The Project* (newsletter), Summer 1988. George Hunt, a patriot and Christian from Colorado, was at the *World Wilderness Congress* meeting in 1988 and has provided many details of what occurred in connection with the setting up of the World Conservation Bank.

Chapter 2: *Beyond Secret Societies: The Supermen of the Illuminati*

1. Richard Smoley, *Gnosis* Magazine, Summer 1995, p. 1.
2. Fritz Springmeier, *The Top 13 Illuminati Bloodlines,* (Self-published book, Portland, Oregon; available by order from Living Truth Publishers, 1708 Patterson Road, Austin, Texas 78733; phone toll free 1-800-234-9673).
3. PBS-TV special, "The World of David Rockefeller," 1980, with Bill Moyers, host.
4. Jacques Attali, *Sigmund Warbung: A Man of Influence* (France: Fayard, 1985). Also see article by Lewis Pauwels, *Figaro* magazine (France), July 16/23, 1988 and August 13/20, 1988.
5. *Ibid.*
6. *Ibid.*
7. A. Ralph Epperson, *The New World Order* (Published in 1990 by Publius Press, 3100 South Philamena Place, Tucson, Arizona 85730), pp. 289-290.

8. Texe Marrs, *Dark Majesty: The Secret Brotherhood and the Magic of A Thousand Points of Light* (Austin, Texas: Living Truth Publishers, 1992).
9. *Ibid.* Also: Bill Clinton's DeMolay connection is examined in *The Dallas Morning News,* article entitled, "DeMolay: Doing Rites By Society," July 5, 1994, Section C.
10. Charles W. Leadbeater, *Ancient Mystic Rites* (Wheaton, Illinois; Madras, India; and London: Theosophical Publishing House, 1986 edition), pp. 184-187.
11. *Scottish Rite Journal,* obituary, August, 1990.
12. Manly P. Hall, *The Phoenix* (Los Angeles: Philosophical Research Society, 1960), pp. 122-123.
13. *Ibid.*
14. *Ibid.*
15. Helena P. Blavatsky, *The Secret Doctrine* (Pasadena, California: Theosophical University Press, 1963); see p. 421 especially.
16. K. Paul Johnson, *The Masters Revealed* (State University of New York Press, 1994).
17. Hermann Rauschning, *Voice of Destruction,* (New York: G. P. Putnam Sons, 1940), p. 81. Also see Trevor Ravenscroft *The Spear of Destiny* (New York: G. P. Putnam & Sons, 1973) p. 250; and Bob Rosio, *Hitler and the New Age* (Lafayette, Louisiana: Huntington House Publishers, 1993).
18. Trevor Ravenscroft, *The Spear of Destiny* (American edition, 1973, by Samuel Weiser, York Beach, Maine, 1973) pp. 250-251.
19. Manly P. Hall, *The Phoenix, op. cit.*
20. *George Washington: A Biography in His Own Words,* Vol. 1, edited by Ralph K. Andrist (New York: Newsweek, Inc., 1972).
21. *The Writings of George Washington,* Vol. 20, (Washington, D.C.: U.S. Government Printing Office, 1941) p. 518.

Chapter 3: *Blood and Dynasty: A Confidential Look at the Men Who Rule the World*

1. Dean Grace, *"A Little Masonic History Book: The One Dollar Bill,"* unpublished manuscript, December 1984 with 1991 update.
2. *Ibid.*
3. *Ibid.*
4. Helena Blavatsky, *The Secret Doctrine,* Vol. 2 (Pasadena, California: Theosophical University Press, 1963, originally published 1888).

5. Manly P. Hall, *The Secret Destiny of America* (Los Angeles: Philosophical Research Society, 1972), p. 45.
6. *Ibid,* pp. 23-24.
7. *Ibid,* p. 59.
8. Dennis L. Cuddy, *President Clinton Will Continue the New World Order* (Oklahoma City: Southwest Radio Church, 1993), p. 40.
9. Joseph Kennedy, quoted in *The New York Times,* July 26, 1936. Also see *Secret Records Revealed,* by Dennis L. Cuddy, published by The Plymouth Rock Foundation, Fisk Mill on Water Street, Marlborough, New Hampshire 03455.
10. C. G. Rakovsky, in *Red Symphony,* quoted in Des Griffin, *Fourth Reich of the Rich,* published by Emissary Publications, 1993, pp. 252-3090.
11. *Ibid.*
12. Christopher Gilbert quoted in *The Dove,* Summer 1992, p. 16.
13. See Dele Olojede, "Dining for Dollars: Mandela Courts NY Backers to Fill ANC Campaign Coffers," *New York Newsday,* July 6, 1993, p. 15.
14. Tim Castle, "Big Names Team Up for Merger Windfall," *The European,* March 5-11, 1992, p. 22.
15. "And Norman's Doing Nicely," *The European,* September 1993.
16. "Patrons on a Generous Scale," *Elan,* insert in *The European* newspaper, February 25-March 3, 1994, p. 10.
17. See O. J. Graham, *The Six-Pointed Star* (New Puritan Library, 1948). Also see Fritz Springmeier, *The Top 13 Illuminati Bloodlines* (Hardcover book available from Living Truth Publishers, 1708 Patterson Road, Austin, Texas 78733).
18. John Ensor Harr and Peter J. Johnson, *The Rockefeller Century* (New York: Charles Scribner's Sons, 1988). Also see: John F. McManus, The Insiders: *Architects of the New World Order* (Appleton, Wisconsin: The John Birch Society, 1992).
19. "First Family Ready to Relax in Rockies," *The Modesto Bee* (Modesto, California); August 11, 1995. Also see *The Albuquerque Journal,* August 14, 1995.
20. "Europe's Hidden King," *Harper and Queen* magazine, March, 1990.
21. *Ibid.*
22. J. R. Church, *Guardians of the Grail* (Oklahoma City: Prophecy in the News, 1989).
23. *Ibid.*, p. 91.
24. *Ibid.*, pp. 93-96.

25. Otto von Habsburg, *Charles V* (New York: Praeger Publishers, 1970), p. xiii-xiv.
26. Martin Yant, "Archduke Says Unified Europe is a Certainty," *Columbus Dispatch*, February 8, 1987, p. 1-D.
27. J. R. Church, *Guardians of the Grail*, pp. 97-98.
28. *Newsweek*, circa 1969, quoted in *Bible Prophecy News*, Vol. 21, No. 2, 1992.
29. *Jerusalem Post*, October 4, 1987; also see *Bible Prophecy News*, Vol. 21, No. 2, 1992, p. 10.
30. *Los Angeles Times* (UPI), October 7, 1968, quoted in *The Antichrist King—Juan Carlos*, by Charles Taylor (Huntington Beach, California: Today in Bible Prophecy, Inc.).
31. Dennis L. Cuddy and Robert Henry Goldsborough, *The Network of Power* (Baltimore, Maryland: The American Research Foundation, 1993), p. 42. And see: *Newsweek*, September 11, 1995, p. 55.
32. *Ibid.*
33. Lawrence Patterson, *Criminal Politics*, July 31, 1995, (Address: P.O. Box 37812, Cincinnati, Ohio 45222).
34. *Ibid.*
35. *Dope, Inc.* (Washington, D.C.: Executive Intelligence Review, 1992).
36. For a synopsis of the incredible influence of the Hambros Bank, see Joseph Wechsberg, *The Merchant Bankers* (New York: Pocket Books, 1966).
37. See *Dope, Inc., op. cit.* Also, see: David Yallop, *In God's Name*.
38. *Wealth & Poverty: An Economic History of the Twentieth Century*, edited by Sidney Pollard (Oxford, England, and New York: Oxford University Press, 1990), p. 243; "ANC Has to Be Included in SA Solution: Harry O," *The Citizen*, November 9, 1985, p. 5; Dele Olojede, "Dining for Dollars: Mandela Courts NY Backers...," *New York Newsday*, July 6, 1993, p. 16; "Ogilvie Thompson and Harry O in Russia," *Business Day*, August 31, 1992, front page; "Rockefeller Plan for $5 Billion Bank in SA," *Business Day*, April 17, 1991, front page; George Nicholas, "Secret Pact Between Mossad and CIA Emerges in D. C. Scandal," *Spotlight* newspaper, July 27, 1991; *Dope, Inc., op. cit.*, and Alyn Denham, "South Africa going Marxist," *Spotlight* newspaper, August 8, 1993.
39. *Ibid.*
40. These investigative audiotape reports are available from Living Truth Publishers, 1708 Patterson Road, Austin, Texas 78733 or phone toll free 1-800-234-9673: *The Last Days of Pope John*

Paul II; All Fall Down: The Plot to Crown the Pope the Prince of Peace; and *Satan 2000: The Unity of World Religion.* The latter item is also available on VHS video.

41. *Ibid.*
42. Alice Bailey, *Esoteric Psychology,* Vol. 1, (New York: Lucis Publishing Co., sixth printing, 1970), p. 325.
43. *Ibid.*

Chapter 4: ***Assemblage of the Gods: The Rise of the Ten Wise Men of the Inner Circle***

1. David Meyer, *The Last Trumpet* newsletter, (P.O. Box 806, Beaver Dam, WI 53916).
2. William Irwin Thompson, *Quest* magazine, Spring, 1991.
3. *Ibid.*
4. *Ibid.*
5. *The Iconoclast,* Yale University student newspaper, October, 1873. (Note: This article from *The Iconoclast* was published in its entirety in the book, *America's Secret Establishment,* by Antony Sutton).
6. Texe Marrs, *Dark Majesty: The Secret Brotherhood and the Magic of a Thousand Points of Light* (Austin, Texas: Living Truth Publishers, 1992).
7. Walter Isaacson and Evan Thomas, *The Wise Men* (New York: Touchstone Books edition, 1986).
8. *Initiator,* 1982, (Published by the Planetary Commission for the World We Choose); and see Texe Marrs, *Dark Majesty, op. cit.,* p. 136.
9. J. C. Cooper, *An Illustrated Encyclopedia of Traditional Symbols* (London: Thames and Hudson, Ltd., 1978).
10. J. E. Cirlot, *A Dictionary of Symbols* (New York: Philosophical Library, Inc., Second Edition, 1971), p. 46.
11. Ed Vallowe, *Biblical Mathematics* (This self-published book may be ordered by mail from Living Truth Publishers, Austin, Texas 78733, or phone toll free 1-800-234-9673).
12. *Ibid.*
13. John Calvin, *Institutes of the Christian Religion,* Vol. 2, p. 1519.

Chapter 5: *"Ordo Ab Chao"—The Great Work of the Illuminati*

1. See Rex Hutchens, *A Bridge to Light* (Washington, D.C.: The Supreme Mother Council, 33° Ancient and Accepted Scottish Rite of Freemasonry, 1988). *Note:* This book is a summary of the book, *Morals and Dogma of the Ancient and Accepted Scottish Rite of Freemasonry,* by Albert Pike, 33°.
2. Albert Pike, *Morals and Dogma of the Ancient and Accepted Scottish Rite of Freemasonry,* Albert Pike 33°, originally published 1871; 1924 edition by L. H. Jenkins, Inc., Richmond, Virginia; available today from The Supreme Mother Council, 33°, House of the Temple, Washington, D.C.
3. Texe Marrs, *Ten Signs of the End of the World,* (Available from Living Truth Publishers, 1708 Patterson Road, Austin, Texas 78733; $20 for video, $10 for audiotape. Add $2 for postage and handling).
4. Albert Gore, Jr., *Earth in the Balance* (New York: Houghton-Mifflin, 1991).
5. Edward Epstein, "Gorbachev to Convene Meeting in S.F. This Fall," *San Francisco Chronicle,* February 3, 1995, p. A13.
6. "Cultivate Generals, Says American Expert," Dr. Samuel Huntington interviewed by Norman Chandler, *The Star* newspaper (Johannesburg, South Africa); "Randy Weaver's Role in the Plot to Discredit Idaho's Conservatism," by Don Rotheringham, *The New American,* December 14, 1992; "Canadian Neo-Nazi Group Created by Britain's MI5?," *Nexus,* December 1994-January 1995, p. 8; "The Intelligence Service Bomb Swindle," *Der Spiegel* magazine (Germany); "Bombs vs. Blitz," *The Hoskins Report,* P.O. Box 997, Lynchburg, Virginia 24505, May 1, 1995, p. 4; *Fascist Terror Stalking America,* 90 minute video by Texe Marrs; and *The Bloodstained Hands of Big Brother Government,* video by Texe Marrs, (Austin, Texas: Living Truth Publishers, 1995).
7. *Ibid:* Texe Marrs' videos.
8. Rex Hutchens, *A Bridge to Light, op. cit.*
9. John Randolph Price, *The Superbeings* (Austin, Texas: Quartus Books, 1981), p. 1.
10. Nesta Webster, *World Revolution* (England).
11. Recommended reading on this subject: Des Griffin, *Descent Into Slavery* (Emissary Publications, 9205 Clackamas Road, Clackamas, Oregon, 97015, 1980); Des Griffin, *Fourth Reich of the Rich,* same publisher, 2d ed., 1993; David Allen Rivera, *Final Warning: A History of the New World Order* (Rivera

Enterprises, P.O. Box 10524, Harrisburg, Pennsylvania 17105); Larry Bates, *The New Economic Disorder* (Creation House Publishers, Altamonte, Florida); and Ken Klein, *The False Prophet* (Winterhaven Publishing House, Eugene, Oregon 97401).

12. William P. Honan, "War Decoding Helped U.S. To Shape U.N.," *New York Times,* April 23, 1995; "Roosevelt Expected and Wanted Japanese Attack," *The Present Truth Ministry* newsletter, P.O. Box 475, Uniontown, Arkansas 72955, March 1995; Charles J. Lewis, Hearst Newspapers, "Pearl Harbor Admiral's Family Seeks Exoneration," *Austin American-Statesman,* April 29, 1995, p. A13; Mike Blair, "Pearl Harbor: Truth Surfaces After 50 Years," *Spotlight* magazine reprint, December 1993. In his exhaustive article, Blair quotes such authoritative books as John Costello, *The Pacific War;* John Toland, *Infamy: Pearl Harbor and its Aftermath;* and George Morgenstern, *Pearl Harbor: The Story of the Secret War.* Also see: *Washington Times-Herald* newspaper (December 4, 1941) and *New York Times,* November 3, 1991.

13. See John Torrell, *The Dove,* Summer 1995, pp. 2-22 (*The Dove* is published by European-American Evangelistic Crusades, P.O. Box 41001, Sacramento, California 95841).

14. See: "Department of Defense Appropriations for 1970"—hearings by the House of Representatives Subcommittee on Department of Defense Appropriations, Part 6, pp. 104-150, June 9, 1969; comments by Dr. Donald MacArthur, Deputy Director, Defense Research and Engineering Office of Secretary of Defense; Also see comments made by Professor Martin Dworkin to the House of Representatives, in *Congressional Record,* July 1, 1969, p. 18077. Also: Dr. Jacob Segal and Dr. Lilli Segal, *AIDS: Its Nature and Origins,* 57-page report, 1986; "Smallpox Vaccine Triggered AIDS," *London Times,* May 11, 1987; Dr. Robert Strecker, *The Strecker Memorandum;* and Dr. Alan Cantwell, *AIDS and the Doctors of Death.*

15. *The Report From Iron Mountain on the Possibility and Desirability of Peace* (New York: Dial Press, 1967) Note: The publisher has taken this book out of print, and it is not available from Dial Press. Copies may possibly be found at public libraries or obtained through rare book services.

16. Donald E. Gibson, "The Role of the Establishment in the Antinuclear Movement," *Sociological Spectrum* (Journal), 10:321-340, 1990; and Donald E. Gibson, "The Environmental Movement: Grass-Roots or Establishment," *Sociological Viewpoints,* pp. 92-124.

17. Emanuel M. Josephson, *The Truth About Rockefeller: Public Enemy No. 1, Studies in Criminal Psychopathy* (Chedney Press, 230 E. 61st St., New York, New York 10021).

18. Texe Marrs, *Big Sister Is Watching You* (Austin, Texas: Living Truth Publishers, 1993).

19. Vital crime statistics are compiled and published annually by both the National Centers for Disease Control and the Federal Bureau of Investigation. These figures show that the homicide rate in the U.S.A. has declined every year since 1988.

20. For information and facts about the Oklahoma City bombing devoid of establishment media bias, see my video and special written report, *Fascist Terror Stalking America,* available from Living Truth Publishers, 1708 Patterson Road, Austin, Texas 78733. For facts on the World Trade Center bombing, see Ralph Blumenthal, "Tapes Depict Proposal to Thwart Bomb Used in Trade Center Blast," *New York Times,* October 28, 1993, p. 1; and see *Los Angeles Time* article on this subject, October 28, 1993.

21. See references in footnote #6 above.

22. Paul M. Barrett, "FBI as Supreme Court Snoop," *Wall Street Journal,* September 1, 1992. Also see: J. B. Campbell, "The FBI—America's No. 1 Terrorist Group," *National Educator,* P.O. Box 333, Fullerton, California 92632, December 1993. Excellent materials detailing America's rapid—and planned—descent into a Gestapo police state are available from: Lawrence Patterson, publisher, *Criminal Politics,* P.O. Box 37812, Cincinatti, Ohio 45222, and Donald S. McAlvany, *The McAlvany Intelligence Advisor,* P.O. Box 84904, Phoenix, Arizona 85071.

23. *Goodwill Meditation Group Report,* 1995, London-Geneva-New York City.

24. James Knox, *American Focus* newsletter, May 1, 1995.

25. *Ibid.*

26. See footnotes 11 and 17 above. Also: my books, *Millennium: Peace, Promises, and the Day They Take Our Money Away* and *Dark Majesty: The Secret Brotherhood and the Magic of A Thousand Points of Light.*

27. *Christians Awake Newsletter,* P.O. Box 3513, West End Street, Birmingham, Alabama 35211.

Chapter 6: *Political Alchemy and Conspiracy: Right-Wing and Left-Wing, Republican and Democrat—They're All the Same!*

1. *U.S. News & World Report,* November 1, 1971.

2. Dennis L. Cuddy, *President Clinton Will Continue the New World Order* (Oklahoma City, Oklahoma: Southwest Radio Church, 1993), p. 13.

3. Gary Allen, *Say No to the New World Order* (South African edition: Concord Press, Pretoria, South Africa). And see Christopher Lydon, *Atlantic Monthly*, July 1977.
4. Laurence Stern, *Washington Post*, May 8, 1976.
5. See my book, *Dark Majesty: The Secret Brotherhood and the Magic of A Thousand Points of Light* (Austin, Texas: Living Truth Publishers, 1992).
6. A. Ralph Epperson, *The New World Order* (Publius Press, 3100 South Philamena Place, Tucson, Arizona 85730, 1990), pp. 289-290.
7. For a complete list of current, top administration officials who are members of either the CFR or the Trilateral Commission, including those in President Bill Clinton's administration, contact: Fund to Restore an Educated Electorate, P.O. Box 33339, Kerrville, Texas 78029.
8. "Sovereignty Sellout," *The New American*, July 11, 1994, pp. 5-9.
9. C. W. F. Hegel, *The Philosophy of History*. Also see *Hegel*, by Peter Singer (London, England: University Press).
10. Helena P. Blavatsky, *The Secret Doctrine* (Wheaton, Illinois: Theosophy University Press, 1888), p. 99.
11. Franklin Sanders, "The Hegelian Counterfeit," *The Moneychanger*, January 1991, p. 4.
12. Alexander Herzen, quoted in James H. Billington, *Fire in the Minds of Men: Origins of the Revolutionary Faith* (New York: Basic Books, Inc., Publishers, 1980), p. 225.
13. *Ibid.*
14. Antony C. Sutton, *America's Secret Establishment: An Introduction to the Order of Skull & Bones* (Liberty House Press, 2027 Iris, Billings, Montana 59102, 1986).
15. *Ibid.*
16. Karl Marx, *Das Kapital*, published in London, England in 1867.
17. John Randolph Price, *The Planetary Commission* (Austin, Texas: Quartus Books, 1984), p. 69.
18. Alice Bailey, *The New International Economic Order*, World Goodwill Commentary Number 14, September 1980.
19. Alice Bailey, *Discipleship in the New Age*, Vol. 2, (New York and London: Lucis Publishing Co., 1955/seventh printing 1986).
20. R. E. McMaster, *The Reaper* newsletter (Address: P.O. Box 84901, Phoenix, Arizona 85071), April 27, 1983, p. 4. And see Texe Marrs, *Big Sister Is Watching You*, pp. 29-30.
21. *Brainwashing: A Synthesis of the Russian Textbook on Psychopolitics* (Burbank, California: American Public Relations Forum).

22. See Texe Marrs' audiotape series, *Black Science* (Available for $12 plus $2 postage and handling from Living Truth Publishers, Austin, Texas 78733).
23. See footnote 21 above.
24. *Ibid.*
25. *New York Times,* October 16, 1992.
26. Taylor Caldwell, "The Middle Class Must Not Fail," *The Review of the News,* May 29, 1974.
27. Alice Bailey, *Discipleship in the New Age,* Vol. 2, *op. cit.,* p. 664.

Chapter 7: *Inside the Magic Circle: Reward and Punishment in the Age of the Illuminati*

1. Thomas Larson, "Frenzied Finance," *Everybody's Magazine,* August, 1904.
2. *Ibid.*
3. Emmanuel Josephson, *The Federal Reserve Conspiracy and the Rockefellers* (New York: Chedney Press, 1968), p. 1.
4. "Banking Man at the Top," *Time* magazine, September 7, 1962.
5. Gerald Jonas, *The Circuit Riders: Rockefeller Money and the Rise of Modern Science* (New York: W. W. Norton and Co., 1989).
6. Emmanuel Josephson, *The Truth About Rockefeller* (New York: Chedney Press).
7. For definitive proof on Perot's insider connections, I recommend my thoroughly documented audiotape exposé, *The Ross Perot That Nobody Knows* (Available for $11 from Living Truth Publishers, 1708 Patterson Road, Austin, Texas 78733). Also see: Allen R. Myerson, "Perot's Computer Business Joins Forces With Swiss Bank Corp.," New York Times News Service, article in *Austin American-Statesman,* September 7, 1995, p. C1.
8. Texe Marrs, *Dark Majesty: The Secret Brotherhood and the Magic of A Thousand Points of Light.* Also see James J. Drummey, *The Establishment's Man* (Appleton, Wisconsin: Western Islands, 1991).
9. *Ibid.*
10. Nesta Webster, *Secret Societies and Subversive Movements* (Omni Publications, P.O. Box 900566, Palmdale, California 93590; first published in England, 1924), pp. 220-221.
11. *Ibid.*

12. For documentation on Cecil Rhodes and his "circles within circles" conspiracy, see the following: Carroll J. Quigley, *The Anglo-American Establishment;* Dan Smoot, *The Invisible Government* (Boston: Western Islands, 1962); Roy Livesey, *Understanding the New World Order* (Chichester, England: New Wine Press, 1989); and M. E. Beirnes, "To Rule the World," *Midnight Cry* newsletter, Tequestra, Florida, 1981.
13. Foster Bailey, *Changing Esoteric Values,* lecture published in London, 1954.
14. *Don Bell Reports,* #55, November 12, 1965. Also see *Intimate Papers of Colonel House,* Vol. 1, p. 209.
15. See Red Beckman's book, *The Law That Never Was,* for documentation and proof that the 16th Amendment to the U.S. Constitution is a sham, having never been legally radified by the state legislatures.
16. Antony Sutton, *America's Secret Establishment* (Billings, Montana: Liberty House Press, 1980).
17. For an intriguing and provocative, as well as in-depth, examination of the Vince Foster affair free of media censorship, see the article by James Norman, "Fostergate," *Media Bypass* magazine, (Address: Media Bypass Magazine, P.O. Box 5326, Evansville, Indiana 47716).
18. "Gingrich's March Through Georgia," *US News & World Report,* July 3, 1995, p. 18.
19. Robert F. Kennedy, quoted in Ann Wilson, *Bill Clinton: Friend or Foe?* (J. W. Publishing).

Chapter 8: *Newt Gingrich and the Illuminati's "Third Wave" Revolution*

1. Franklin Sanders, *The Moneychanger,* P.O. Box 341753, Memphis, Tennessee 38184.
2. Adolf Hitler, *Mein Kampf* (American edition by Houghton-Mifflin Co., New York, 1971; originally published in 1927 in Germany by Verlag Frz., Eher Nachf G.M.B.H).
3. Vera Stanley Alder, *When Humanity Comes of Age* (New York: Samuel Weiser, Inc., 1974), pp. 190-193.
4. Manly P. Hall, *The Phoenix,* 2d. ed., (Los Angeles: The Philosophical Research Society, Inc., 1960) p. 105.
5. *Ibid.,* p. 108.
6. *Ibid.,* p. 106.
7. *Ibid.,* pp. 122-123.
8. Manly P. Hall, *Lectures on Ancient Philosophy* (Los Angeles: The Philosophical Research Society), p. 433.

9. *Ibid.*
10. See Cathy Burns, *Hidden Secrets of Masonry* and Reginald C. Haupt, Jr., *Gods of the Lodge.*
11. C. William Smith, "God's Plan for America," *The New Age* magazine, September, 1950.
12. *Ibid.*
13. *Ibid.*
14. According to the *Annual Report of the Council on Foreign Relations,* Newt Gingrich became a member in 1990.
15. Alvin and Heidi Toffler, *Creating A New Civilization* (Atlanta, Georgia: Turner Publishing, Inc., 1995).
16. *Ibid.*, p. 11.
17. *Ibid.*, p. 19.
18. *Ibid.*, pp. 20-21.
19. *Ibid.*, p. 33.
20. *Ibid.*
21. *Ibid.*, p. 84.
22. *Ibid.*, pp. 90-91.
23. Alvin and Heidi Toffler, *Power Shift* (New York: Bantam Books, 1990).
24. *Ibid.*, p. 376.
25. *Ibid.*
26. *Ibid.*, pp. 374-379.
27. Alvin and Heidi Toffler, *Creating A New Civilization, op. cit.*, p. 9.
28. *Ibid.*, p. 8.
29. Dennis L. Cuddy, "Newtonian Politics and Morality," *Christian World Report,* March 1995, p. 8.
30. Newt Gingrich, quoted in *Washington Post,* January 3, 1985.
31. Carl H. Claudy, *Masonic Harvest* (Washington D.C.: The Temple Publishers, 1948), p. 376.
32. *Ibid.*
33. Alice Bailey, *The Beacon,* September/October 1975, pp. 145-148.
34. *Ibid.*
35. Texe Marrs, *Mystery Mark of the New Age* (Westchester, Illinois: Crossway Books, 1988).
36. *The New Group of World Servers,* World Goodwill, New York, New York. Also see *Building and Bridging: The New Group of*

World Servers, published by the School for Esoteric Studies, New York, New York.

37. *Ibid.*
38. Alice Bailey, quoted in *Ibid.*
39. *Ibid.*
40. *Ibid.*
41. *Ibid.*

Chapter 9: *The Meteoric Rise of Wicked Bill Clinton: A Classic Case Study of Illuminati Influence*

1. "Sovereignty Sellout," *The New American,* July 11, 1994, pp. 5-9. Also see *Washington Post,* August 5, 1993, and *New York Times,* August 18, 1993.
2. Texe Marrs, "Bush and Clinton: Bilderberger Twins?," *Flashpoint* newsletter, May 1992. Also see Texe Marrs, *Dark Majesty, op. cit.,* pp. 101-102.
3. Democrat Party nominee William J. Clinton's speech was published in its entirety in the *New York Times.*
4. Carrol J. Quigley, *Tragedy and Hope: A History of the World in Our Time* (New York: Macmillan, 1966).
5. *World Goodwill,* bulletin number 4, 1991.
6. *Ibid.*
7. *Ibid.*
8. Tom Carney, *Thoughtline* newsletter, February 1992, published by Arcana Workshops, Manhattan Beach, California.
9. *Ibid.*
10. Daniel Wattenberg, *The American Spectator,* August, 1992. Also see Texe Marrs, *Big Sister Is Watching You,* pp. 53-56.
11. Albert Gore, Jr., *Earth in the Balance: Ecology and the Human Spirit* (New York: Houghton-Mifflin Co., 1991), p. 263.
12. *Ibid.*
13. *Ibid.,* p. 264.
14. *Ibid.,* p. 265.
15. *Ibid.*
16. *Ibid.,* p. 263.
17. *Ibid.*
18. Texe Marrs, *Mystery Mark of the New Age* (Westchester, Illinois: Crossway Books, 1988).

Chapter 10: *The One-Eyed Infidel and the Naked Man on a White Horse*

1. *The European*, November 18-24, 1994: see *Elan* magazine insert, p. 6.
2. Neal Wilgus, *The Illuminoids: Secret Societies and Political Paranoia* (Santa Fe, New Mexico: Sun Publishing, 1978).
3. Trevor Ravenscroft, *The Spear of Destiny* (York Beach, Maine: Samuel Weiser, Inc., 1982 ed.; first published in Great Britain in 1973).
4. The occult teachings of Edgar Cayce are examined in my book, *New Age Cults and Religions* (Austin, Texas: Living Truth Publishers, 1708 Patterson Road, Austin, Texas 78733).
5. Alice Bailey, *Lecture on Telepathy* (New York: Lucis Trust Publishing).
6. *Ibid.*
7. Sir John Sinclair, *The Alice Bailey Inheritance* (Wellingborough, Northamptonshire, England: Turnstone Press Ltd., 1984), p. 118.
8. Arthur Schlessinger, *Foreign Affairs*, 1995.
9. *The New International Economic Order*, published by World Goodwill, New York, New York, September 1980.

Chapter 11: *Circle of Intrigue: The Colossal Plot of the Solar Serpent*

1. Albert Mackey, *An Encyclopedia of Freemasonry*, Vol. 1, (Chicago: The Masonic History Co., copyright 1873 and 1927), p. 151.
2. Hans Biedermann, *Dictionary of Symbolism* (New York: Penguin Books, 1994), pp. 36-37.
3. Manly P. Hall, *Secret Teachings of all Ages* (Los Angeles: Philosophical Research Society, 1966), p. IXXXVI.
4. Stanislas de Rola, *Alchemy: The Secret Art* (London, England: Thames Hudson, 1973), p. 33.
5. *Ibid.*
6. J. C. Cooper, *An Illustrated Encyclopedia of Traditional Symbols* (London, England: Thames & Hudson, 1978), p. 36.
7. Hans Biedermann, *Dictionary of Symbolism, op. cit.*, p. 70.
8. *Ibid.*
9. *Ibid.*
10. Manly P. Hall, *Secret Teachings of All Ages, op. cit.*, p. LXXXXVII.

11. Alexander Hislop, *The Two Babylons* (Loizeaux Brothers: 1959 ed.; originally published 1836 in England), p. 87.
12. *Ibid.*
13. *Ibid.*
14. *Ibid.*
15. Samuel Marrs, *The Angels Laughed* (Yesherun Publications, P.O. Box 720849, Dallas, Texas 75372). Also see G. S. Gaskell, *Dictionary of Scripture and Myth* (New York: Dorset Press, 1988), p. 158.
16. Milton, *Camus,* p. 50-3.
17. Albert Pike, *Morals and Dogma, op.cit.*, p. 31.
18. *Ibid.*, p. 623.
19. Ottoman Sufi, "Doctrine of the Soul," *History of Ottoman Poetry,* Vol. 1, p. 52.
20. Alexander Hislop, *The Two Babylons, op. cit.*, p. 226.
21. *Ibid.*, p. 227.
22. *Ibid.*
23. *Ibid.*
24. *Ibid.*, p. 194.
25. *Ibid.*
26. *Ibid.*, p. 227.
27. Manly P. Hall, *Secret Teachings of all Ages, op. cit.*, p. CLXXVII; and see Jennings, *The Rosicrucians: Their Rites and Mysteries.*
28. Stanislas de Rola, *Alchemy: The Secret Art, op. cit.*, p. 10.
29. *Ibid.*
30. *Ibid.*, p. 9.

Chapter 12: *A "Code of Hell"—The Lawless Quest for Global Dominion*

1. Carroll J. Quigley, *The Anglo-American Establishment,* 1981.
2. Disraeli, quoted in Nesta Webster's, *Secret Societies and Subversive Movements, op. cit.*, p. 71.
3. Woodrow Wilson, *The New Freedom,* 1913.
4. Red Beckman, *The Law That Never Was.*
5. Nesta Webster, *Secret Societies and Subversive Movements, op. cit.*, p. 266.
6. See Gaetan Delaforge, *The Templar Tradition in the Age of Aquarius* (Putney, Vermont: Threshold Books, 1987); John J.

Robinson, *Born in Blood: The Lost Secrets of Masonry* (New York: M. Evans and Company, 1989); and Michael Baigent and Richard Leigh, *The Temple and the Lodge* (New York: Arcade Publishing/Little, Brown and Co., 1989).

7. *Ibid.* Also see Texe Marrs, *The Masonic Plot Against America,* 60 minute audiotape (Available for $11 from Living Truth Publishers, Austin, Texas 78733).
8. Henri Martin, *History of France,* Vol. XVI.
9. *Ibid.*
10. Nesta Webster, *Secret Societies and Subversive Movements, op. cit.,* pp. 215-217.
11. *Ibid,* pp. 13, 14, 104-106. Webster further quotes the source *Nachtrag von...Originalschriften.*
12. *Ibid,* p. 76. Also: *Nachtrag* I.
13. *Ibid;* also: *Nachtrag von...Originalschriften,* II. 45.
14. *Ibid,* pp. 143, 163. Also: *Neusten Arbeiten des Spartacus and Philo.*
15. Lombard de Langres, *Histoire des Jacobins* (1820), p. 31.
16. See Texe Marrs, *The Masonic Plot Against America* (Audiotape: order for $12 from Living Truth Publishers, Austin, Texas 78733). Also see Charles Beard, *An Economic Interpretation of the Constitution.*
17. Few Americans today know their history well enough to realize that the current U.S. Constitution was not this nation's first. The first Constitution was the *Articles of Confederation.* The illuminists and their wealthy co-conspirators despised the *Articles* because it provided a *weak* central government and prevented a centralization of police power, banking, currency, and finance.
18. Alexis de Tocqueville, *Democracy in America.*
19. Taylor Caldwell, in *The Review of the News,* May 29, 1974. Reprinted in *The New American,* May 1, 1995.
20. James Smith, "Rich-Poor Gap Worsening in U.S.," *Toronto Star,* July 25, 1995.
21. *Ibid.*

Chapter 13: *Mind Control and the Gruesome Reality of the World Conspiracy*

1. See Des Griffin, *Descent Into Slavery, op. cit.*
2. Antony Sutton, *America's Secret Establishment, op. cit.,* p. 3.

3. Winston Churchill, *The Illustrated Sunday Herald*, London, England, February 8, 1920.
4. A. K. Chesterton: *The New Unhappy Lords: An Exposure of Power Politics, op. cit.*
5. *Ibid.*
6. R. E. McMaster, Jr., *The Power of Total Perspective* (Published by A. N. International, Inc., P.O. Box 84901, Phoenix, Arizona 85071). Note: R. E. McMaster, Jr., is publisher of the investment and political newsletter, *The Reaper*, same address as for his book.
7. *Ibid.*
8. *Ibid.*
9. *Ibid.*
10. Jean Raspail, *Camp of the Saints*, quoted in Earl Jones, *Intelligence Newsletter*, July/August, 1995, p. 2, published by Christian Crusade for Truth, HC 66, Box 39, Deming, New Mexico 88030.
11. Smedley, *War is a Racket*.
12. Walter Bernays, *Propaganda* (1928).
13. Mikhail Gorbachev, *Perestroika: New Thinking For Our Country and the World* (New York: Harper & Row, 1981).

Chapter 14: *Pain, Death, and the Armageddon Script*

1. José Arguelles, interviewed by Jose-Alexis Viereck, *Meditation*, Summer 1987, Vol. II, No. 3, pp. 6-19. Also see Antero Alli, "A Post-Convergence Interview with José Arguelles," *Magical Blend*, Issue 18, 1988, pp. 17-20; and see the book, *The Crystal Papers*, by José Arguelles.
2. *Ibid.*
3. *Ibid.*
4. *Ibid.*
5. *Ibid.*
6. *Ibid.*
7. Barbara Marx Hubbard, *The Hunger of Eve*.
8. Barbara Marx Hubbard, *The Book of Co-Creation: An Evolutionary Interpretation of the New Testament*. (Also revised and retitled, in a later edition, as *The Book of Co-Creation: The Revelation—Our Crisis is a Birth*, (Sonoma, CA: The Foundation for Conscious Evolution, 1993).
9. *Ibid.*

10. Vera Stanley Alder.
11. John Randolph Price.
12. Peter Lemesurier, *The Armageddon Script.*
13. *Ibid.*
14. See Joseph J. Carr, *The Twisted Cross* (Lafayette, Louisiana: Huntington House, Inc., 1985).
15. George Orwell, *1984* (New York: New American Library/Signet Paperback edition, 1983; originally copyrighted 1949).

Appendix: *The World Conspiracy—An Insider Membership List*

1. Resources and references used to compile this *Insider Membership List* include the following: *The New American* magazine, issues dated May 15, 1995 and December 26, 1994; directory provided by the Trilateral Commission; list by Ronald Weber, St. Louis, Missouri; *Annual Report of the Council on Foreign Relations; The Moneychanger*, February, 1993; *The CFR/Trilateral/New World Order Connection*, chart by Fund to Restore an Educated Electorate, P.O. Box 33339, Kerrville, Texas 78029; Fritz Springmeier, *The Top 13 Illuminati Bloodlines* and *Be Wise As a Serpent; Bulletin*, Committee to Restore the Constitution, September 1994; *Spotlight* newspaper, issues dated June 29, 1992 and July 10, 1995; and Texe Marrs' books, *Dark Majesty, Millennium*, and *Big Sister Is Watching You*. For further research: A recent publication which does an excellent job of listing key members of the Bilderbergers, CFR, TLC, Skull & Bones Society, and Committee of 300 is the book, *Who's Who of the Elite*, by Robert Gaylon Ross, Sr., published by RIE, HCR 1, Box 516, Spicewood Texas 78669.

For Our Newsletter

Texe Marrs offers a *free* newsletter about Bible prophecy and world events, secret societies, the New Age movement, cults, and the occult challenge to Christianity. If you would like to receive this newsletter, please write to:

Living Truth Ministries
1708 Patterson Road
Austin, Texas 78733

About the Author

Well-known author of the #1 national bestseller, *Dark Secrets of The New Age*, **Texe Marrs** has also written 35 other books for such major publishers as Simon & Schuster, John Wiley, Prentice Hall/Arco, Stein & Day, and Dow Jones-Irwin. His books have sold over a million copies.

Texe Marrs was assistant professor of aerospace studies, teaching American defense policy, strategic weapons systems, and related subjects at the University of Texas at Austin for five years. He has also taught international affairs, political science, and psychology for two other universities. A graduate *summa cum laude* from Park College, Kansas City, Missouri, he earned his Master's degree at North Carolina State University.

As a career USAF officer (now retired), he commanded communications-electronics and engineering units. He holds a number of military decorations including the Vietnam Service Medal, and served in Germany, Italy, and throughout Asia.

President of Living Truth Publishers in Austin, Texas, Texe Marrs is a frequent guest on radio and TV talk shows throughout the U.S.A. and Canada. His monthly newsletter, *Flashpoint*, is distributed around the world, and he is also heard globally on his international shortwave radio program, *World of Prophecy*.